Garfield
Cooks Up Trouble

BY JIM DAVIS

Ballantine Books • New York

A Ballantine Books Trade Paperback Original

Published in the United States by Ballantine Books, an imprint of Random House,
a division of Penguin Random House LLC, New York.

BALLANTINE and the HOUSE colophon are registered trademarks of Penguin Random House LLC.

ISBN 978-0-425-28562-6
Ebook ISBN 978-0-425-28563-3

Printed in China on acid-free paper

randomhousebooks.com

9 8 7 6 5 4 3 2 1

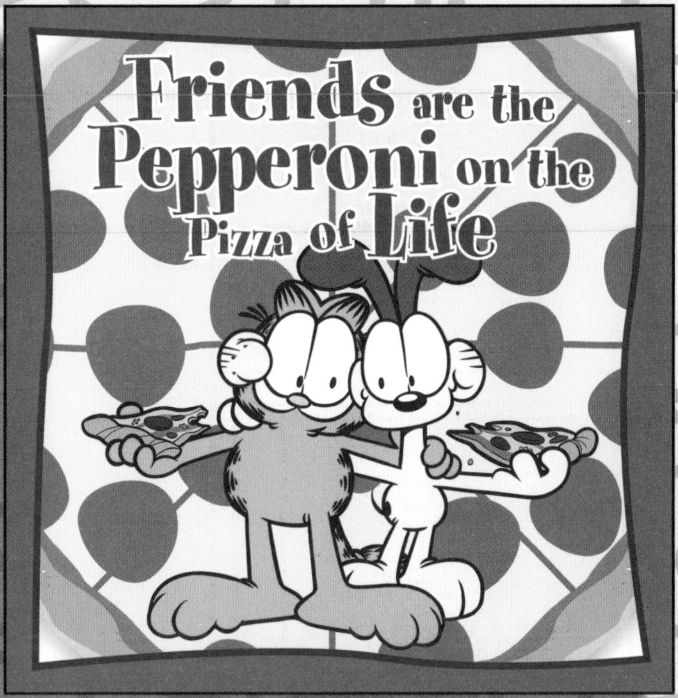
Friends are the Pepperoni on the Pizza of Life

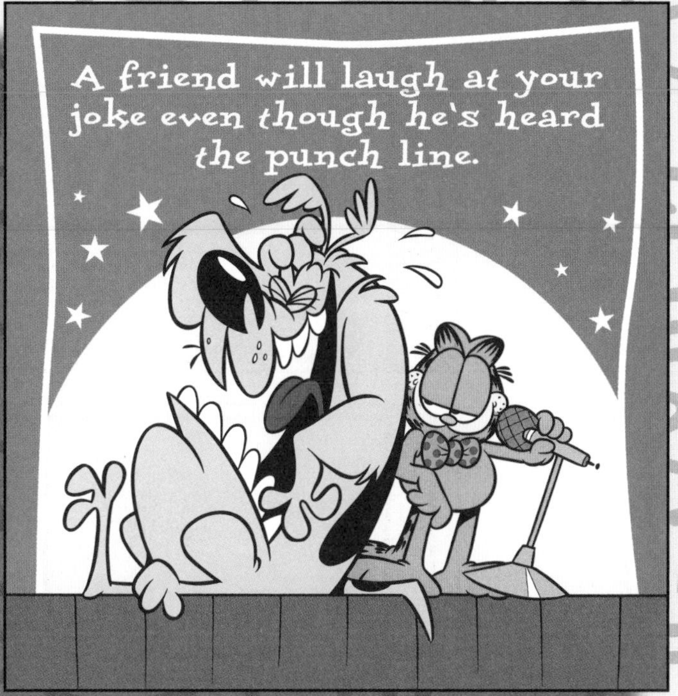
A friend will laugh at your joke even though he's heard the punch line.

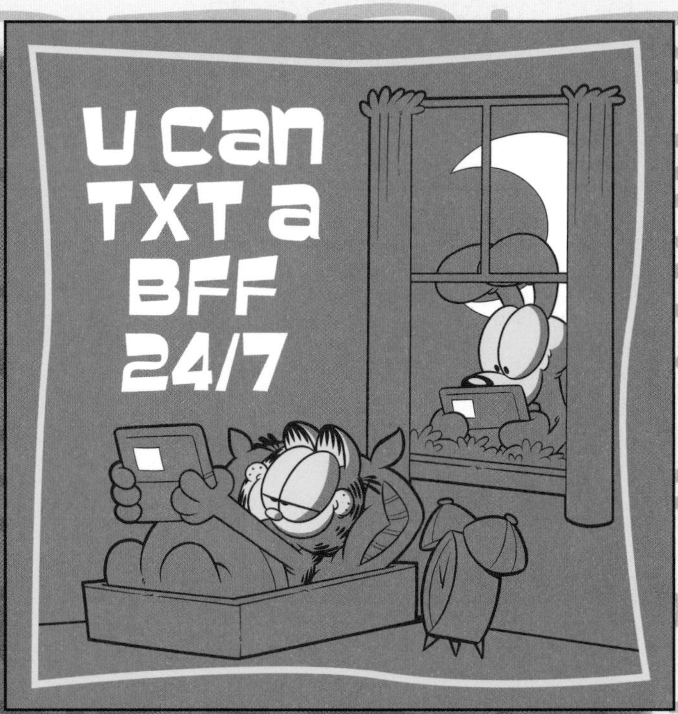
U can TXT a BFF 24/7

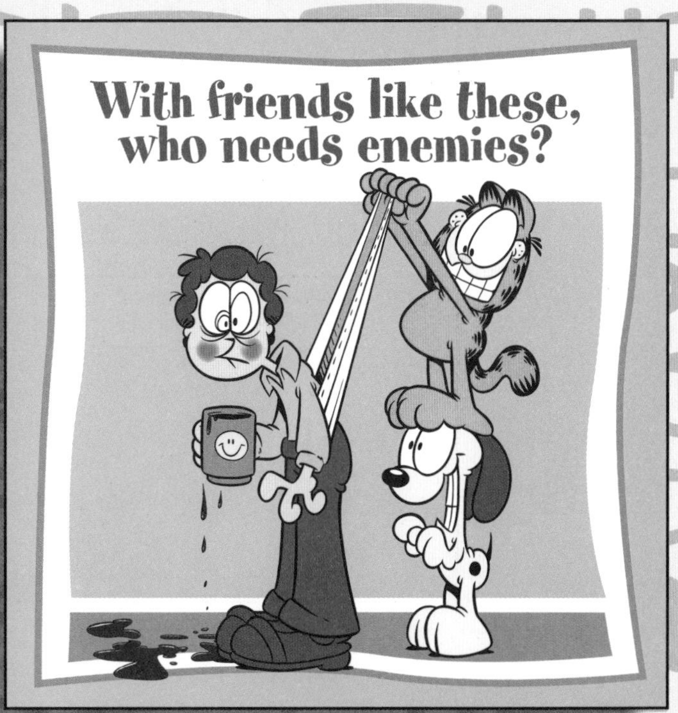
With friends like these, who needs enemies?

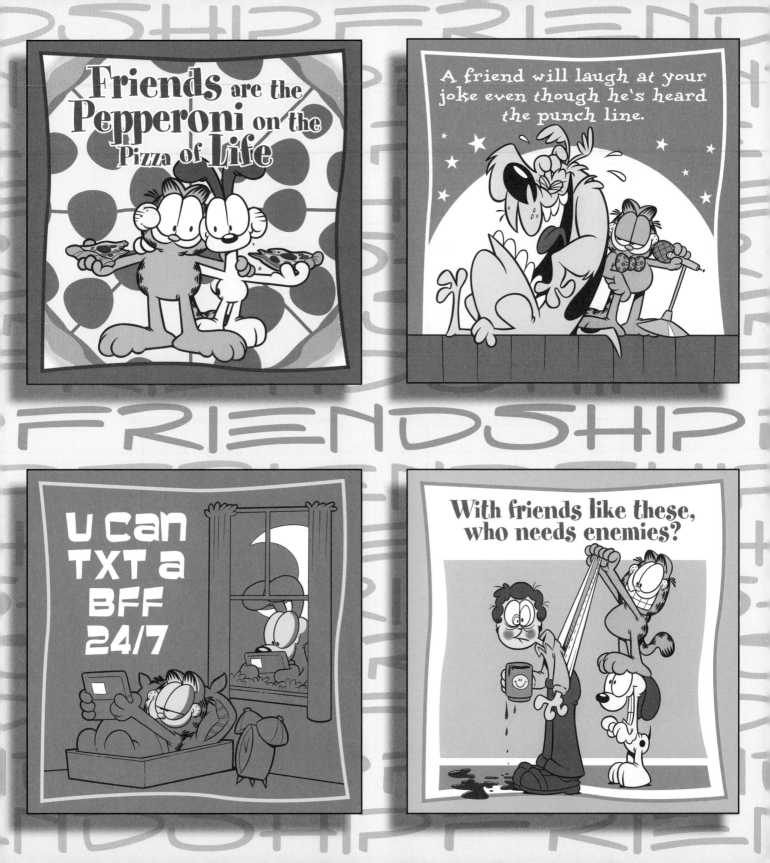

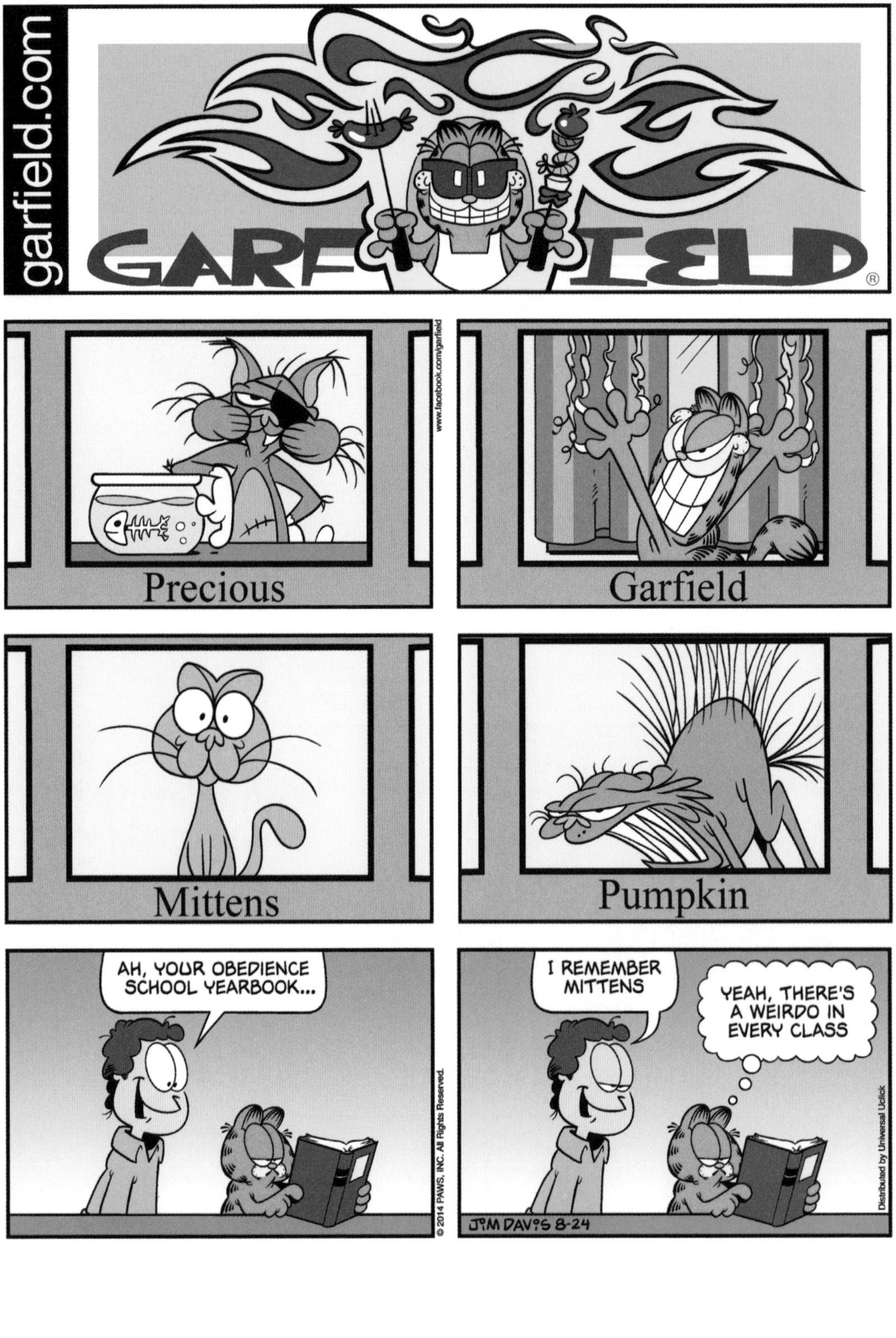
garfield.com
GARFIELD®
www.facebook.com/garfield
Precious
Garfield
Mittens
Pumpkin
AH, YOUR OBEDIENCE SCHOOL YEARBOOK...
I REMEMBER MITTENS
YEAH, THERE'S A WEIRDO IN EVERY CLASS
© 2014 PAWS, INC. All Rights Reserved.
JIM DAVIS 8-24
Distributed by Universal Uclick

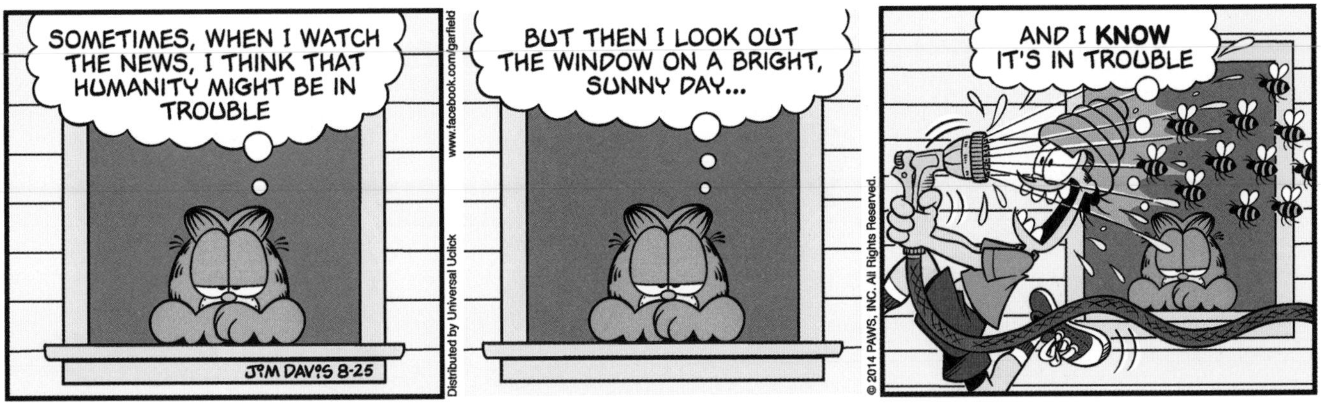
SOMETIMES, WHEN I WATCH THE NEWS, I THINK THAT HUMANITY MIGHT BE IN TROUBLE
JIM DAVIS 8-25
Distributed by Universal Uclick www.facebook.com/garfield
BUT THEN I LOOK OUT THE WINDOW ON A BRIGHT, SUNNY DAY...
© 2014 PAWS, INC. All Rights Reserved.
AND I **KNOW** IT'S IN TROUBLE

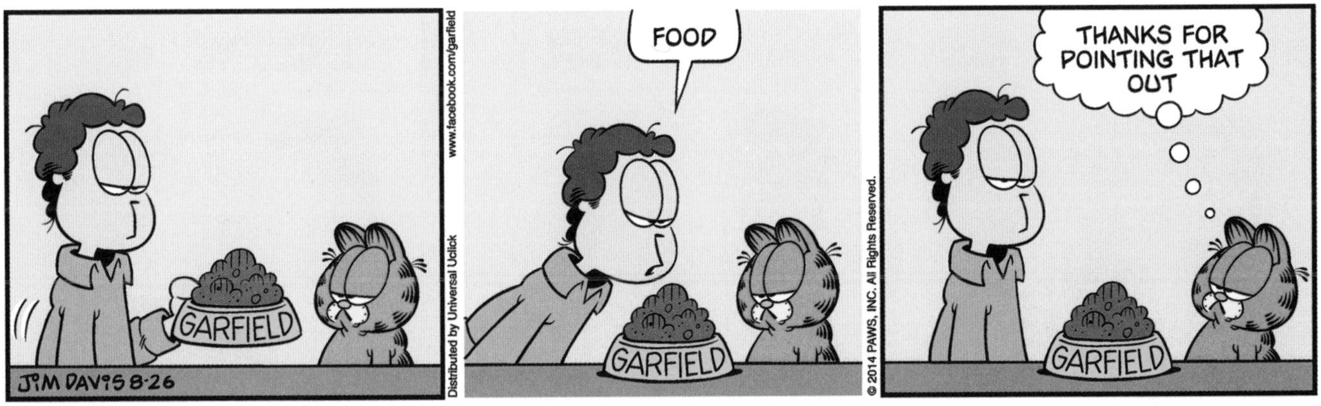
GARFIELD
JIM DAVIS 8-26
Distributed by Universal Uclick www.facebook.com/garfield
FOOD
GARFIELD
© 2014 PAWS, INC. All Rights Reserved.
THANKS FOR POINTING THAT OUT
GARFIELD

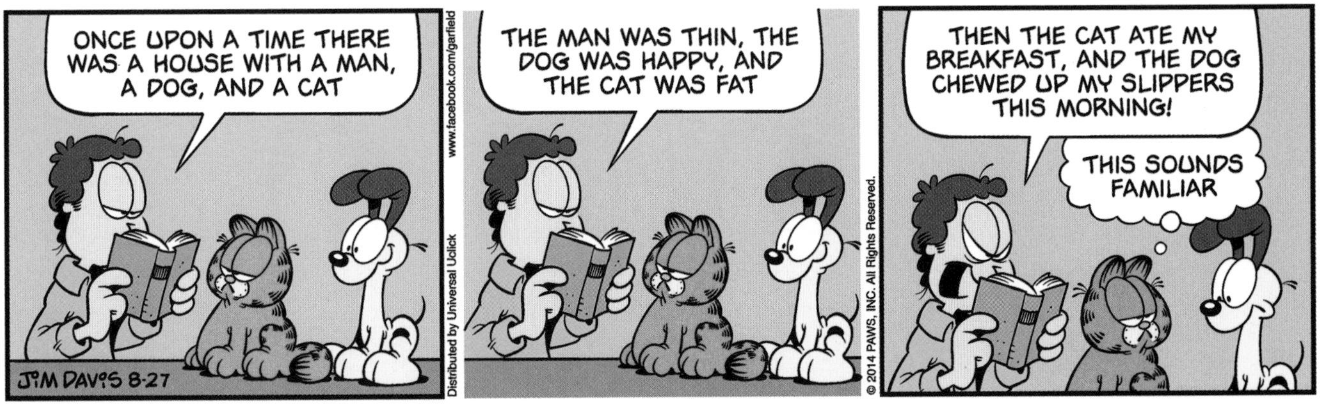
ONCE UPON A TIME THERE WAS A HOUSE WITH A MAN, A DOG, AND A CAT
JIM DAVIS 8-27
Distributed by Universal Uclick www.facebook.com/garfield
THE MAN WAS THIN, THE DOG WAS HAPPY, AND THE CAT WAS FAT
© 2014 PAWS, INC. All Rights Reserved.
THEN THE CAT ATE MY BREAKFAST, AND THE DOG CHEWED UP MY SLIPPERS THIS MORNING!
THIS SOUNDS FAMILIAR

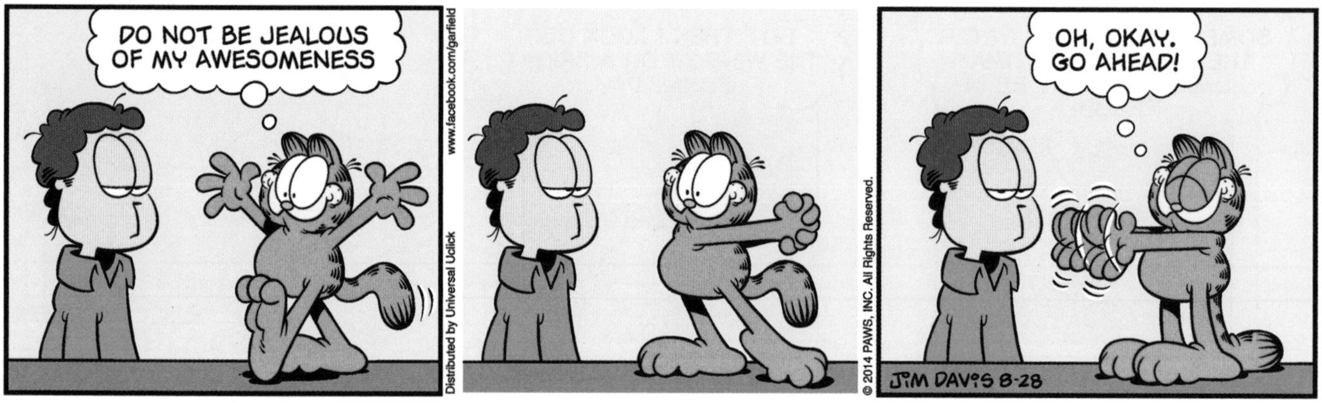
DO NOT BE JEALOUS OF MY AWESOMENESS
OH, OKAY. GO AHEAD!
JIM DAVIS 8-28
Distributed by Universal Uclick www.facebook.com/garfield
© 2014 PAWS, INC. All Rights Reserved.

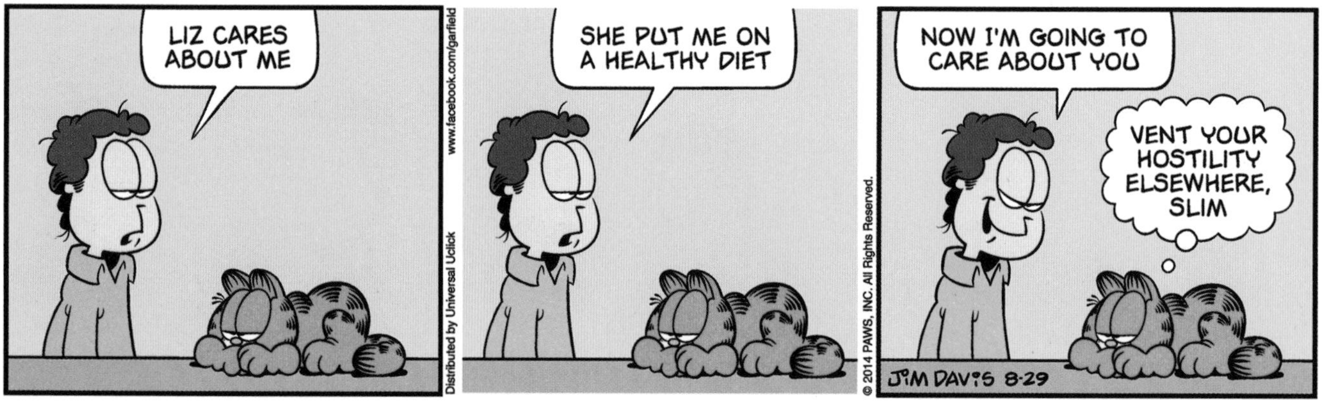
LIZ CARES ABOUT ME
SHE PUT ME ON A HEALTHY DIET
NOW I'M GOING TO CARE ABOUT YOU
VENT YOUR HOSTILITY ELSEWHERE, SLIM
JIM DAVIS 8-29
Distributed by Universal Uclick www.facebook.com/garfield
© 2014 PAWS, INC. All Rights Reserved.

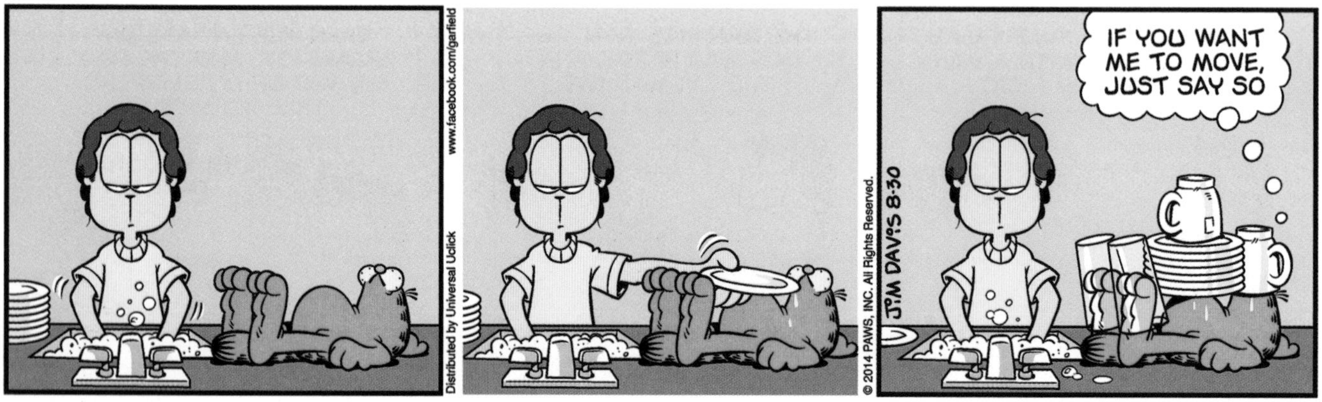
IF YOU WANT ME TO MOVE, JUST SAY SO
JIM DAVIS 8-30
Distributed by Universal Uclick www.facebook.com/garfield
© 2014 PAWS, INC. All Rights Reserved.

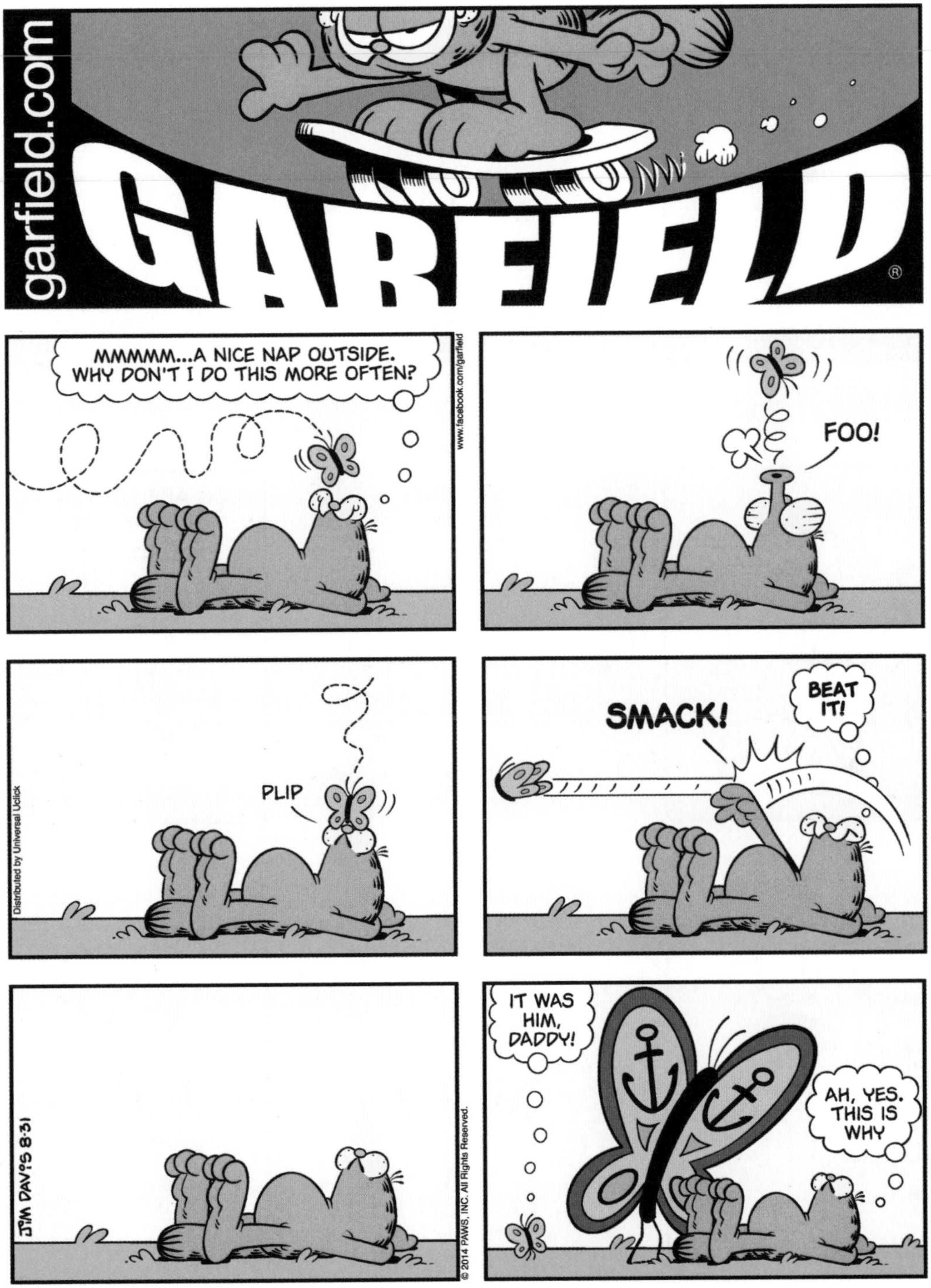
garfield.com
GARFIELD®
MMMMM...A NICE NAP OUTSIDE. WHY DON'T I DO THIS MORE OFTEN?
www.facebook.com/garfield
FOO!
Distributed by Universal Uclick
PLIP
SMACK!
BEAT IT!
JIM DAVIS 8-31
© 2014 PAWS, INC. All Rights Reserved.
IT WAS HIM, DADDY!
AH, YES. THIS IS WHY

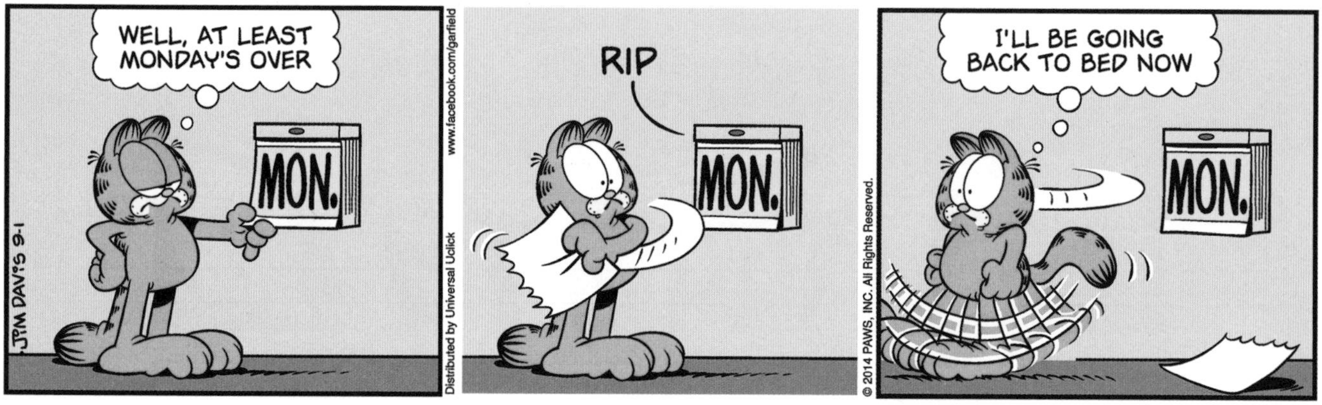

WELL, AT LEAST MONDAY'S OVER
MON.
JIM DAVIS 9-1
Distributed by Universal Uclick
www.facebook.com/garfield
RIP
MON.
© 2014 PAWS, INC. All Rights Reserved.
I'LL BE GOING BACK TO BED NOW
MON.

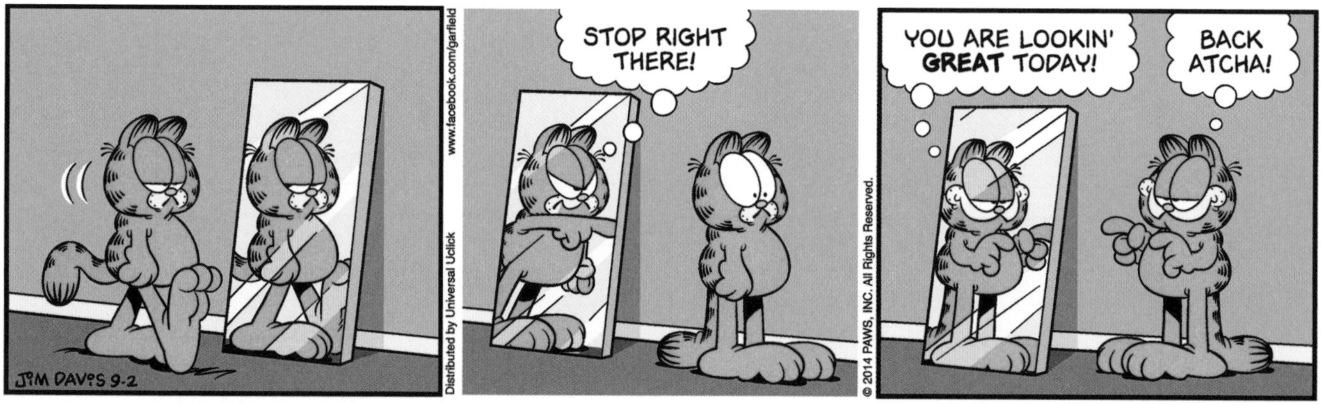

JIM DAVIS 9-2
Distributed by Universal Uclick
www.facebook.com/garfield
STOP RIGHT THERE!
© 2014 PAWS, INC. All Rights Reserved.
YOU ARE LOOKIN' GREAT TODAY!
BACK ATCHA!

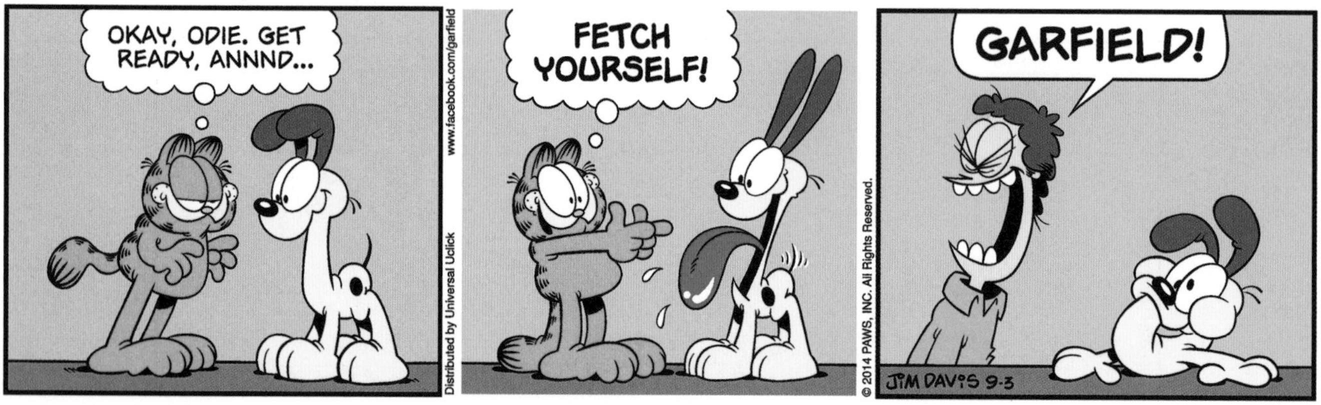

OKAY, ODIE. GET READY, ANNND...
Distributed by Universal Uclick
www.facebook.com/garfield
FETCH YOURSELF!
© 2014 PAWS, INC. All Rights Reserved.
GARFIELD!
JIM DAVIS 9-3

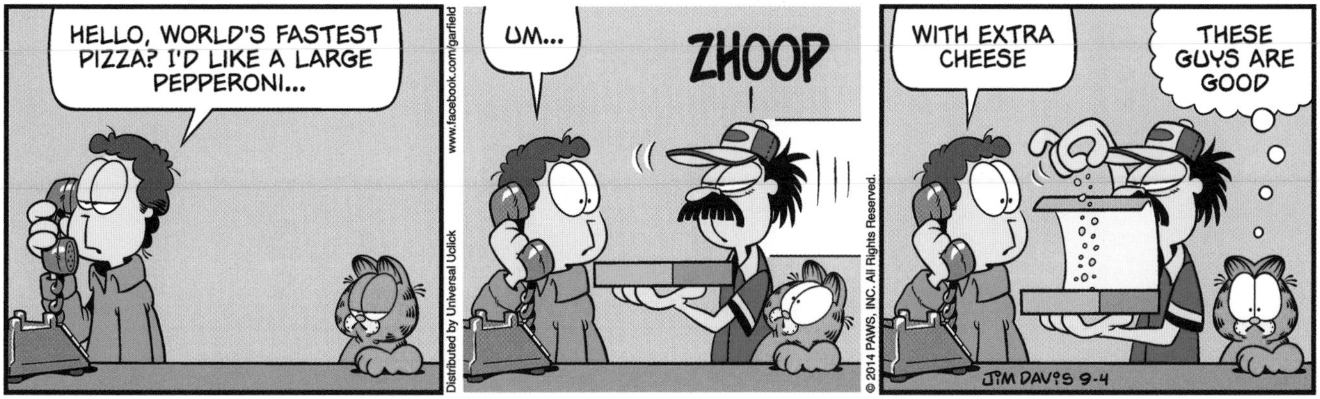
HELLO, WORLD'S FASTEST PIZZA? I'D LIKE A LARGE PEPPERONI...
Distributed by Universal Uclick
www.facebook.com/garfield
UM...
ZHOOP
© 2014 PAWS, INC. All Rights Reserved.
WITH EXTRA CHEESE
THESE GUYS ARE GOOD
JIM DAVIS 9-4

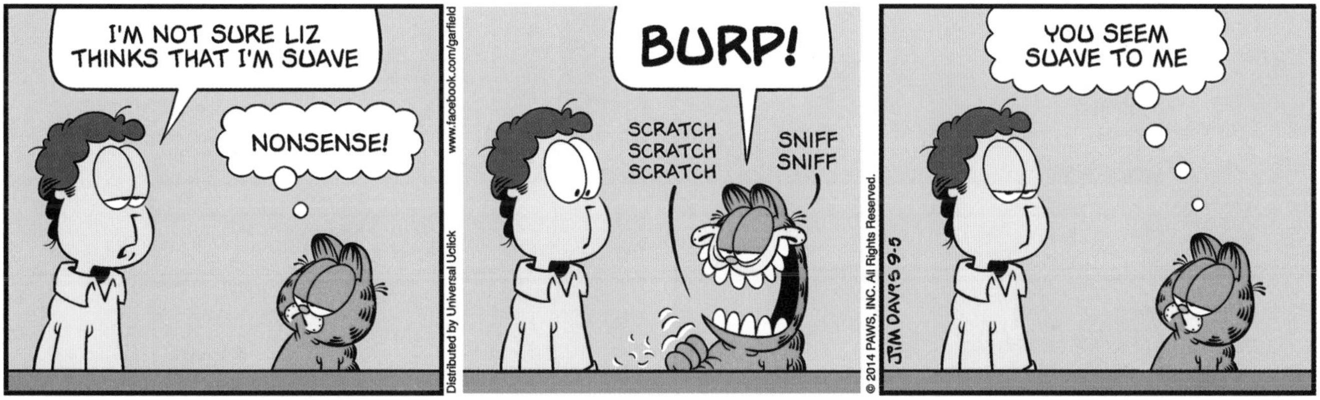
I'M NOT SURE LIZ THINKS THAT I'M SUAVE
NONSENSE!
Distributed by Universal Uclick
www.facebook.com/garfield
BURP!
SCRATCH SCRATCH SCRATCH
SNIFF SNIFF
© 2014 PAWS, INC. All Rights Reserved.
JIM DAVIS 9-5
YOU SEEM SUAVE TO ME

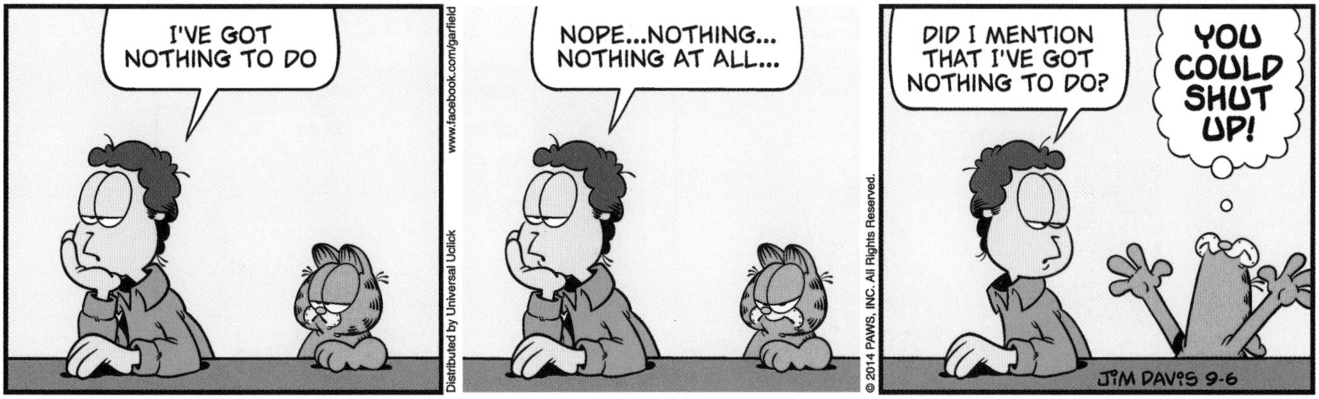
I'VE GOT NOTHING TO DO
Distributed by Universal Uclick
www.facebook.com/garfield
NOPE...NOTHING... NOTHING AT ALL...
© 2014 PAWS, INC. All Rights Reserved.
DID I MENTION THAT I'VE GOT NOTHING TO DO?
YOU COULD SHUT UP!
JIM DAVIS 9-6

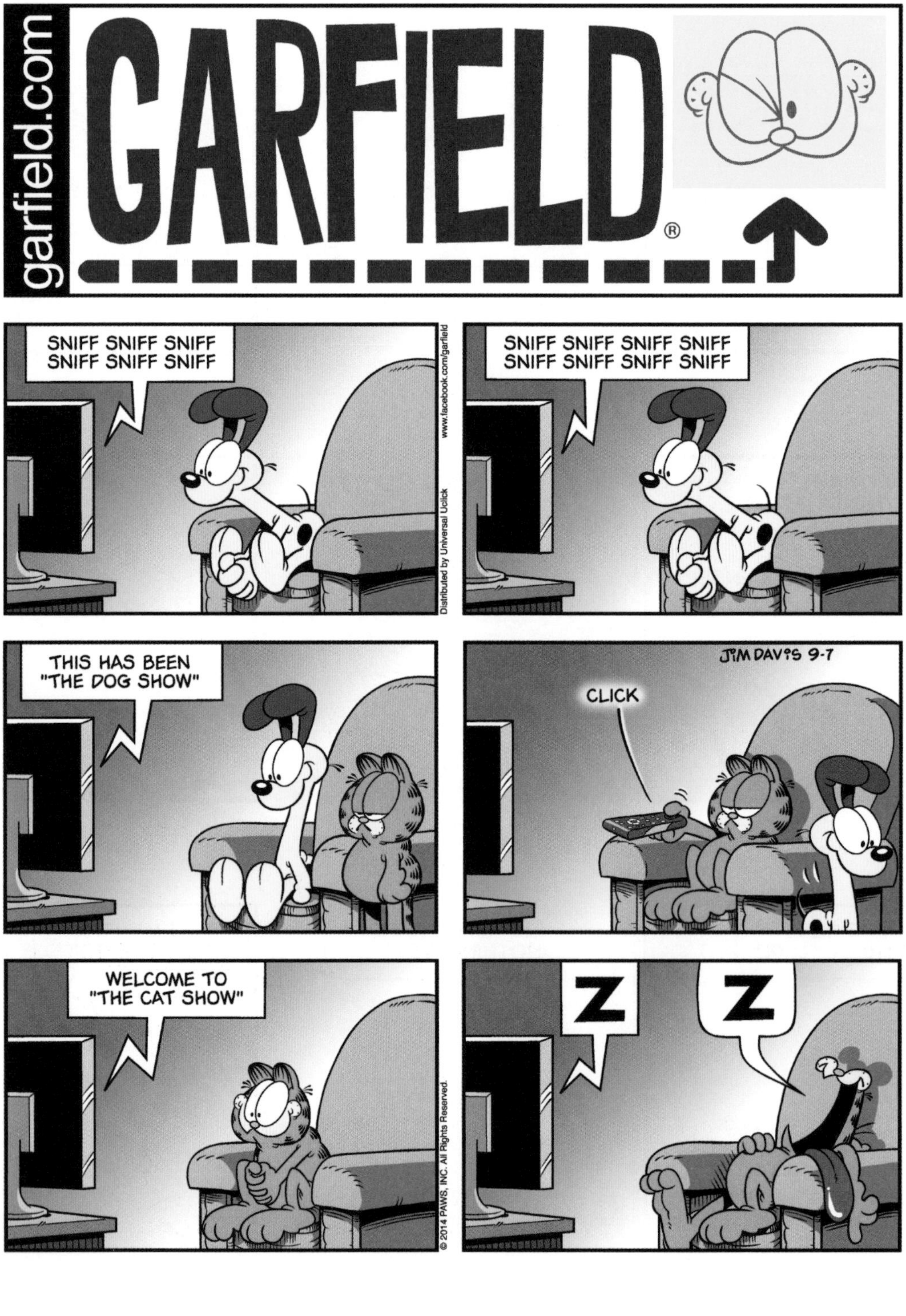
garfield.com
GARFIELD®
SNIFF SNIFF SNIFF SNIFF SNIFF SNIFF
SNIFF SNIFF SNIFF SNIFF SNIFF SNIFF SNIFF SNIFF
Distributed by Universal Uclick www.facebook.com/garfield
THIS HAS BEEN "THE DOG SHOW"
JIM DAVIS 9-7
CLICK
WELCOME TO "THE CAT SHOW"
© 2014 PAWS, INC. All Rights Reserved.
Z
Z

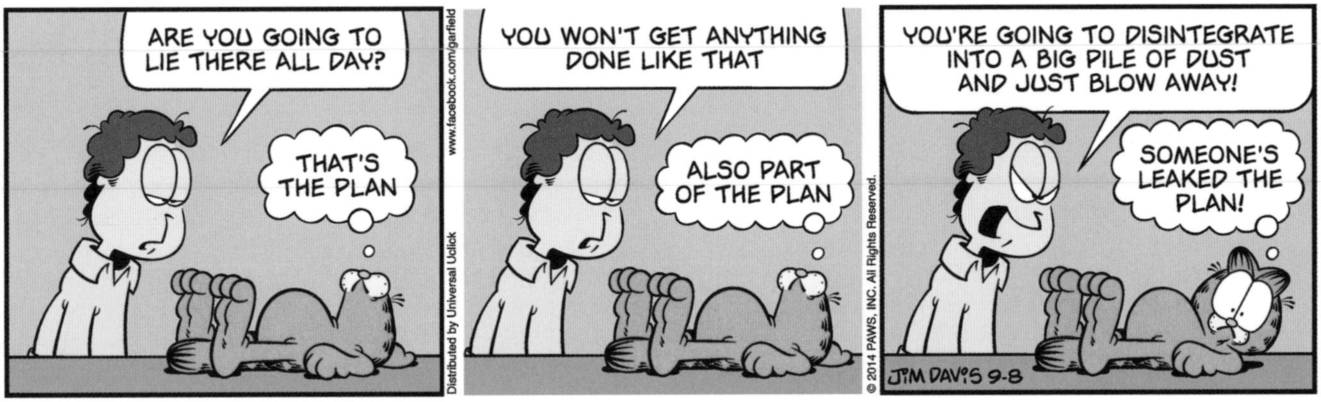
ARE YOU GOING TO LIE THERE ALL DAY?
THAT'S THE PLAN
Distributed by Universal Uclick
www.facebook.com/garfield
YOU WON'T GET ANYTHING DONE LIKE THAT
ALSO PART OF THE PLAN
© 2014 PAWS, INC. All Rights Reserved.
YOU'RE GOING TO DISINTEGRATE INTO A BIG PILE OF DUST AND JUST BLOW AWAY!
SOMEONE'S LEAKED THE PLAN!
JIM DAVIS 9-8

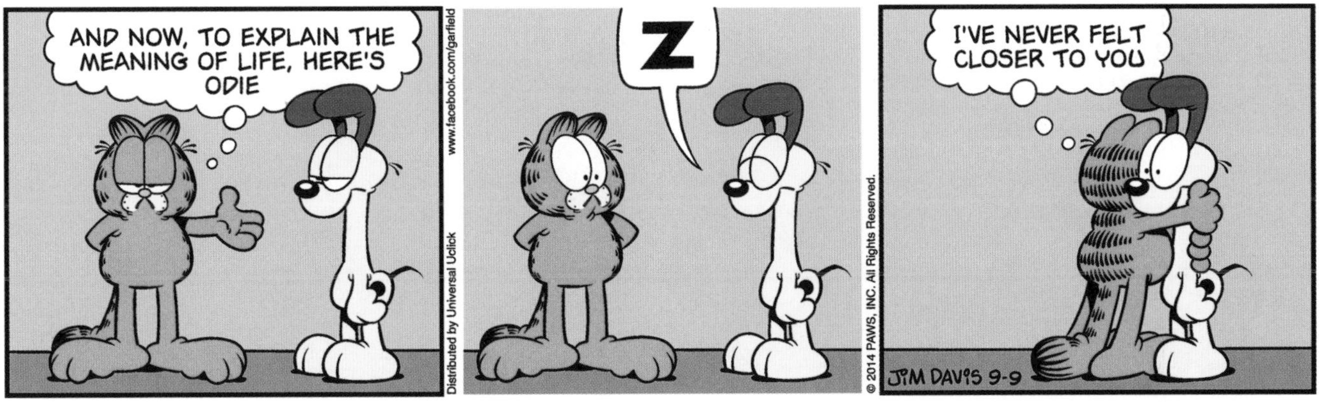
AND NOW, TO EXPLAIN THE MEANING OF LIFE, HERE'S ODIE
Distributed by Universal Uclick
www.facebook.com/garfield
Z
© 2014 PAWS, INC. All Rights Reserved.
I'VE NEVER FELT CLOSER TO YOU
JIM DAVIS 9-9

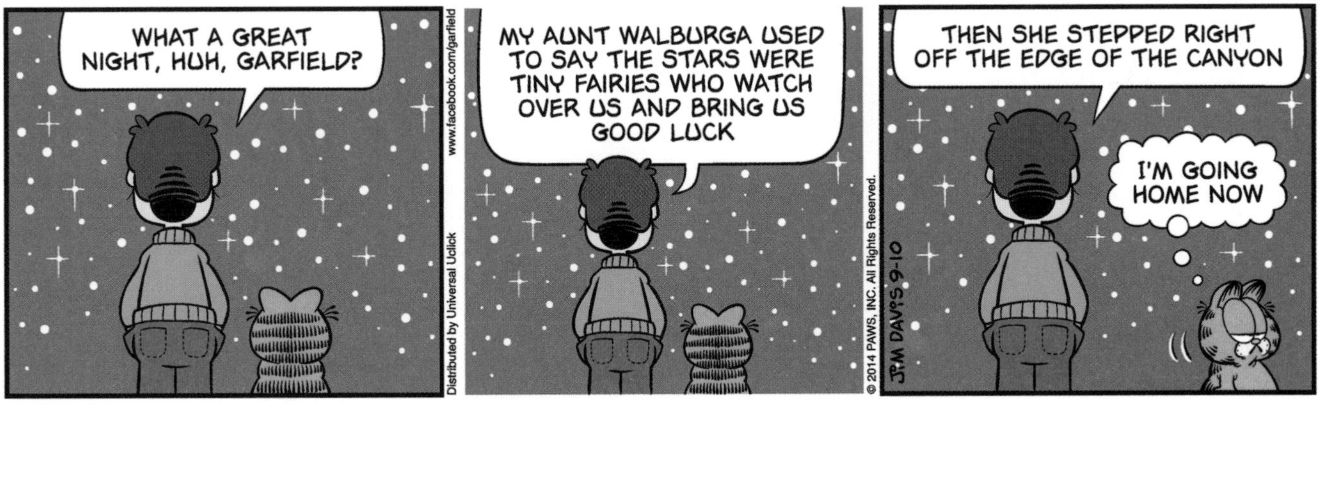
WHAT A GREAT NIGHT, HUH, GARFIELD?
Distributed by Universal Uclick
www.facebook.com/garfield
MY AUNT WALBURGA USED TO SAY THE STARS WERE TINY FAIRIES WHO WATCH OVER US AND BRING US GOOD LUCK
© 2014 PAWS, INC. All Rights Reserved.
JIM DAVIS 9-10
THEN SHE STEPPED RIGHT OFF THE EDGE OF THE CANYON
I'M GOING HOME NOW

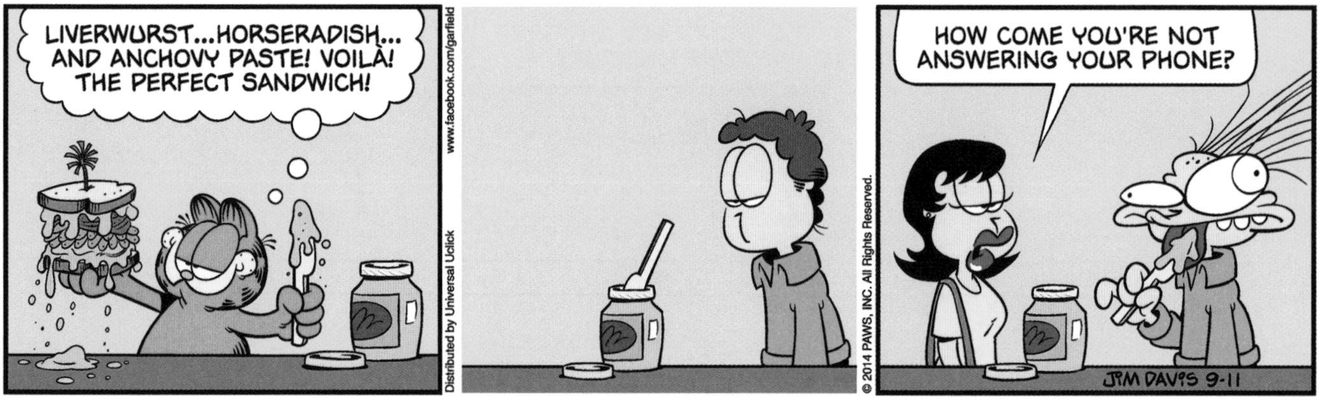
LIVERWURST...HORSERADISH... AND ANCHOVY PASTE! VOILÀ! THE PERFECT SANDWICH!
www.facebook.com/garfield
Distributed by Universal Uclick
© 2014 PAWS, INC. All Rights Reserved.
HOW COME YOU'RE NOT ANSWERING YOUR PHONE?
JIM DAVIS 9-11

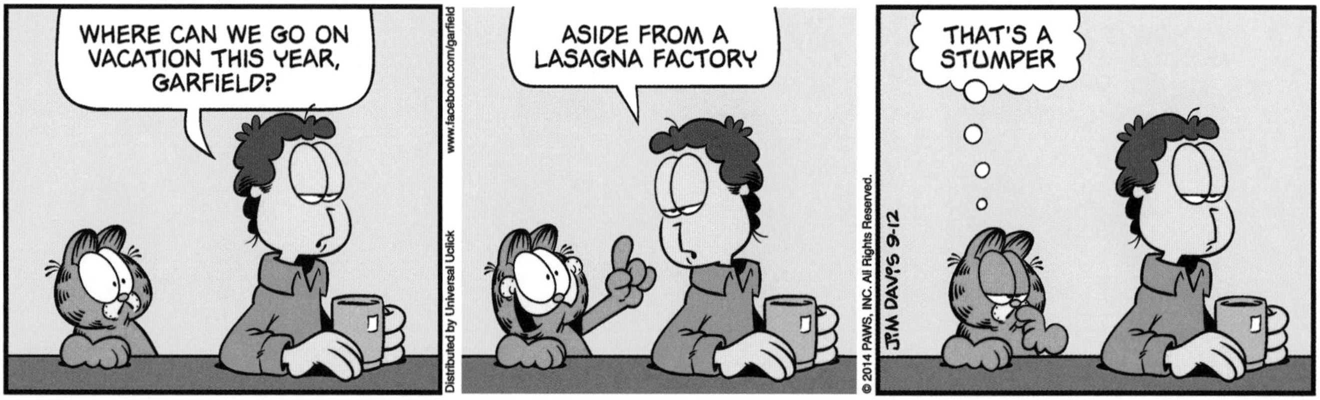
WHERE CAN WE GO ON VACATION THIS YEAR, GARFIELD?
www.facebook.com/garfield
Distributed by Universal Uclick
ASIDE FROM A LASAGNA FACTORY
© 2014 PAWS, INC. All Rights Reserved.
JIM DAVIS 9-12
THAT'S A STUMPER

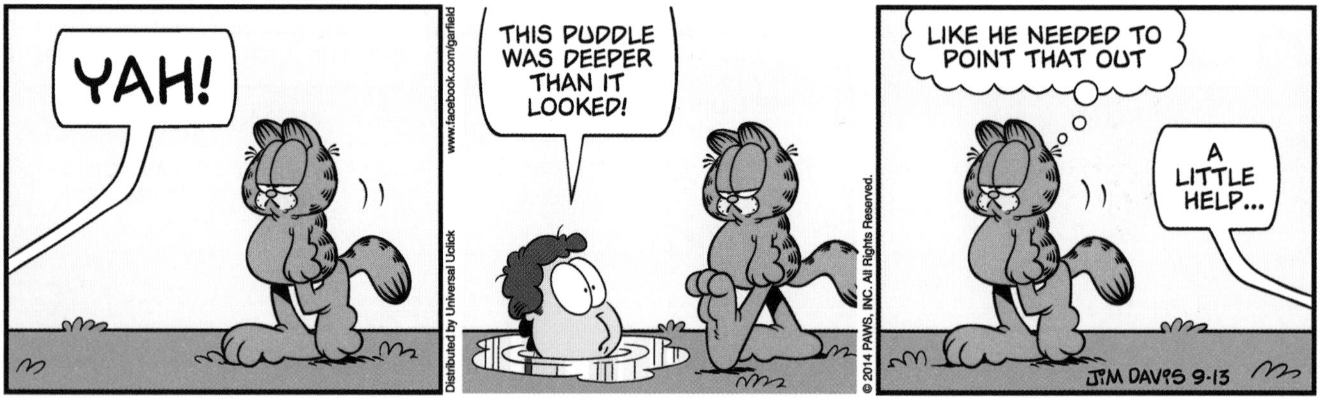
YAH!
www.facebook.com/garfield
Distributed by Universal Uclick
THIS PUDDLE WAS DEEPER THAN IT LOOKED!
© 2014 PAWS, INC. All Rights Reserved.
LIKE HE NEEDED TO POINT THAT OUT
A LITTLE HELP...
JIM DAVIS 9-13

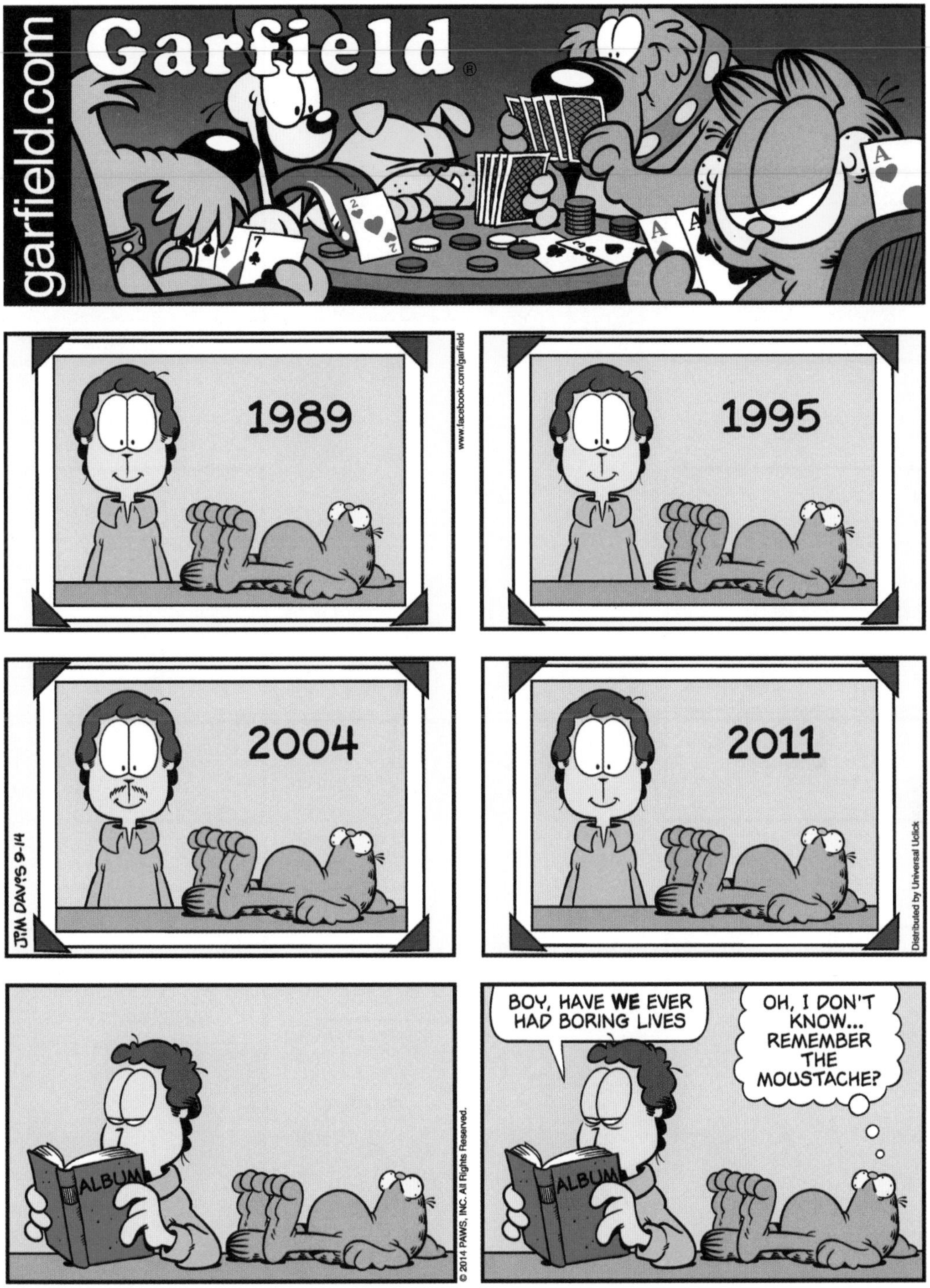
garfield.com
Garfield®
www.facebook.com/garfield
1989
1995
2004
2011
JIM DAVIS 9-14
Distributed by Universal Uclick
ALBUM
© 2014 PAWS, INC. All Rights Reserved.
BOY, HAVE WE EVER HAD BORING LIVES
OH, I DON'T KNOW... REMEMBER THE MOUSTACHE?

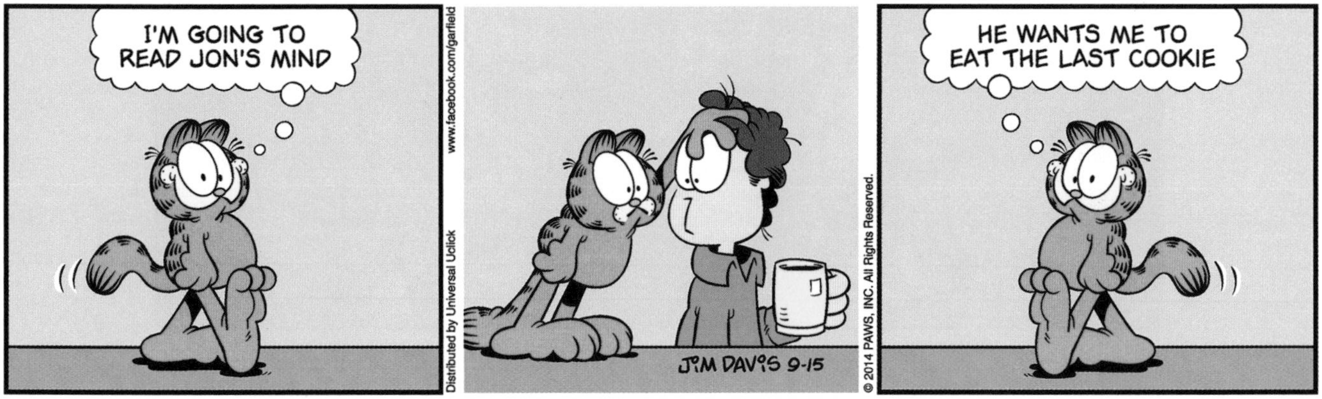
I'M GOING TO READ JON'S MIND
JIM DAVIS 9-15
HE WANTS ME TO EAT THE LAST COOKIE
www.facebook.com/garfield
Distributed by Universal Uclick
© 2014 PAWS, INC. All Rights Reserved.

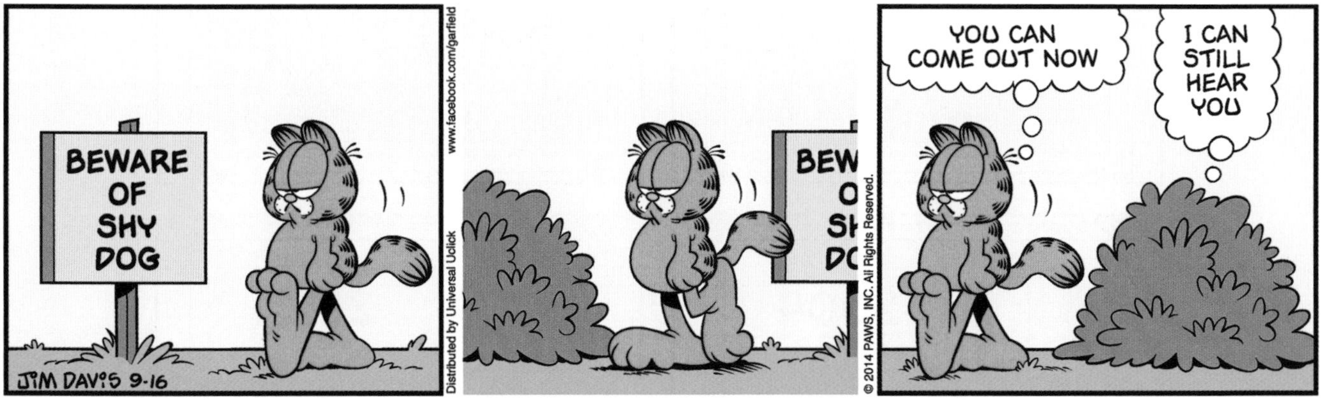
BEWARE OF SHY DOG
JIM DAVIS 9-16
YOU CAN COME OUT NOW
I CAN STILL HEAR YOU
www.facebook.com/garfield
Distributed by Universal Uclick
© 2014 PAWS, INC. All Rights Reserved.

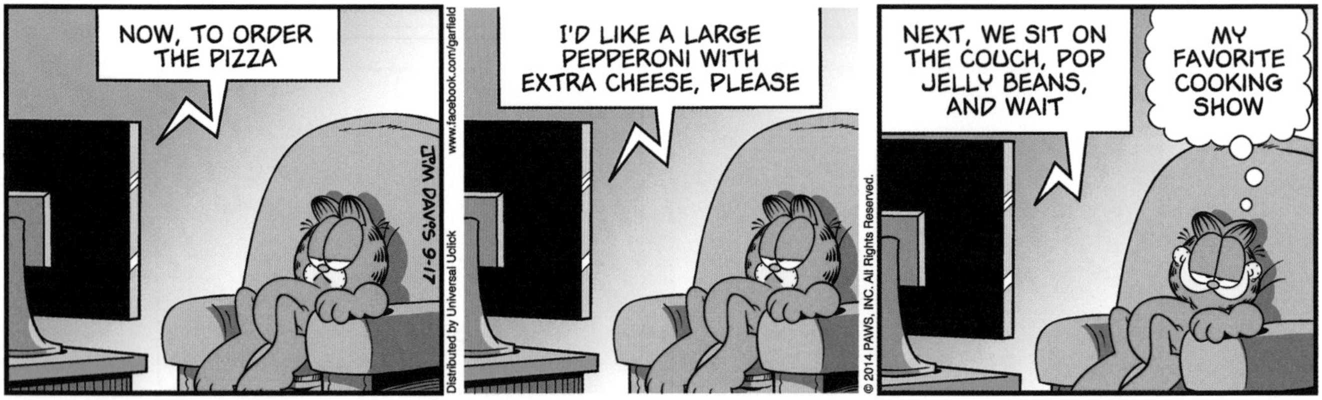
NOW, TO ORDER THE PIZZA
JIM DAVIS 9-17
I'D LIKE A LARGE PEPPERONI WITH EXTRA CHEESE, PLEASE
NEXT, WE SIT ON THE COUCH, POP JELLY BEANS, AND WAIT
MY FAVORITE COOKING SHOW
www.facebook.com/garfield
Distributed by Universal Uclick
© 2014 PAWS, INC. All Rights Reserved.

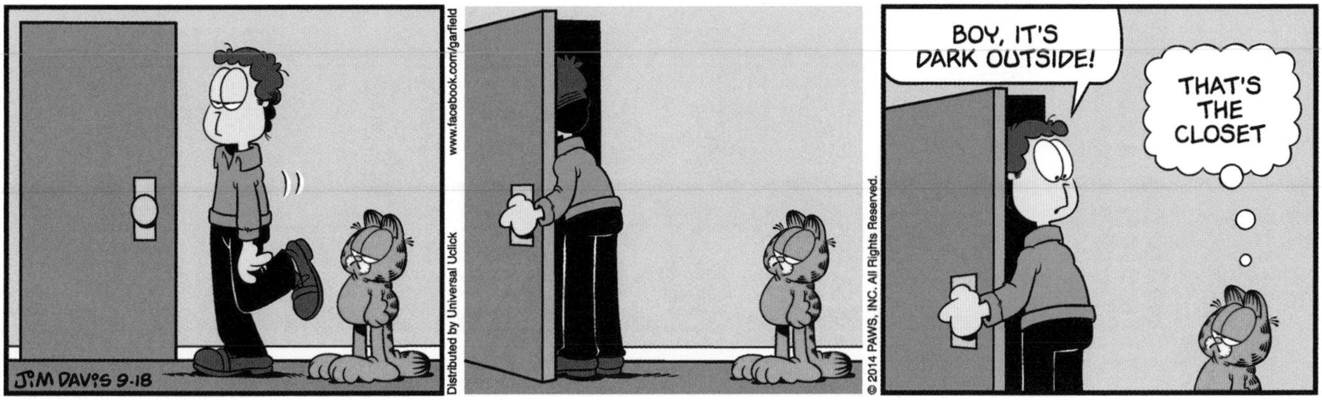
JIM DAVIS 9-18
Distributed by Universal Uclick
www.facebook.com/garfield
© 2014 PAWS, INC. All Rights Reserved.
BOY, IT'S DARK OUTSIDE!
THAT'S THE CLOSET

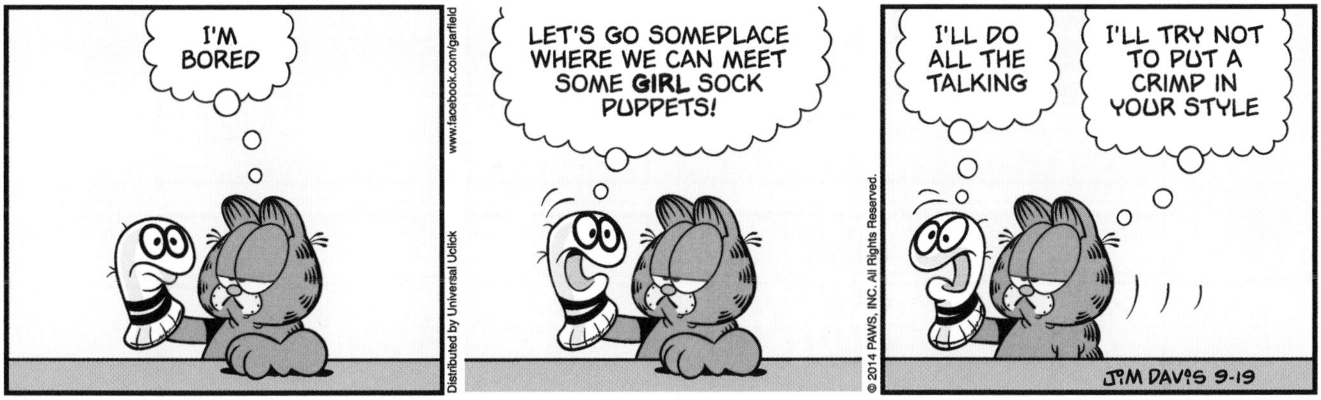
I'M BORED
Distributed by Universal Uclick
www.facebook.com/garfield
LET'S GO SOMEPLACE WHERE WE CAN MEET SOME **GIRL** SOCK PUPPETS!
© 2014 PAWS, INC. All Rights Reserved.
I'LL DO ALL THE TALKING
I'LL TRY NOT TO PUT A CRIMP IN YOUR STYLE
JIM DAVIS 9-19

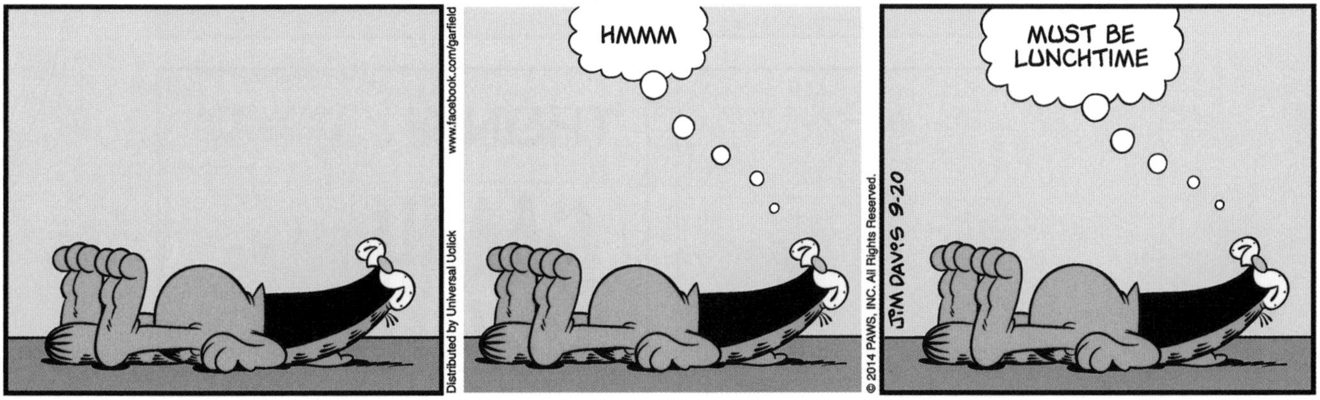
Distributed by Universal Uclick
www.facebook.com/garfield
HMMM
© 2014 PAWS, INC. All Rights Reserved.
JIM DAVIS 9-20
MUST BE LUNCHTIME

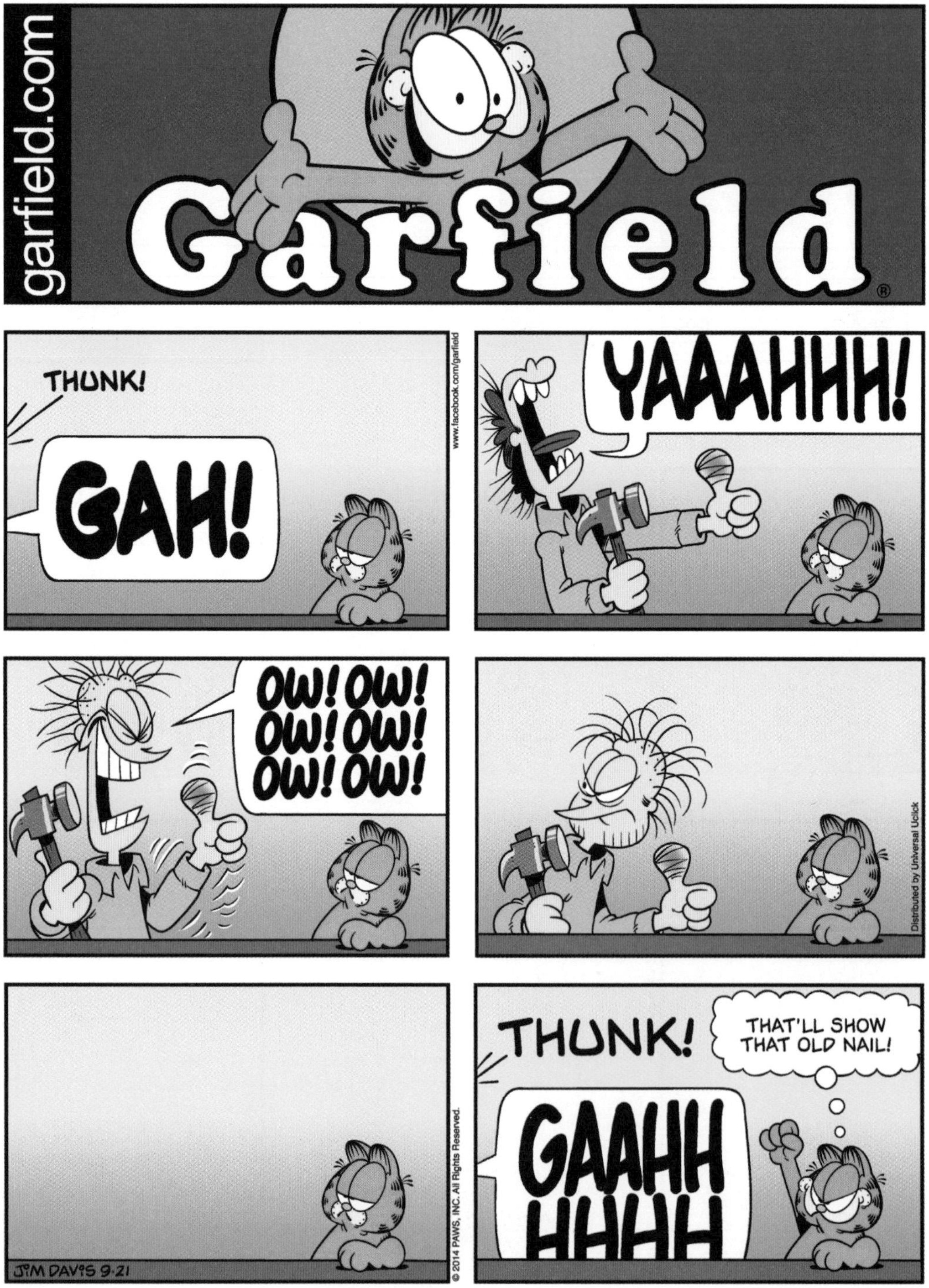
garfield.com
Garfield®
www.facebook.com/garfield
THUNK!
GAH!
YAAAHHH!
OW! OW!
OW! OW!
OW! OW!
Distributed by Universal Uclick
JIM DAVIS 9-21
© 2014 PAWS, INC. All Rights Reserved.
THUNK!
GAAHH
HHHH
THAT'LL SHOW
THAT OLD NAIL!

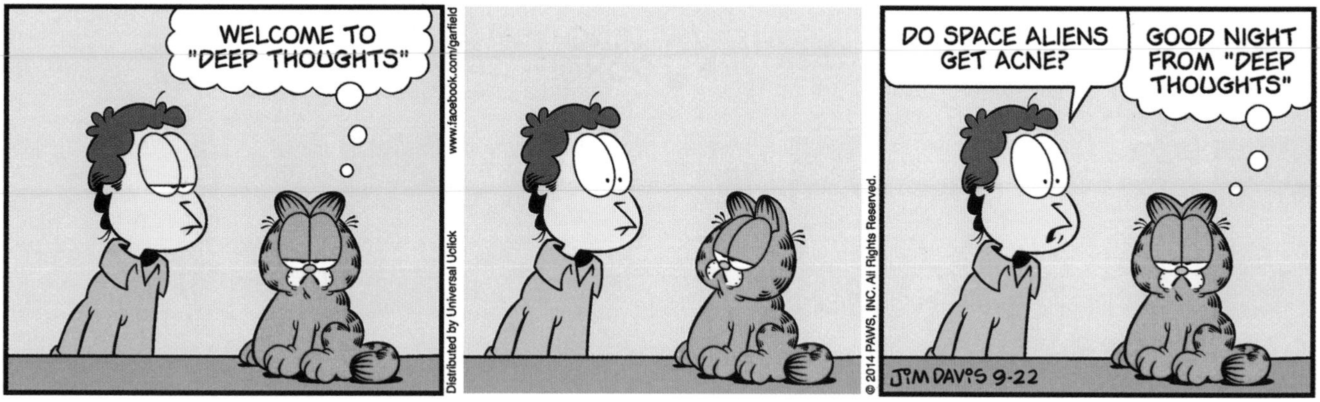
WELCOME TO "DEEP THOUGHTS"
www.facebook.com/garfield
Distributed by Universal Uclick
DO SPACE ALIENS GET ACNE?
GOOD NIGHT FROM "DEEP THOUGHTS"
© 2014 PAWS, INC. All Rights Reserved.
JIM DAVIS 9-22

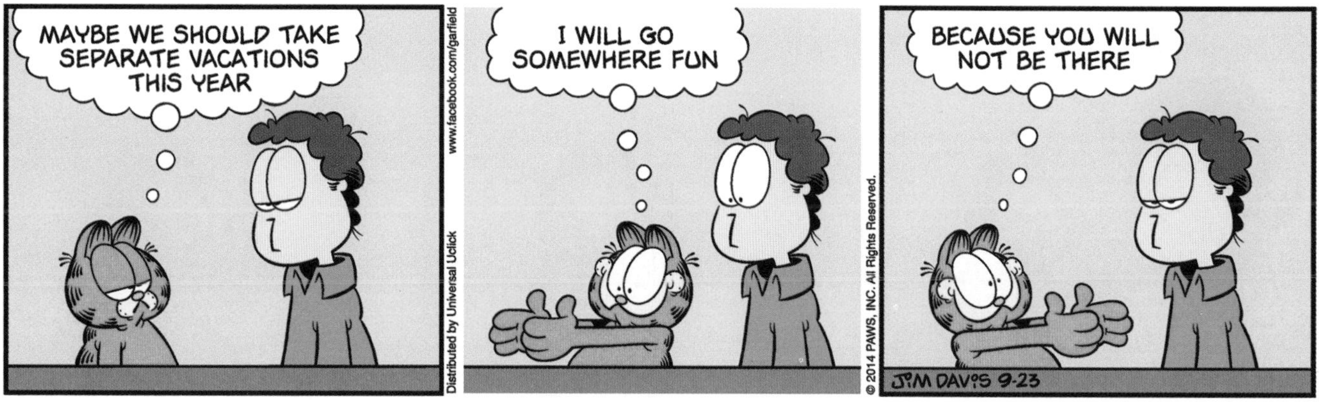
MAYBE WE SHOULD TAKE SEPARATE VACATIONS THIS YEAR
www.facebook.com/garfield
Distributed by Universal Uclick
I WILL GO SOMEWHERE FUN
BECAUSE YOU WILL NOT BE THERE
© 2014 PAWS, INC. All Rights Reserved.
JIM DAVIS 9-23

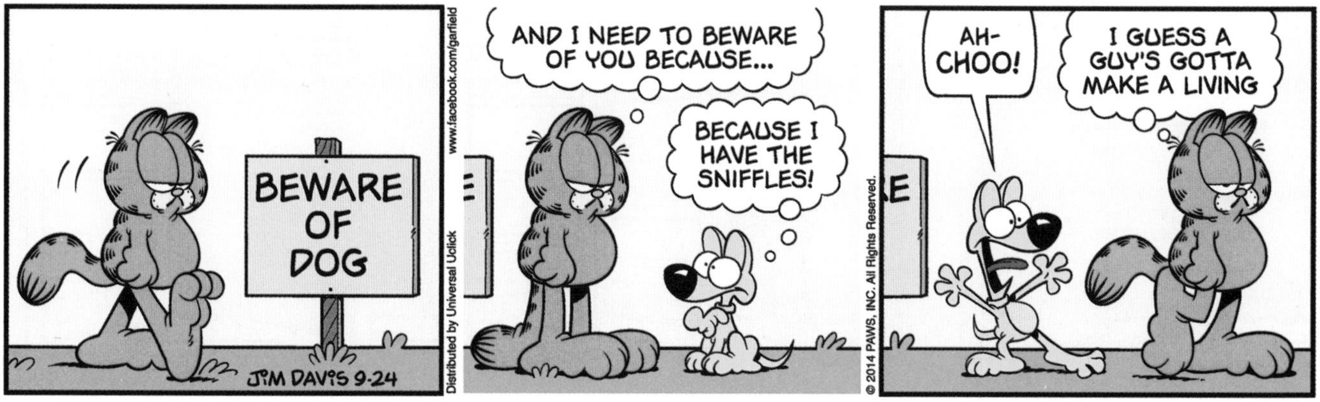
BEWARE OF DOG
JIM DAVIS 9-24
www.facebook.com/garfield
Distributed by Universal Uclick
AND I NEED TO BEWARE OF YOU BECAUSE...
BECAUSE I HAVE THE SNIFFLES!
© 2014 PAWS, INC. All Rights Reserved.
AH-CHOO!
I GUESS A GUY'S GOTTA MAKE A LIVING

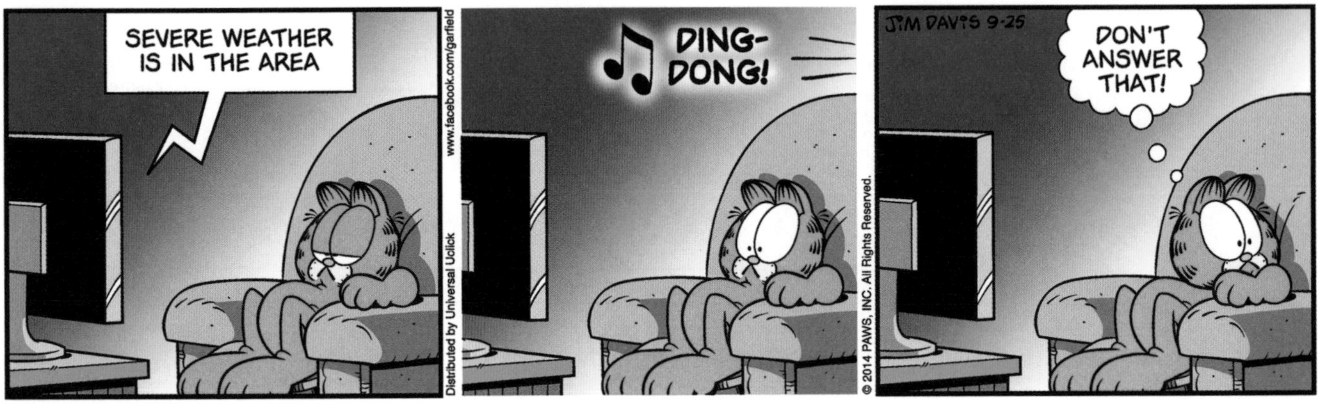
SEVERE WEATHER IS IN THE AREA
Distributed by Universal Uclick
www.facebook.com/garfield
DING-DONG!
© 2014 PAWS, INC. All Rights Reserved.
JIM DAVIS 9-25
DON'T ANSWER THAT!

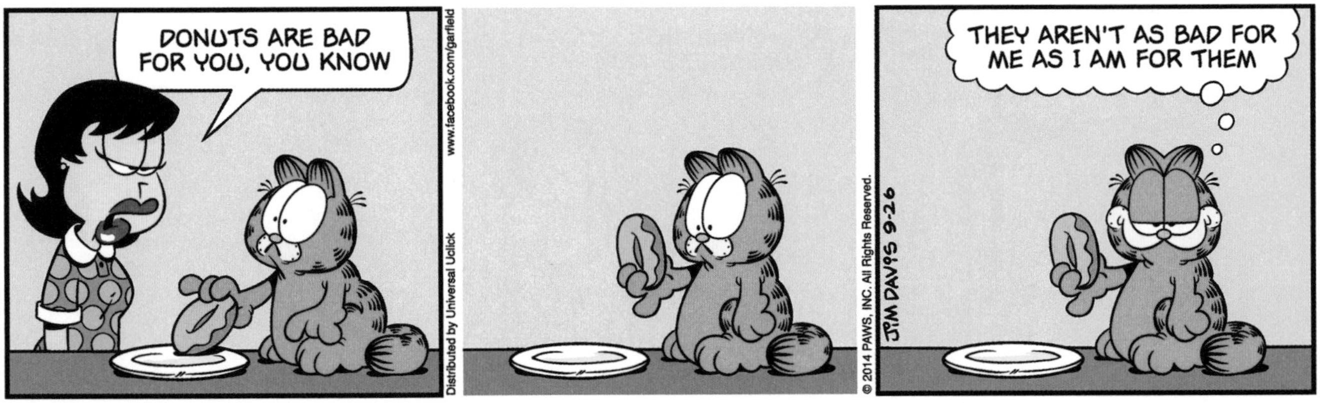
DONUTS ARE BAD FOR YOU, YOU KNOW
Distributed by Universal Uclick
www.facebook.com/garfield
© 2014 PAWS, INC. All Rights Reserved.
JIM DAVIS 9-26
THEY AREN'T AS BAD FOR ME AS I AM FOR THEM

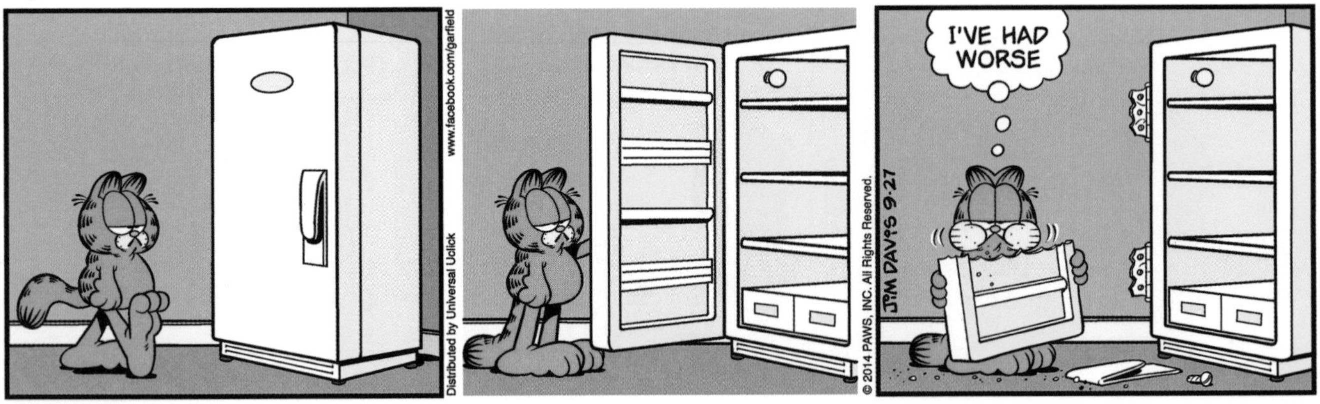
Distributed by Universal Uclick
www.facebook.com/garfield
© 2014 PAWS, INC. All Rights Reserved.
JIM DAVIS 9-27
I'VE HAD WORSE

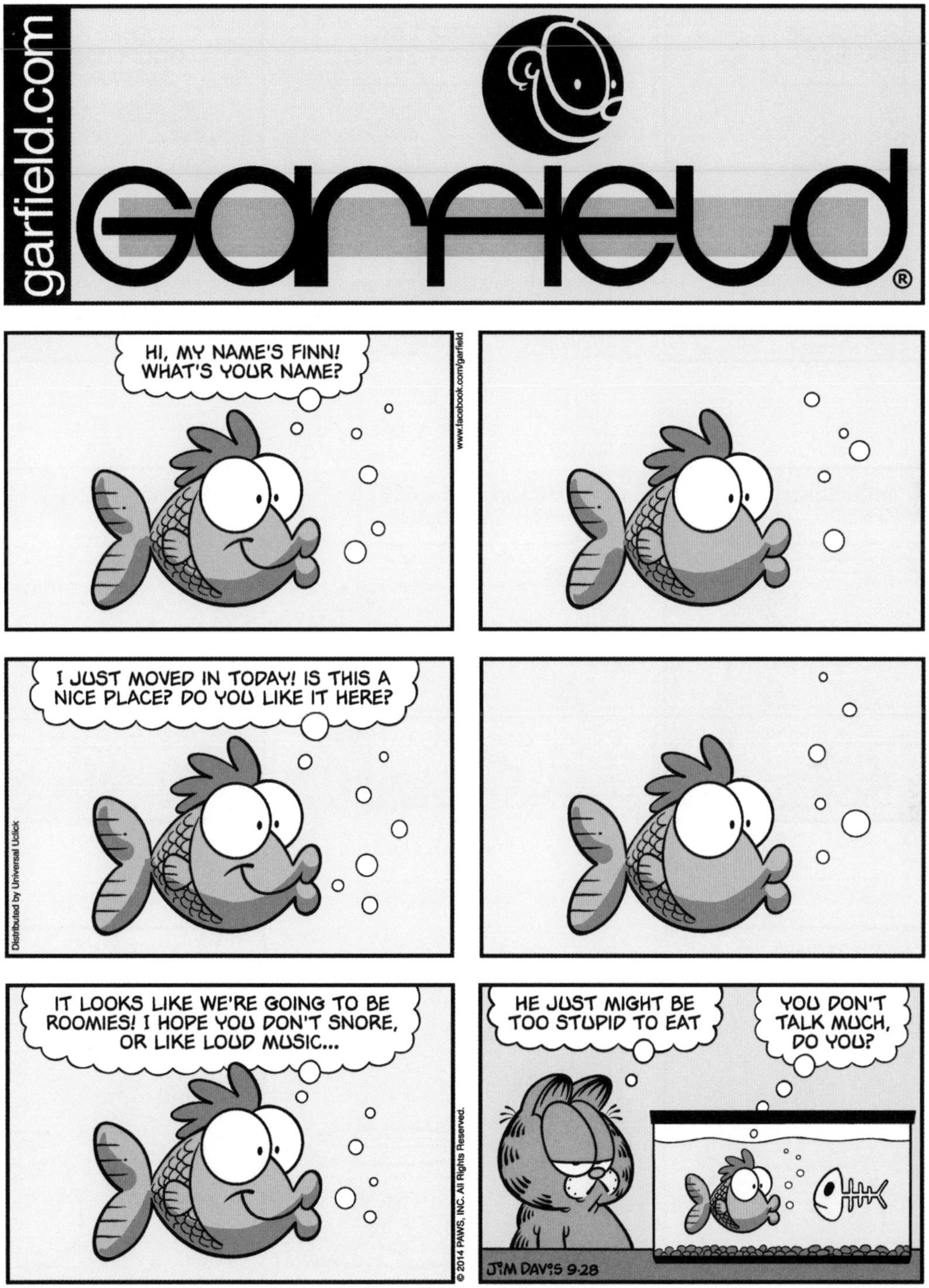
garfield.com
GARFIELD®
HI, MY NAME'S FINN! WHAT'S YOUR NAME?
www.facebook.com/garfield
I JUST MOVED IN TODAY! IS THIS A NICE PLACE? DO YOU LIKE IT HERE?
Distributed by Universal Uclick
IT LOOKS LIKE WE'RE GOING TO BE ROOMIES! I HOPE YOU DON'T SNORE, OR LIKE LOUD MUSIC...
© 2014 PAWS, INC. All Rights Reserved.
HE JUST MIGHT BE TOO STUPID TO EAT
YOU DON'T TALK MUCH, DO YOU?
JIM DAVIS 9-28

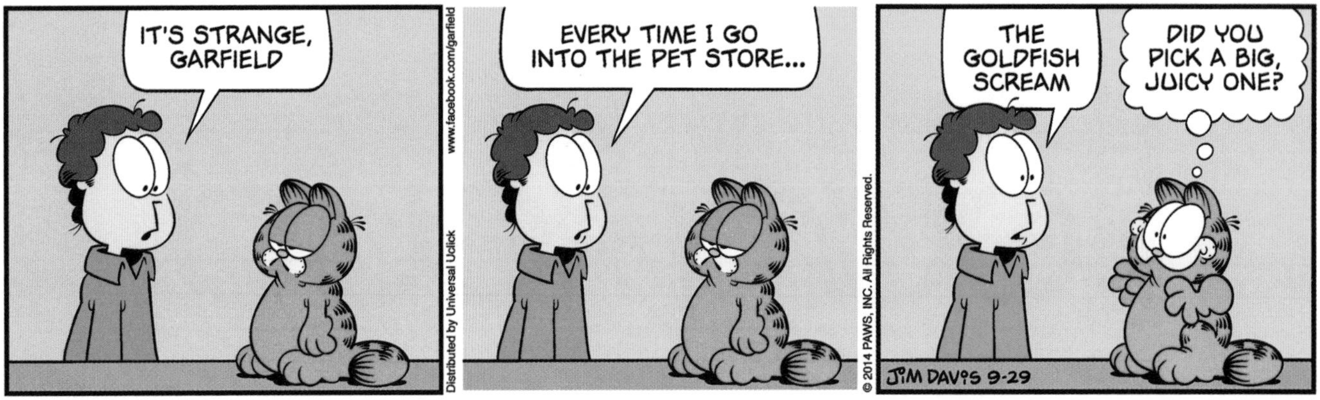
IT'S STRANGE, GARFIELD
EVERY TIME I GO INTO THE PET STORE...
THE GOLDFISH SCREAM
DID YOU PICK A BIG, JUICY ONE?
JIM DAVIS 9-29
Distributed by Universal Uclick
www.facebook.com/garfield
© 2014 PAWS, INC. All Rights Reserved.

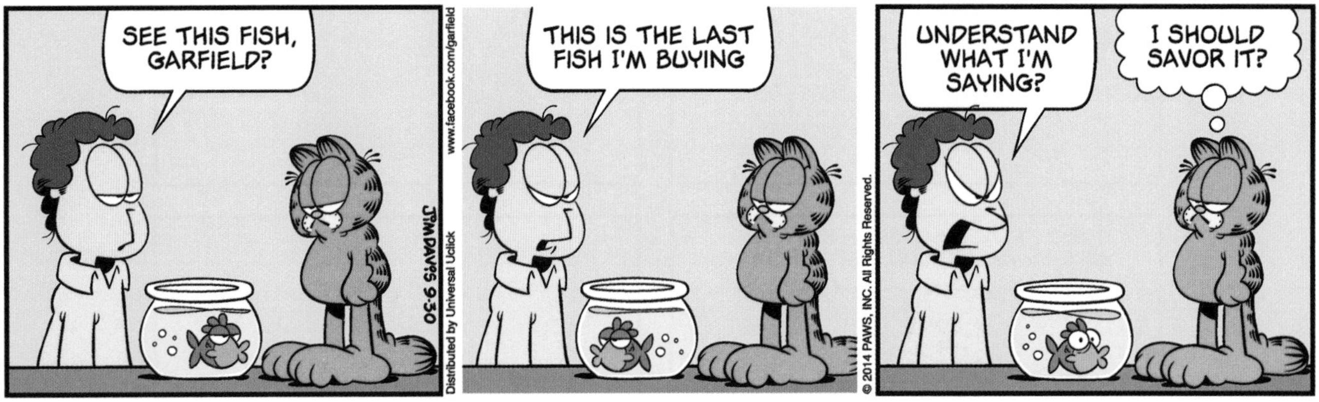
SEE THIS FISH, GARFIELD?
THIS IS THE LAST FISH I'M BUYING
UNDERSTAND WHAT I'M SAYING?
I SHOULD SAVOR IT?
JIM DAVIS 9-30
Distributed by Universal Uclick
www.facebook.com/garfield
© 2014 PAWS, INC. All Rights Reserved.

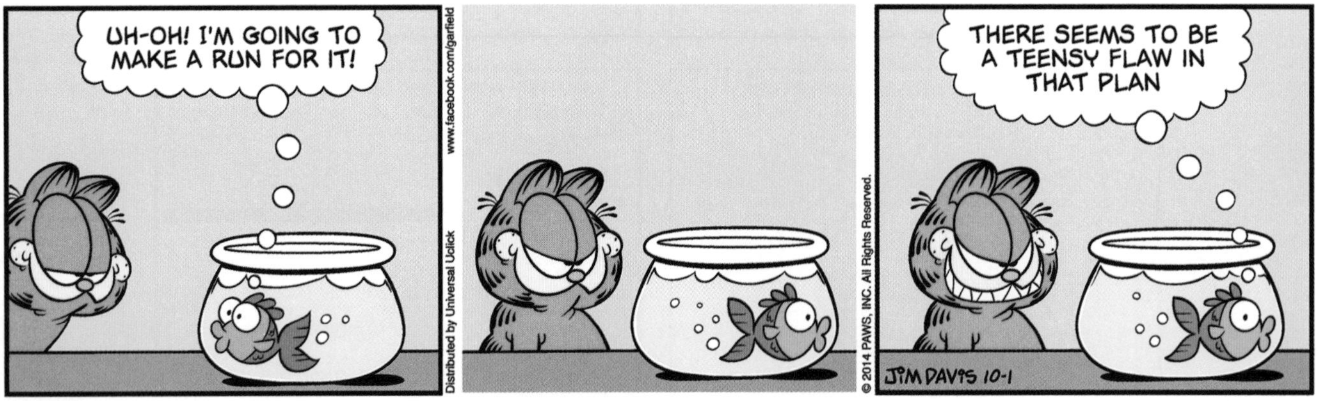
UH-OH! I'M GOING TO MAKE A RUN FOR IT!
THERE SEEMS TO BE A TEENSY FLAW IN THAT PLAN
JIM DAVIS 10-1
Distributed by Universal Uclick
www.facebook.com/garfield
© 2014 PAWS, INC. All Rights Reserved.

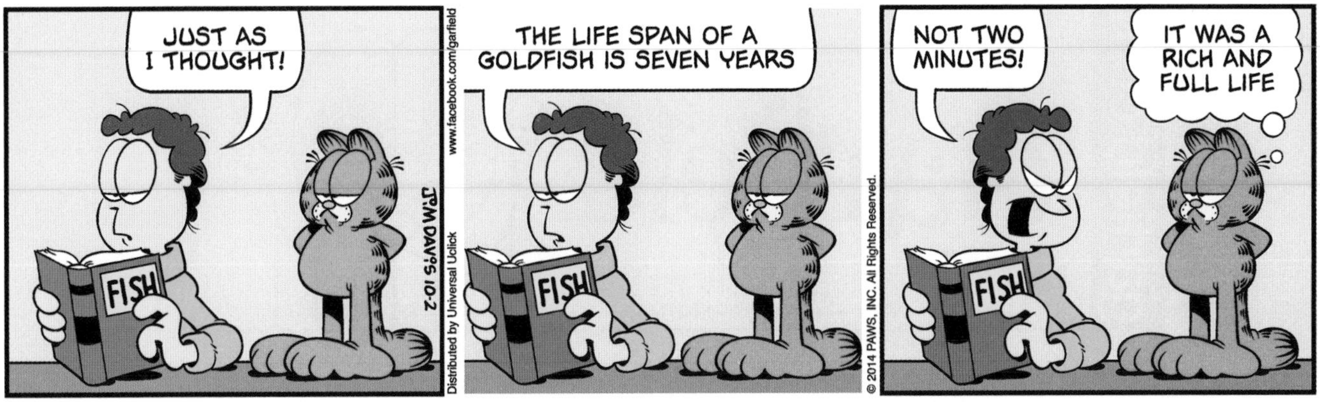
JUST AS I THOUGHT!
THE LIFE SPAN OF A GOLDFISH IS SEVEN YEARS
NOT TWO MINUTES!
IT WAS A RICH AND FULL LIFE
FISH
JIM DAVIS 10-2
www.facebook.com/garfield
Distributed by Universal Uclick
© 2014 PAWS, INC. All Rights Reserved.

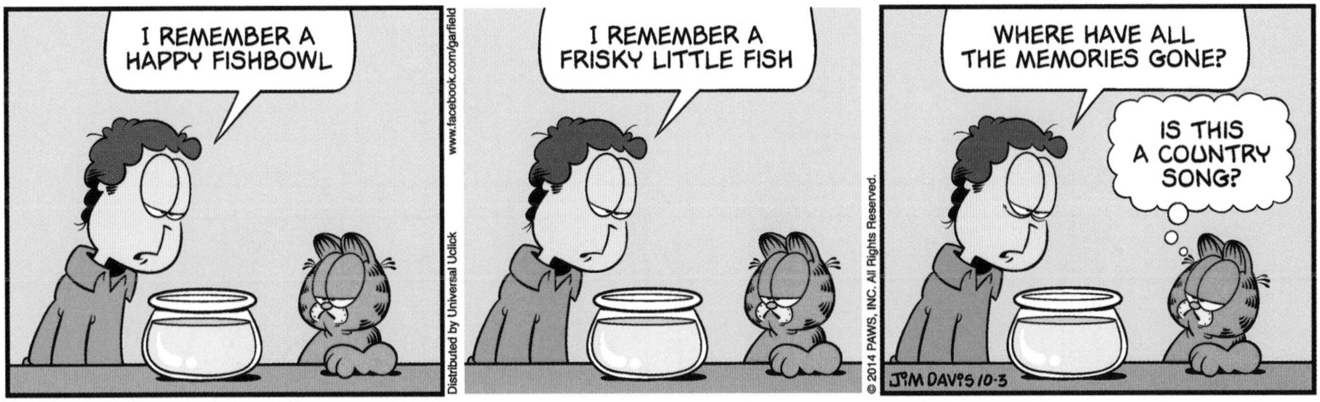
I REMEMBER A HAPPY FISHBOWL
I REMEMBER A FRISKY LITTLE FISH
WHERE HAVE ALL THE MEMORIES GONE?
IS THIS A COUNTRY SONG?
JIM DAVIS 10-3
www.facebook.com/garfield
Distributed by Universal Uclick
© 2014 PAWS, INC. All Rights Reserved.

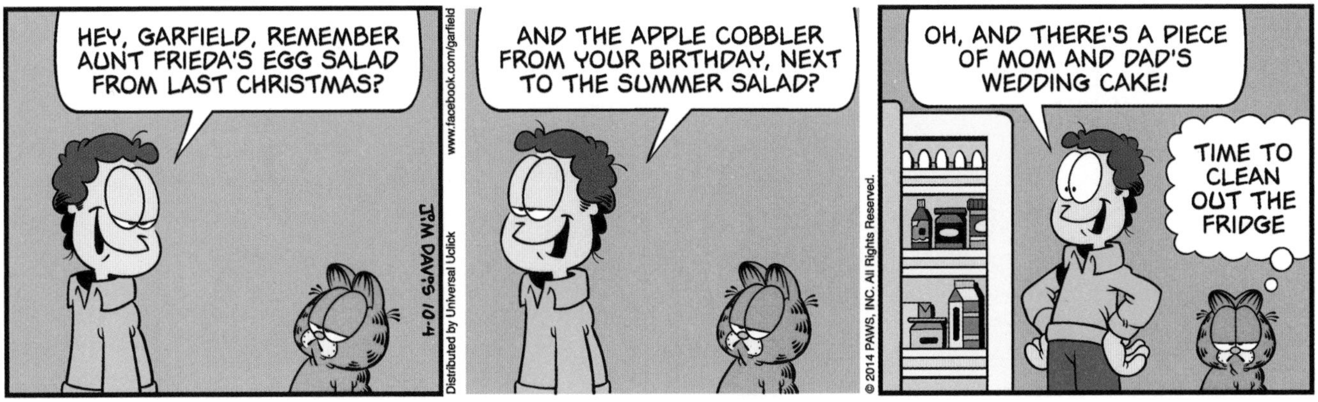
HEY, GARFIELD, REMEMBER AUNT FRIEDA'S EGG SALAD FROM LAST CHRISTMAS?
AND THE APPLE COBBLER FROM YOUR BIRTHDAY, NEXT TO THE SUMMER SALAD?
OH, AND THERE'S A PIECE OF MOM AND DAD'S WEDDING CAKE!
TIME TO CLEAN OUT THE FRIDGE
JIM DAVIS 10-4
www.facebook.com/garfield
Distributed by Universal Uclick
© 2014 PAWS, INC. All Rights Reserved.

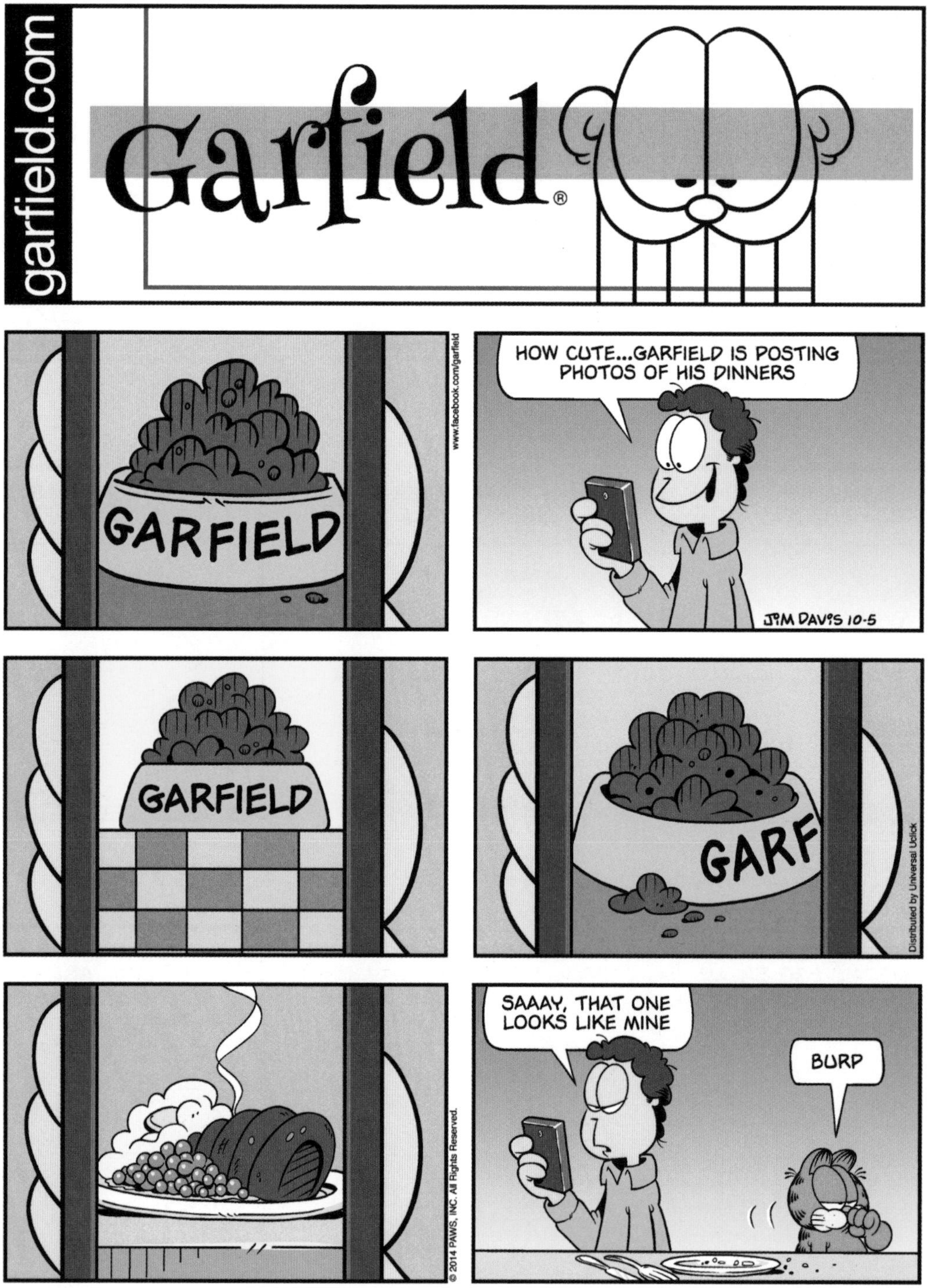
garfield.com
Garfield
GARFIELD
www.facebook.com/garfield
HOW CUTE...GARFIELD IS POSTING PHOTOS OF HIS DINNERS
JIM DAVIS 10-5
GARFIELD
GARF
Distributed by Universal Uclick
© 2014 PAWS, INC. All Rights Reserved.
SAAAY, THAT ONE LOOKS LIKE MINE
BURP

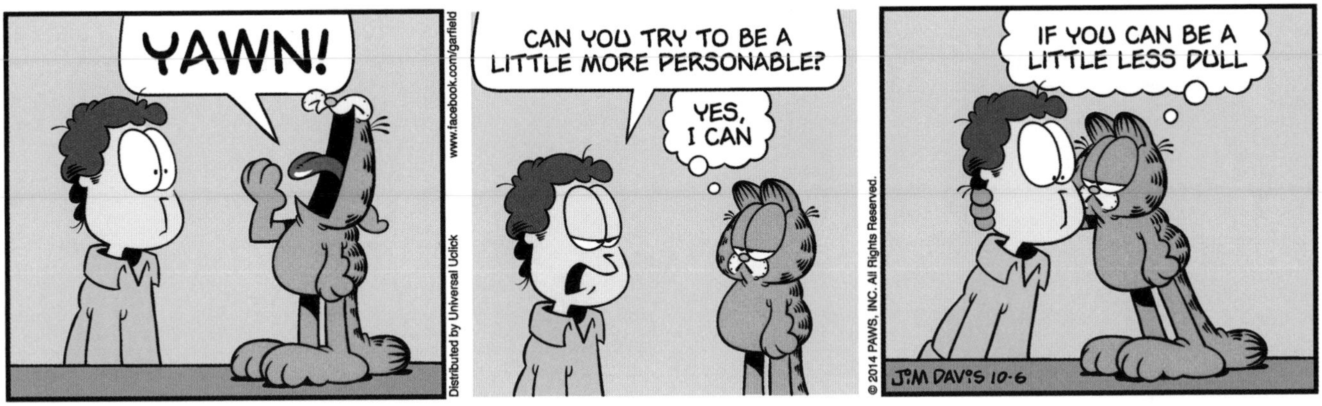
YAWN!
www.facebook.com/garfield
Distributed by Universal Uclick
CAN YOU TRY TO BE A LITTLE MORE PERSONABLE?
YES, I CAN
© 2014 PAWS, INC. All Rights Reserved.
IF YOU CAN BE A LITTLE LESS DULL
JIM DAVIS 10-6

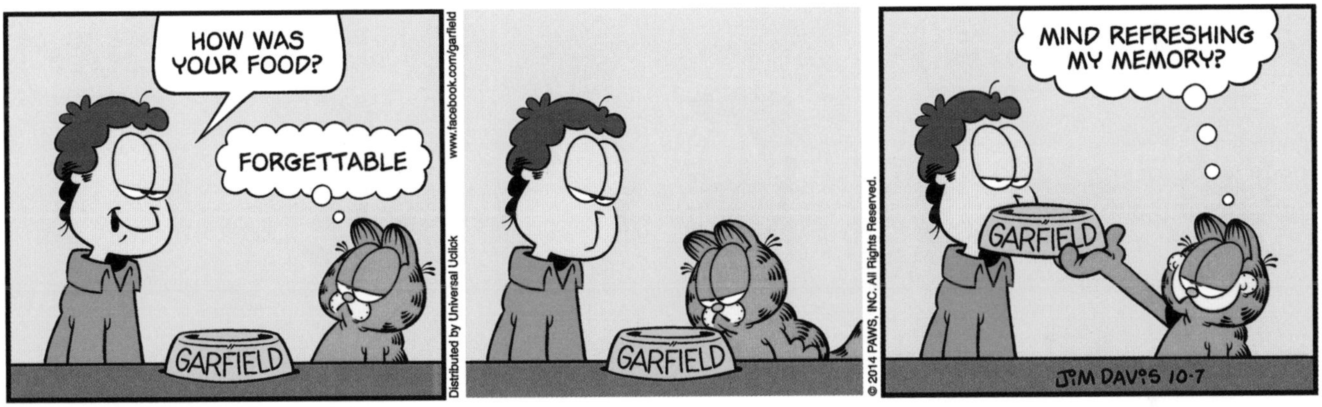
HOW WAS YOUR FOOD?
FORGETTABLE
GARFIELD
Distributed by Universal Uclick
www.facebook.com/garfield
GARFIELD
© 2014 PAWS, INC. All Rights Reserved.
MIND REFRESHING MY MEMORY?
GARFIELD
JIM DAVIS 10-7

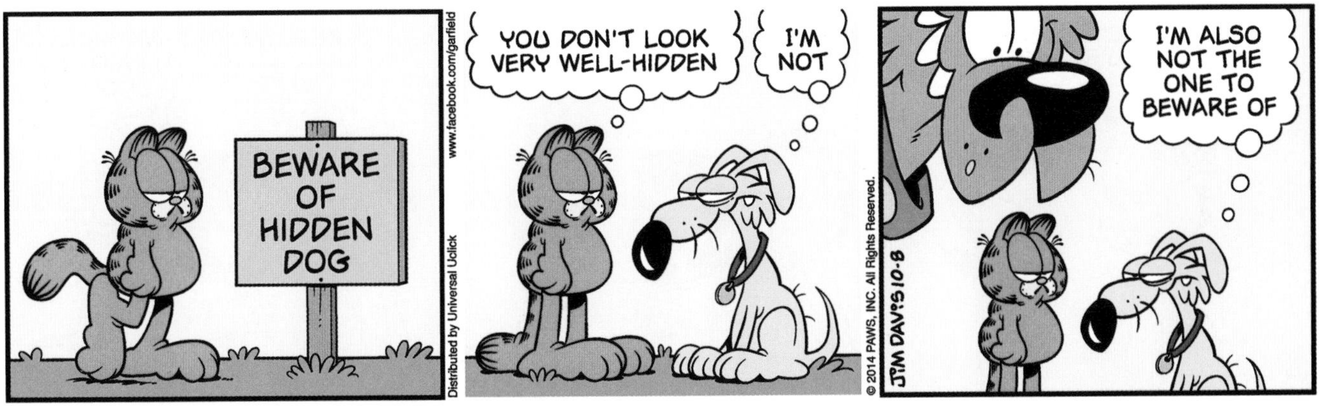
BEWARE OF HIDDEN DOG
www.facebook.com/garfield
Distributed by Universal Uclick
YOU DON'T LOOK VERY WELL-HIDDEN
I'M NOT
© 2014 PAWS, INC. All Rights Reserved.
JIM DAVIS 10-8
I'M ALSO NOT THE ONE TO BEWARE OF

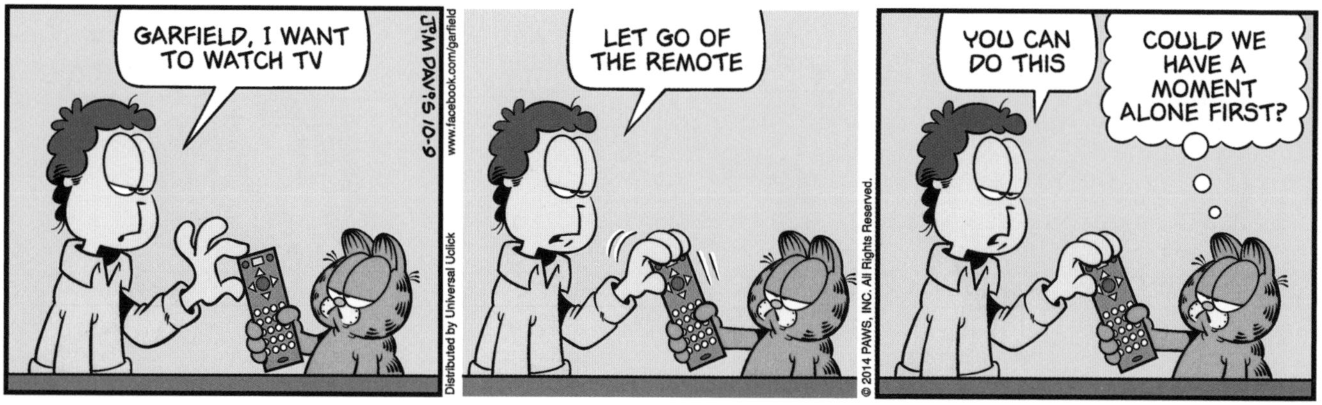
GARFIELD, I WANT TO WATCH TV
JIM DAVIS 10-9
www.facebook.com/garfield
Distributed by Universal Uclick
LET GO OF THE REMOTE
© 2014 PAWS, INC. All Rights Reserved.
YOU CAN DO THIS
COULD WE HAVE A MOMENT ALONE FIRST?

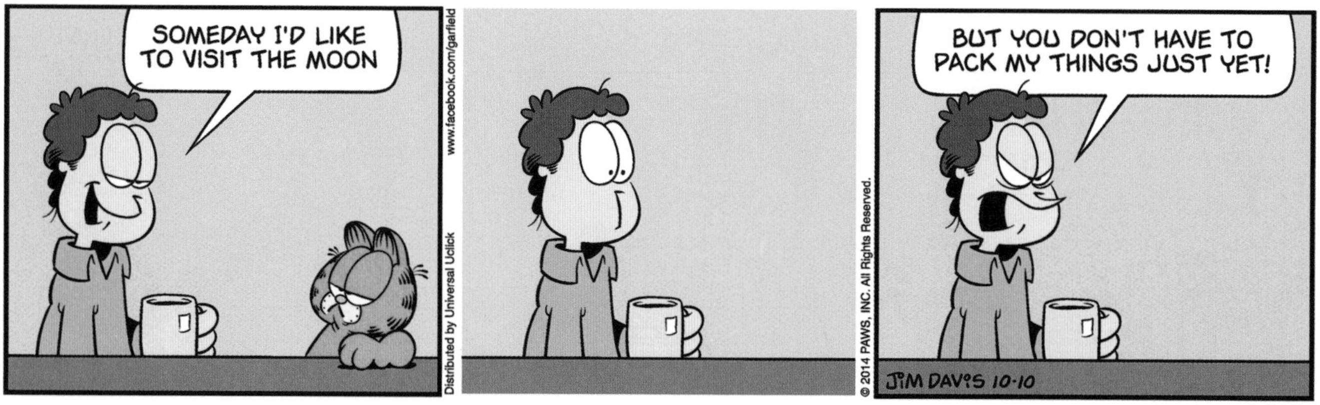
SOMEDAY I'D LIKE TO VISIT THE MOON
www.facebook.com/garfield
Distributed by Universal Uclick
© 2014 PAWS, INC. All Rights Reserved.
BUT YOU DON'T HAVE TO PACK MY THINGS JUST YET!
JIM DAVIS 10-10

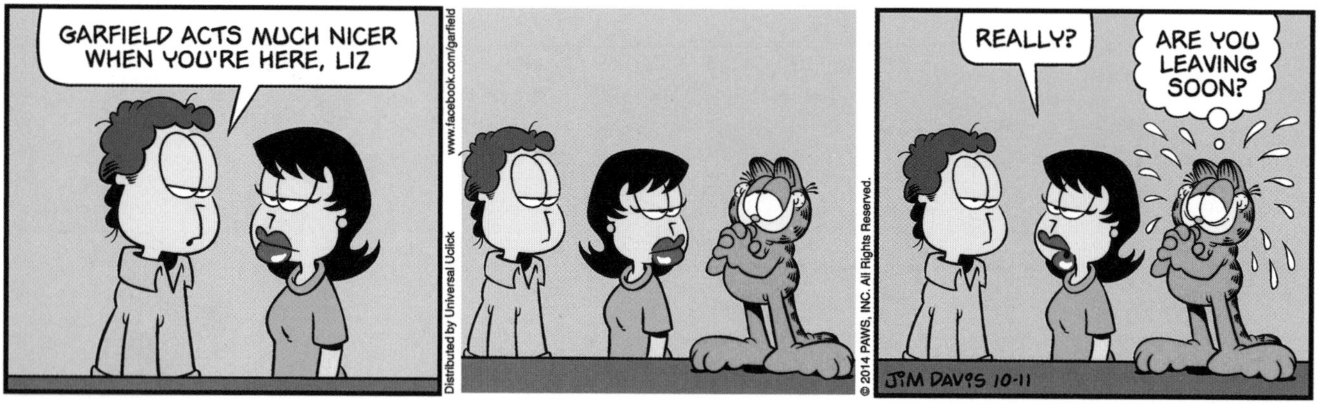
GARFIELD ACTS MUCH NICER WHEN YOU'RE HERE, LIZ
www.facebook.com/garfield
Distributed by Universal Uclick
© 2014 PAWS, INC. All Rights Reserved.
REALLY?
ARE YOU LEAVING SOON?
JIM DAVIS 10-11

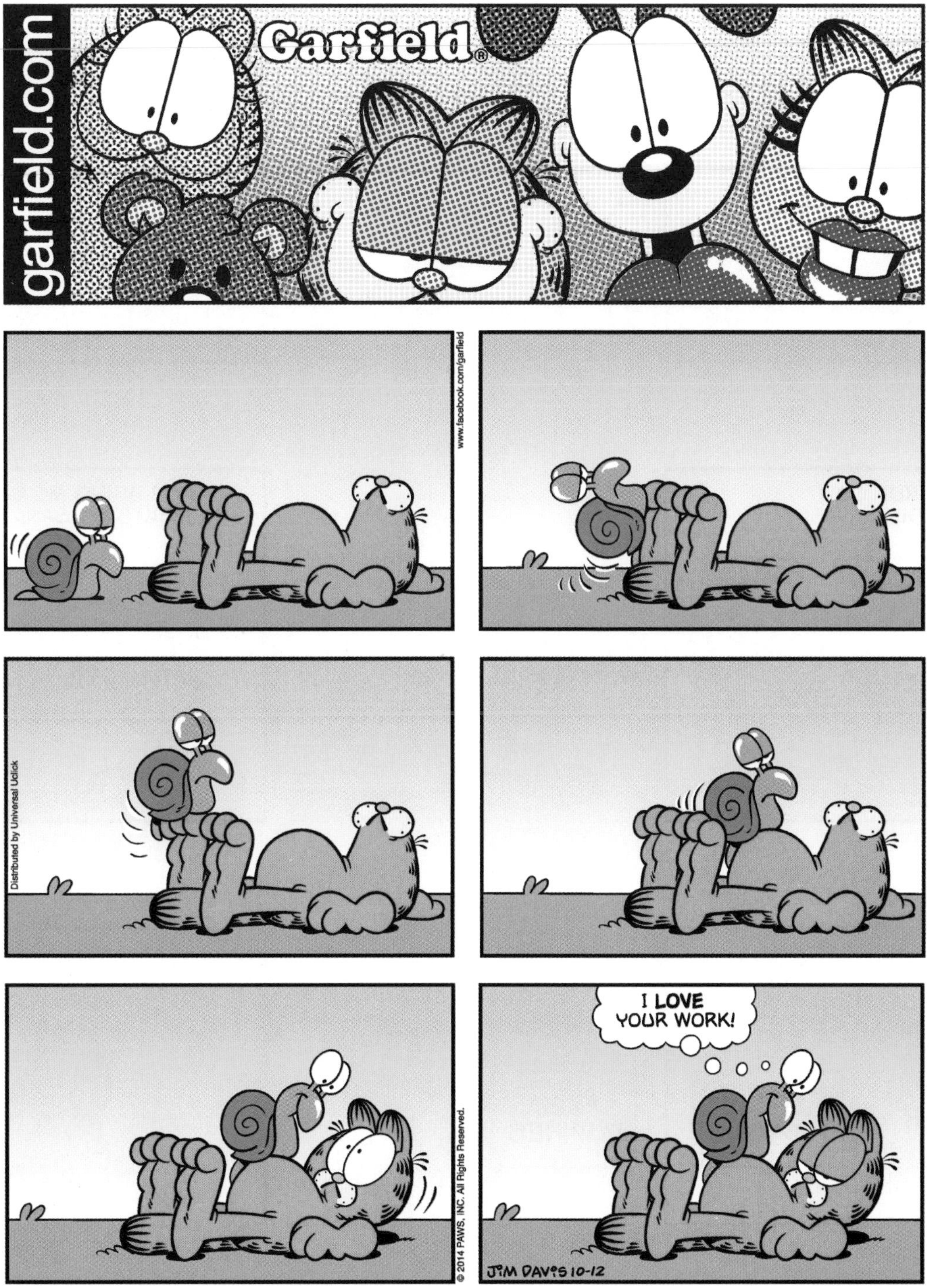
garfield.com
Garfield®
www.facebook.com/garfield
Distributed by Universal Uclick
I LOVE YOUR WORK!
© 2014 PAWS, INC. All Rights Reserved.
JIM DAVIS 10-12

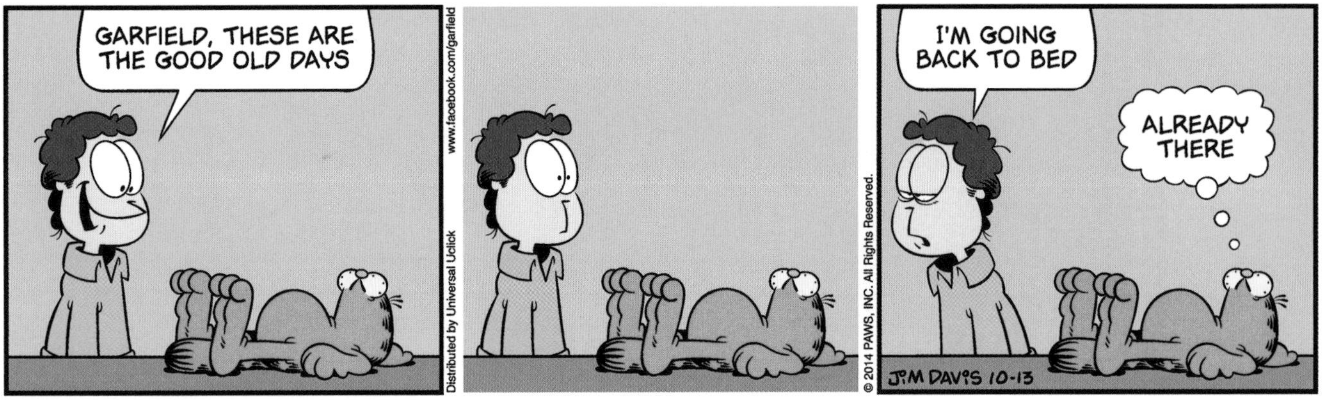
GARFIELD, THESE ARE THE GOOD OLD DAYS
Distributed by Universal Uclick www.facebook.com/garfield
I'M GOING BACK TO BED
ALREADY THERE
© 2014 PAWS, INC. All Rights Reserved.
JIM DAVIS 10-13

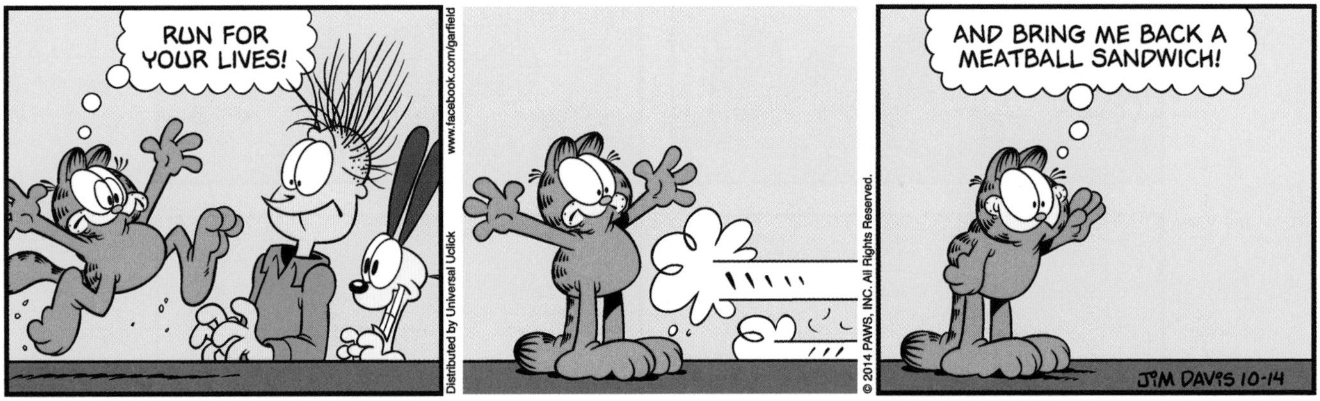
RUN FOR YOUR LIVES!
Distributed by Universal Uclick www.facebook.com/garfield
AND BRING ME BACK A MEATBALL SANDWICH!
© 2014 PAWS, INC. All Rights Reserved.
JIM DAVIS 10-14

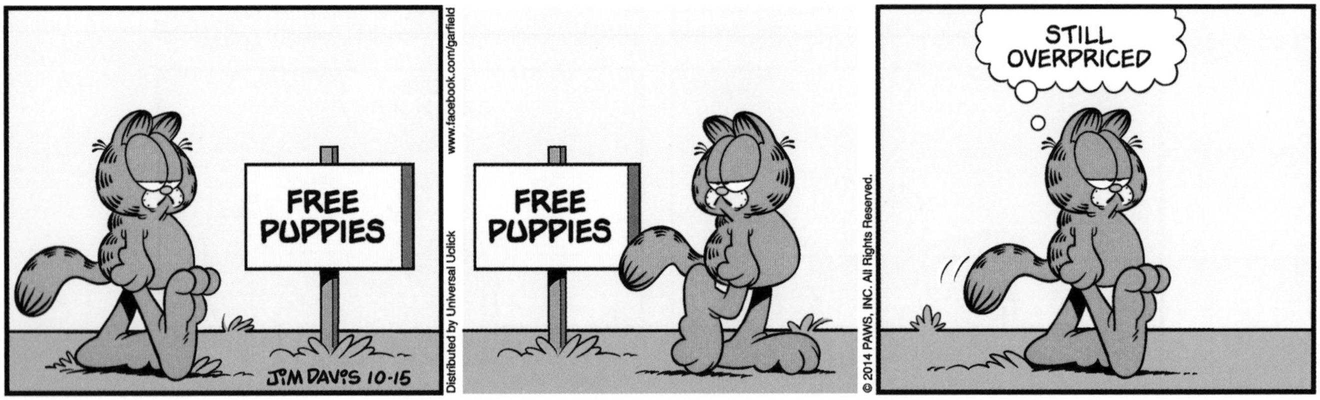
FREE PUPPIES
JIM DAVIS 10-15
Distributed by Universal Uclick www.facebook.com/garfield
FREE PUPPIES
© 2014 PAWS, INC. All Rights Reserved.
STILL OVERPRICED

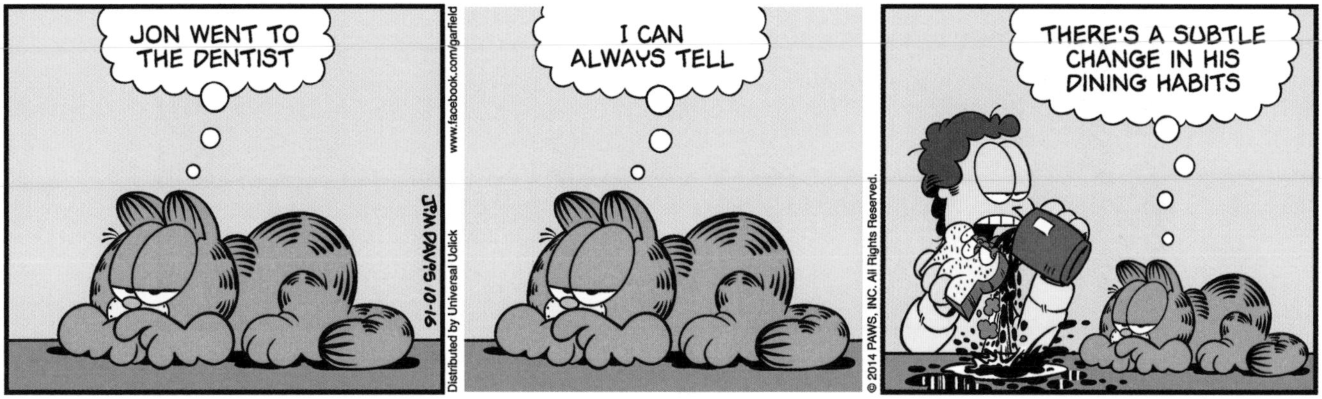
JON WENT TO THE DENTIST
I CAN ALWAYS TELL
THERE'S A SUBTLE CHANGE IN HIS DINING HABITS
JIM DAVIS 10-16
www.facebook.com/garfield
Distributed by Universal Uclick
© 2014 PAWS, INC. All Rights Reserved.

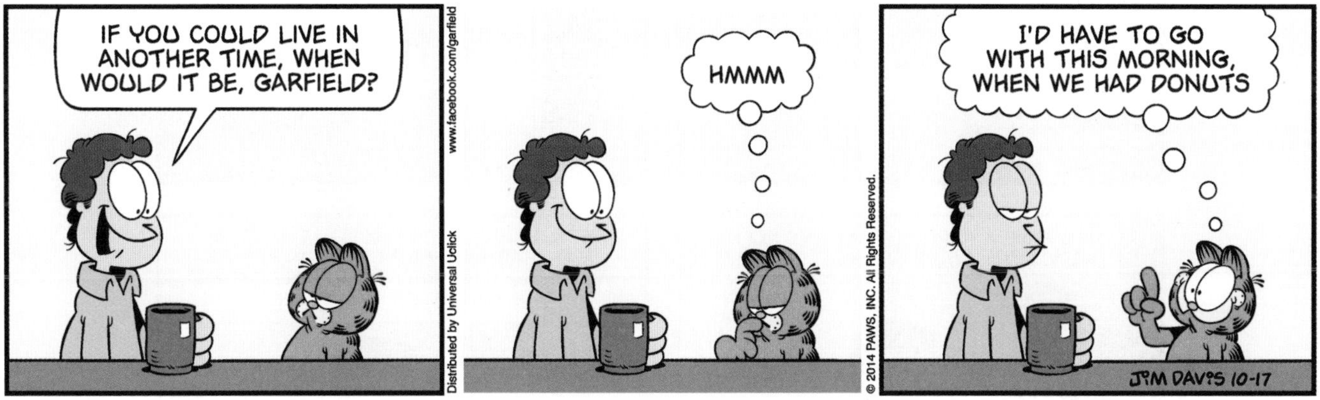
IF YOU COULD LIVE IN ANOTHER TIME, WHEN WOULD IT BE, GARFIELD?
HMMM
I'D HAVE TO GO WITH THIS MORNING, WHEN WE HAD DONUTS
JIM DAVIS 10-17
www.facebook.com/garfield
Distributed by Universal Uclick
© 2014 PAWS, INC. All Rights Reserved.

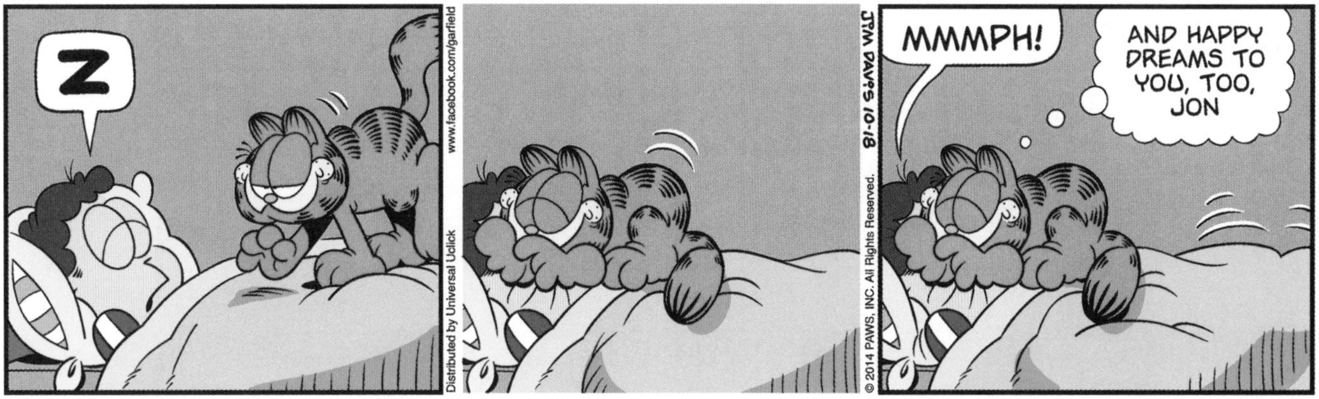
Z
MMMPH!
AND HAPPY DREAMS TO YOU, TOO, JON
JIM DAVIS 10-18
www.facebook.com/garfield
Distributed by Universal Uclick
© 2014 PAWS, INC. All Rights Reserved.

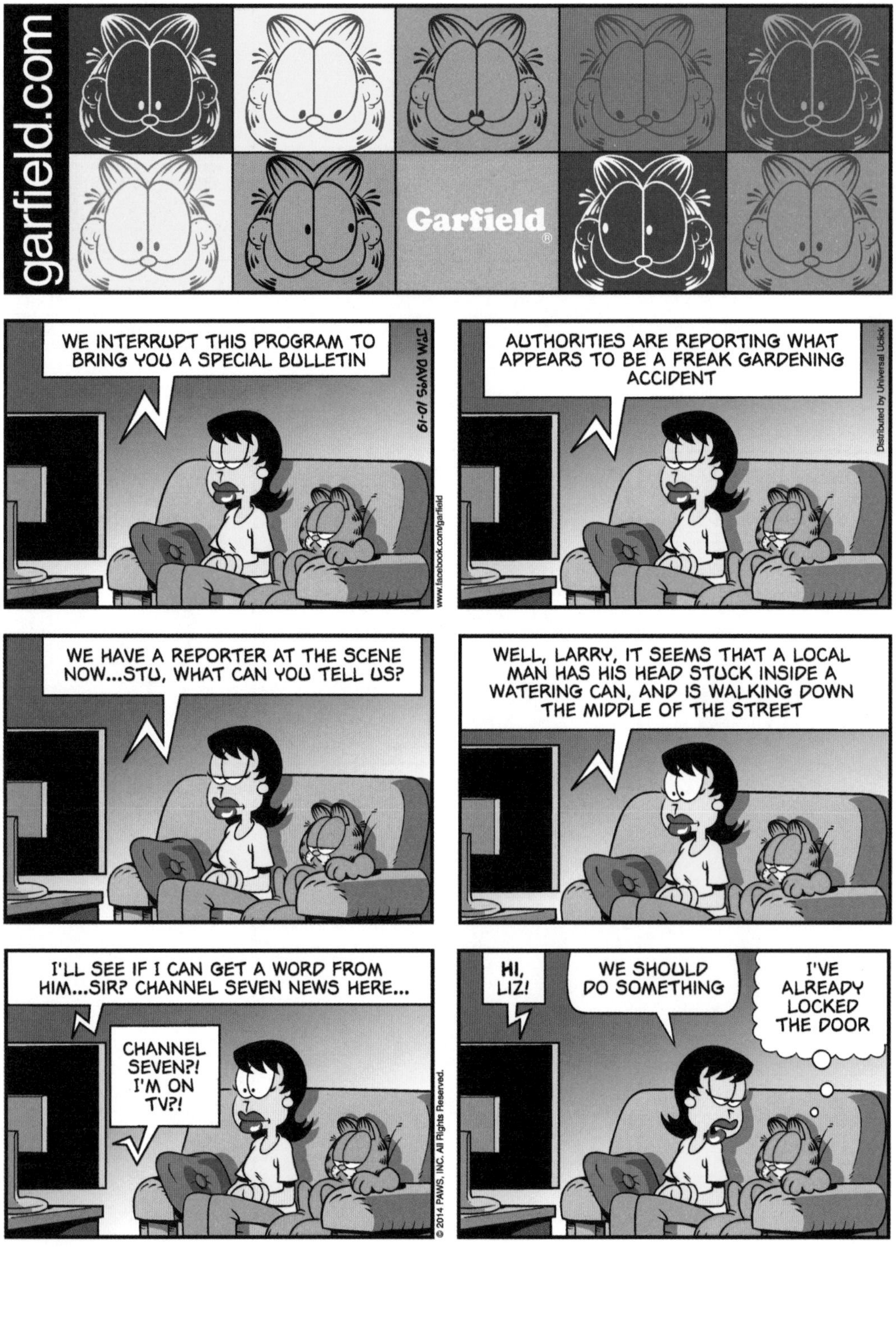
garfield.com
Garfield®
JIM DAVIS 10-19
www.facebook.com/garfield
WE INTERRUPT THIS PROGRAM TO BRING YOU A SPECIAL BULLETIN
AUTHORITIES ARE REPORTING WHAT APPEARS TO BE A FREAK GARDENING ACCIDENT
Distributed by Universal Uclick
WE HAVE A REPORTER AT THE SCENE NOW...STU, WHAT CAN YOU TELL US?
WELL, LARRY, IT SEEMS THAT A LOCAL MAN HAS HIS HEAD STUCK INSIDE A WATERING CAN, AND IS WALKING DOWN THE MIDDLE OF THE STREET
I'LL SEE IF I CAN GET A WORD FROM HIM...SIR? CHANNEL SEVEN NEWS HERE...
CHANNEL SEVEN?! I'M ON TV?!
© 2014 PAWS, INC. All Rights Reserved.
HI, LIZ!
WE SHOULD DO SOMETHING
I'VE ALREADY LOCKED THE DOOR

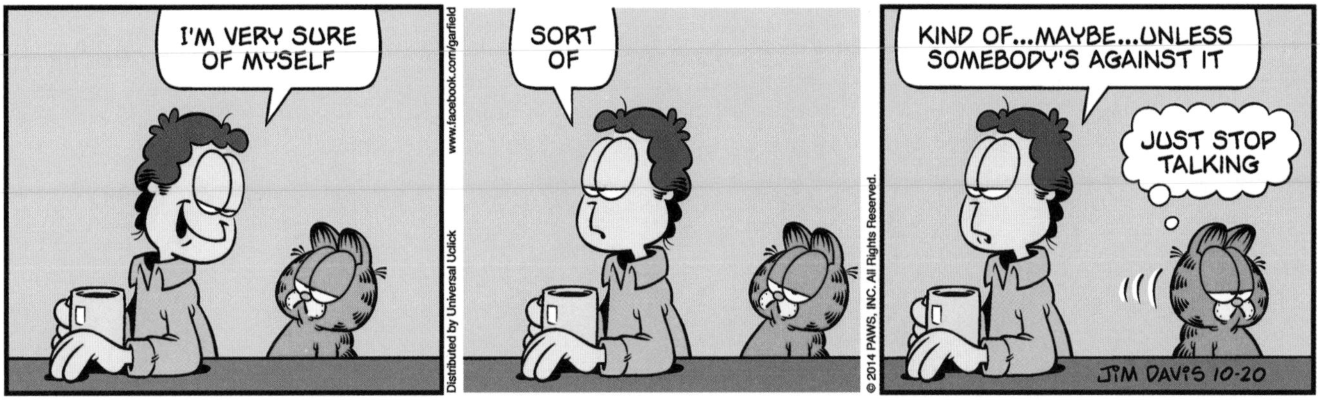
I'M VERY SURE OF MYSELF
SORT OF
KIND OF...MAYBE...UNLESS SOMEBODY'S AGAINST IT
JUST STOP TALKING
JIM DAVIS 10-20
www.facebook.com/garfield
Distributed by Universal Uclick
© 2014 PAWS, INC. All Rights Reserved.

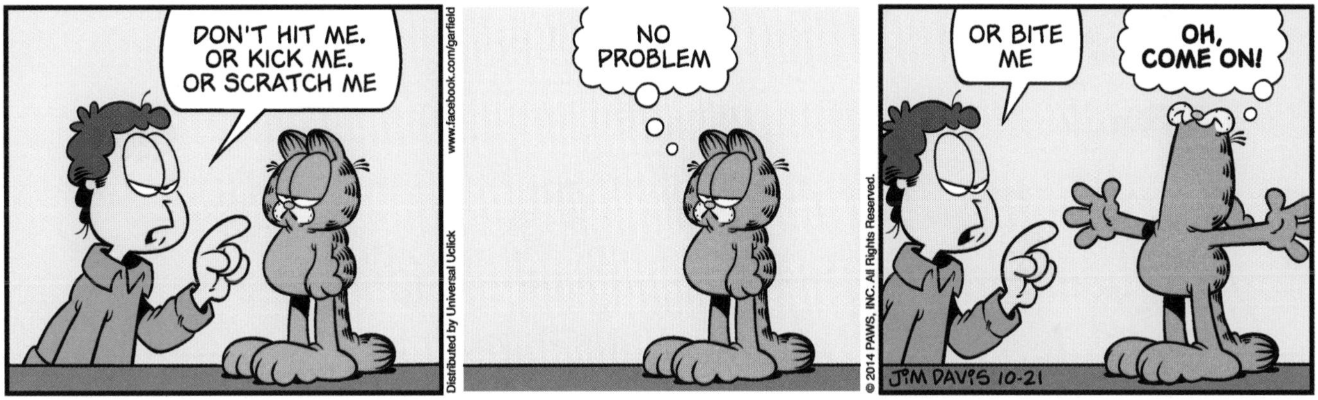
DON'T HIT ME. OR KICK ME. OR SCRATCH ME
NO PROBLEM
OR BITE ME
OH, COME ON!
JIM DAVIS 10-21
www.facebook.com/garfield
Distributed by Universal Uclick
© 2014 PAWS, INC. All Rights Reserved.

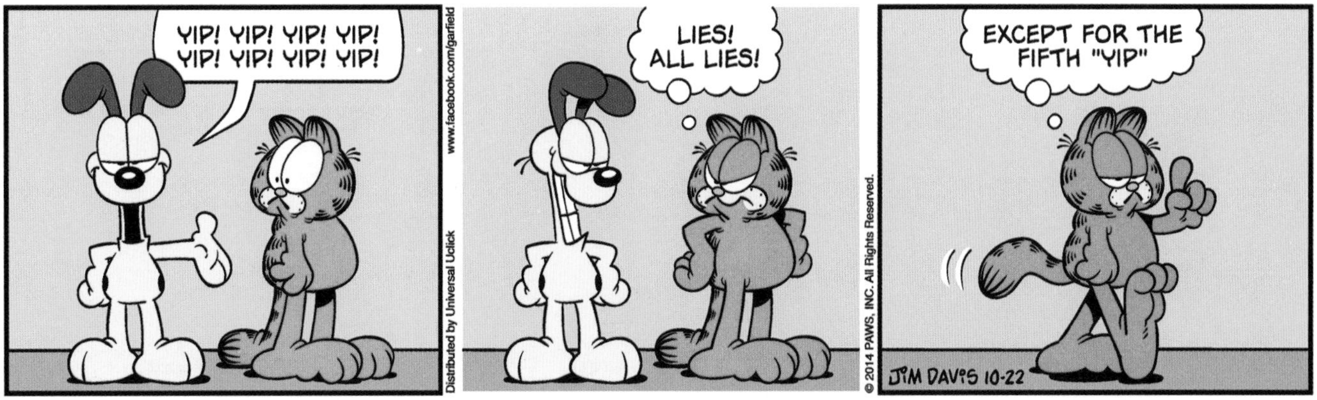
YIP! YIP! YIP! YIP! YIP! YIP! YIP! YIP!
LIES! ALL LIES!
EXCEPT FOR THE FIFTH "YIP"
JIM DAVIS 10-22
www.facebook.com/garfield
Distributed by Universal Uclick
© 2014 PAWS, INC. All Rights Reserved.

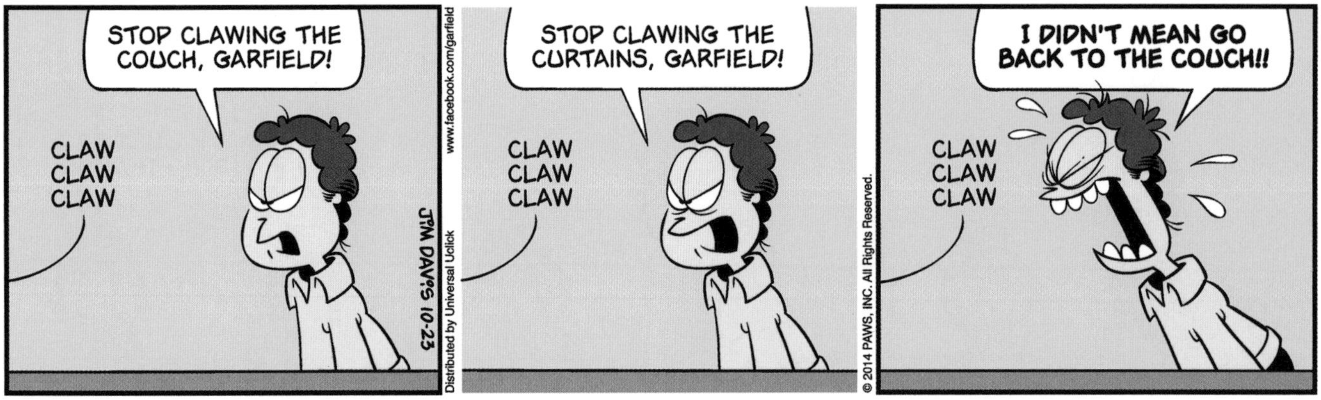
STOP CLAWING THE COUCH, GARFIELD!
CLAW CLAW CLAW
JIM DAVIS 10-23
Distributed by Universal Uclick www.facebook.com/garfield
STOP CLAWING THE CURTAINS, GARFIELD!
CLAW CLAW CLAW
© 2014 PAWS, INC. All Rights Reserved.
I DIDN'T MEAN GO BACK TO THE COUCH!!
CLAW CLAW CLAW

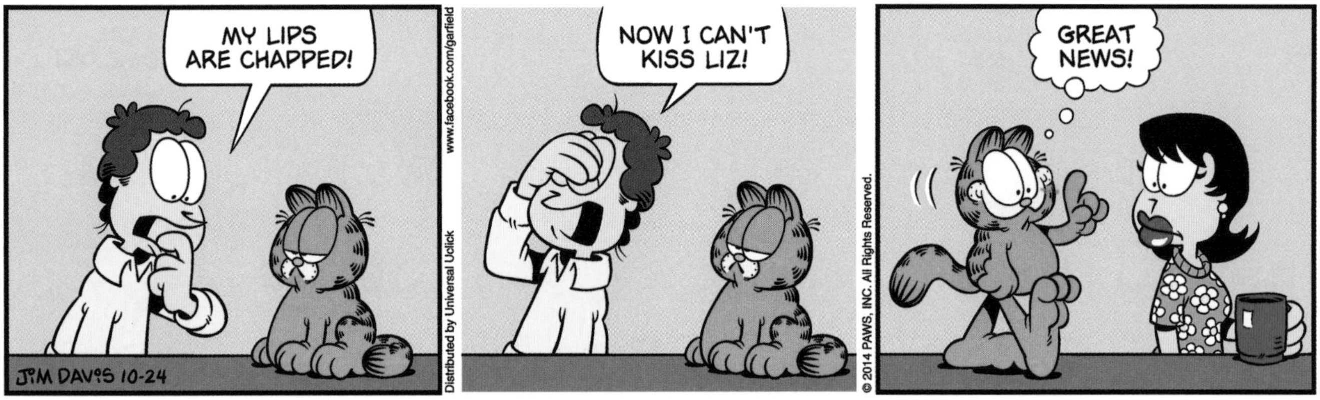
MY LIPS ARE CHAPPED!
JIM DAVIS 10-24
Distributed by Universal Uclick www.facebook.com/garfield
NOW I CAN'T KISS LIZ!
© 2014 PAWS, INC. All Rights Reserved.
GREAT NEWS!

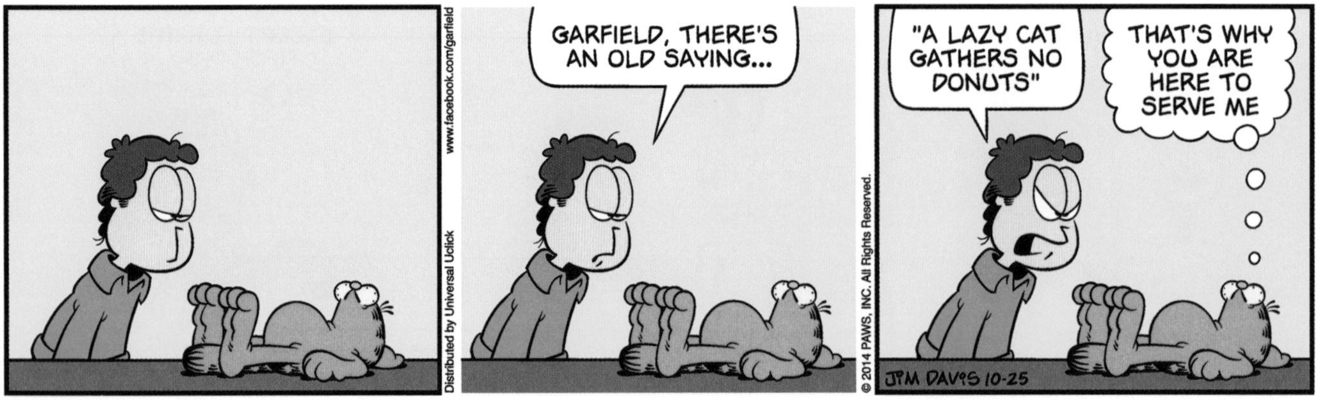
Distributed by Universal Uclick www.facebook.com/garfield
GARFIELD, THERE'S AN OLD SAYING...
© 2014 PAWS, INC. All Rights Reserved.
"A LAZY CAT GATHERS NO DONUTS"
THAT'S WHY YOU ARE HERE TO SERVE ME
JIM DAVIS 10-25

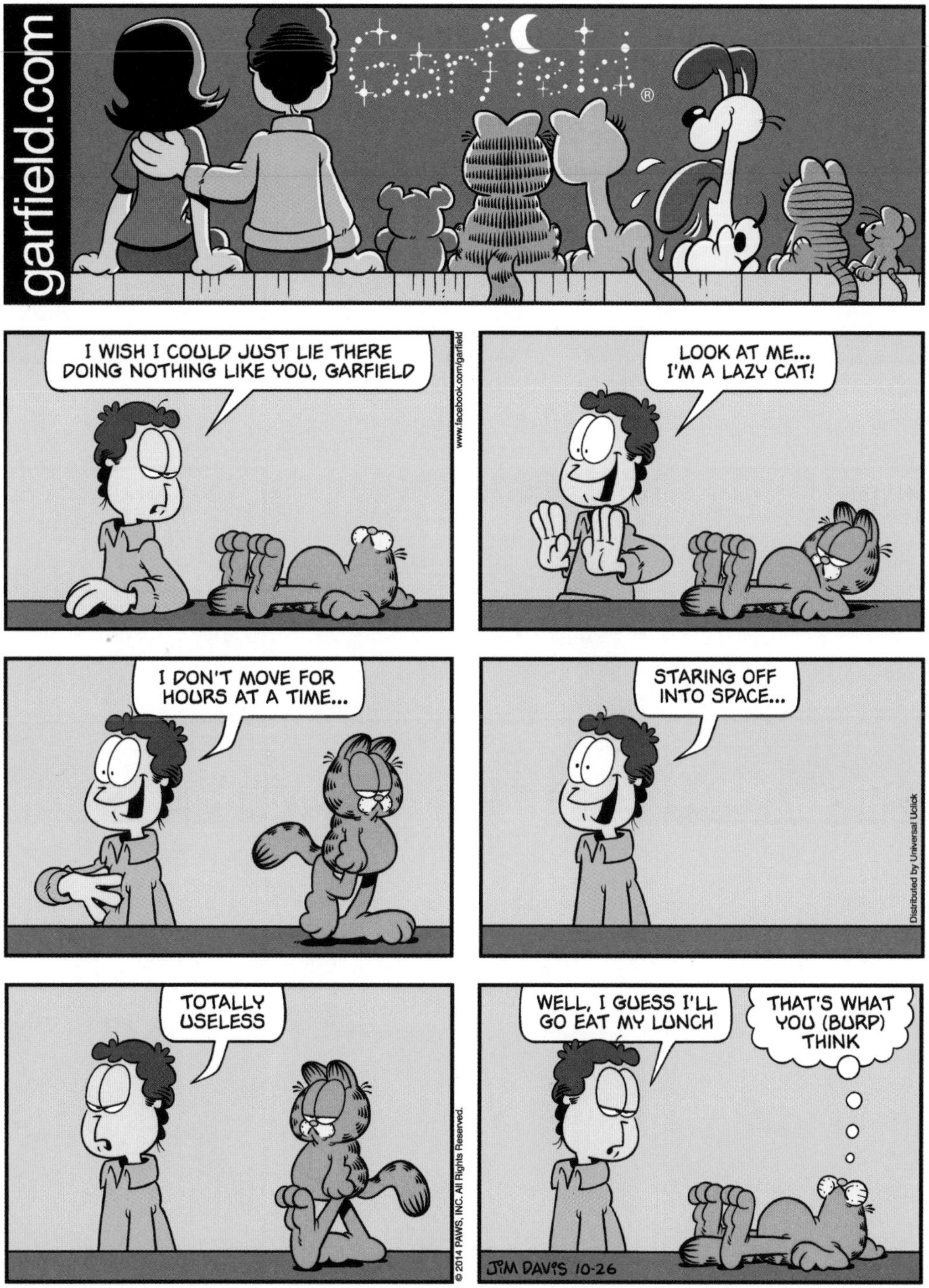
garfield.com
Garfield
I WISH I COULD JUST LIE THERE DOING NOTHING LIKE YOU, GARFIELD
www.facebook.com/garfield
LOOK AT ME... I'M A LAZY CAT!
I DON'T MOVE FOR HOURS AT A TIME...
STARING OFF INTO SPACE...
Distributed by Universal Uclick
TOTALLY USELESS
© 2014 PAWS, INC. All Rights Reserved.
WELL, I GUESS I'LL GO EAT MY LUNCH
THAT'S WHAT YOU (BURP) THINK
JIM DAVIS 10-26

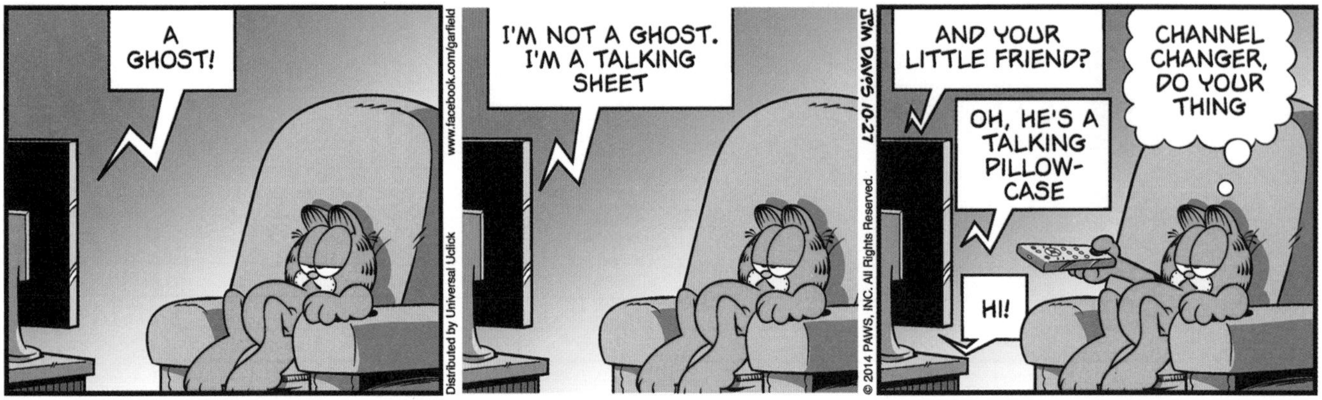
A GHOST!
I'M NOT A GHOST. I'M A TALKING SHEET
AND YOUR LITTLE FRIEND?
OH, HE'S A TALKING PILLOW-CASE
HI!
CHANNEL CHANGER, DO YOUR THING
JIM DAVIS 10-27
© 2014 PAWS, INC. All Rights Reserved.
Distributed by Universal Uclick www.facebook.com/garfield

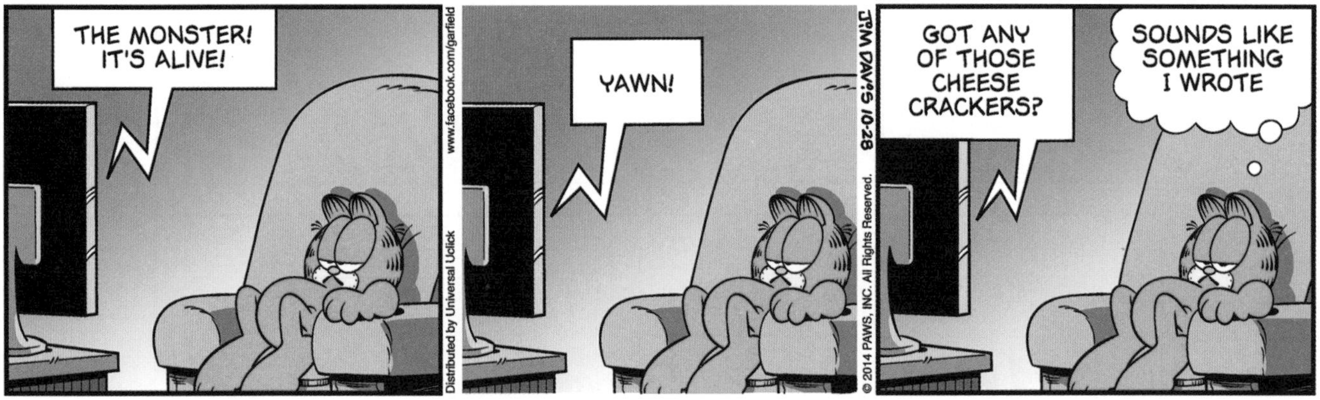
THE MONSTER! IT'S ALIVE!
YAWN!
GOT ANY OF THOSE CHEESE CRACKERS?
SOUNDS LIKE SOMETHING I WROTE
JIM DAVIS 10-28
© 2014 PAWS, INC. All Rights Reserved.
Distributed by Universal Uclick www.facebook.com/garfield

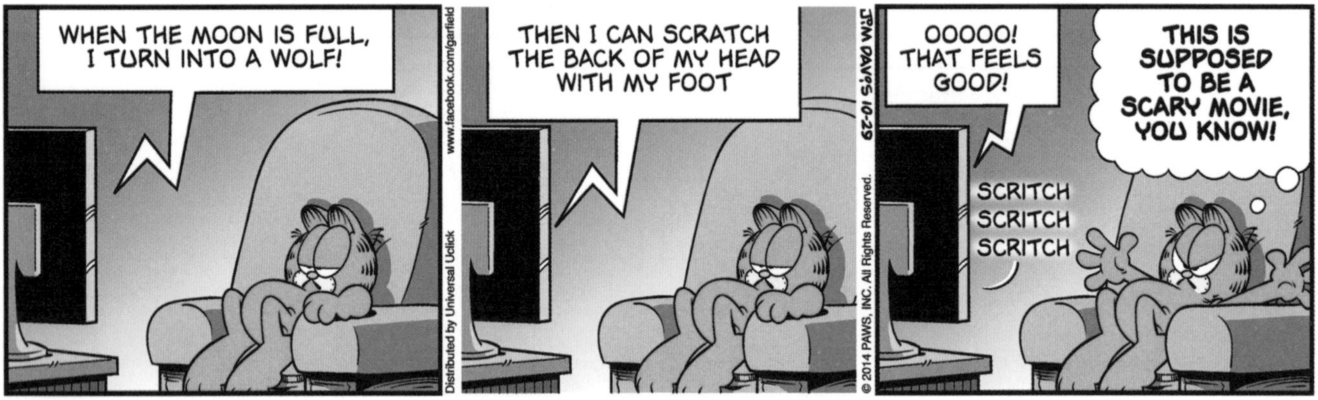
WHEN THE MOON IS FULL, I TURN INTO A WOLF!
THEN I CAN SCRATCH THE BACK OF MY HEAD WITH MY FOOT
OOOOO! THAT FEELS GOOD!
SCRITCH SCRITCH SCRITCH
THIS IS SUPPOSED TO BE A SCARY MOVIE, YOU KNOW!
JIM DAVIS 10-29
© 2014 PAWS, INC. All Rights Reserved.
Distributed by Universal Uclick www.facebook.com/garfield

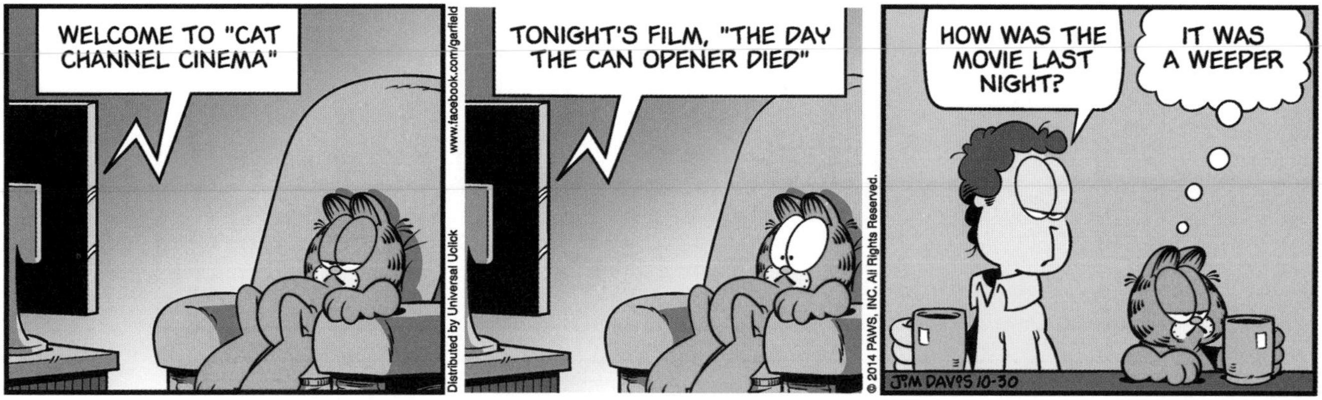
WELCOME TO "CAT CHANNEL CINEMA"
TONIGHT'S FILM, "THE DAY THE CAN OPENER DIED"
HOW WAS THE MOVIE LAST NIGHT?
IT WAS A WEEPER
JIM DAVIS 10-30
Distributed by Universal Uclick
www.facebook.com/garfield
© 2014 PAWS, INC. All Rights Reserved.

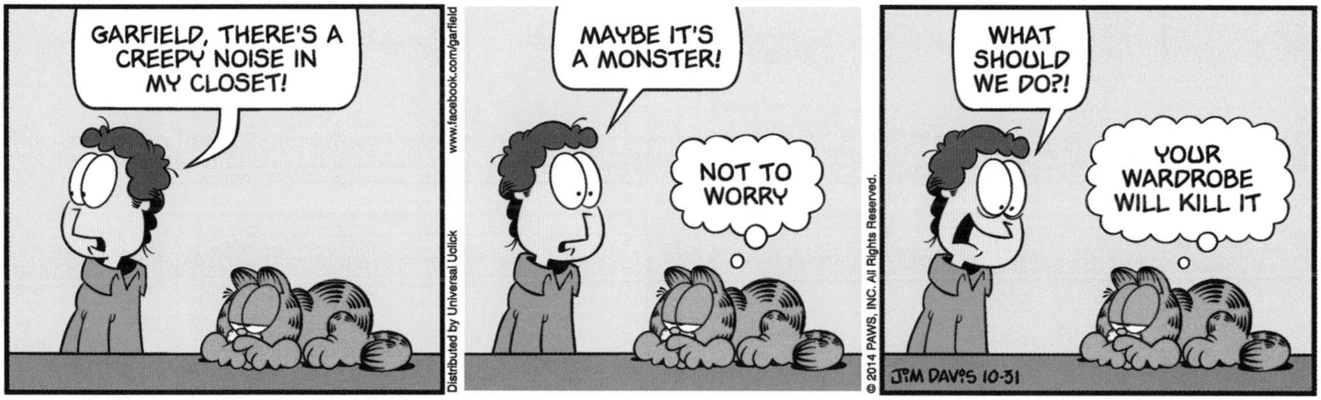
GARFIELD, THERE'S A CREEPY NOISE IN MY CLOSET!
MAYBE IT'S A MONSTER!
NOT TO WORRY
WHAT SHOULD WE DO?!
YOUR WARDROBE WILL KILL IT
JIM DAVIS 10-31
Distributed by Universal Uclick
www.facebook.com/garfield
© 2014 PAWS, INC. All Rights Reserved.

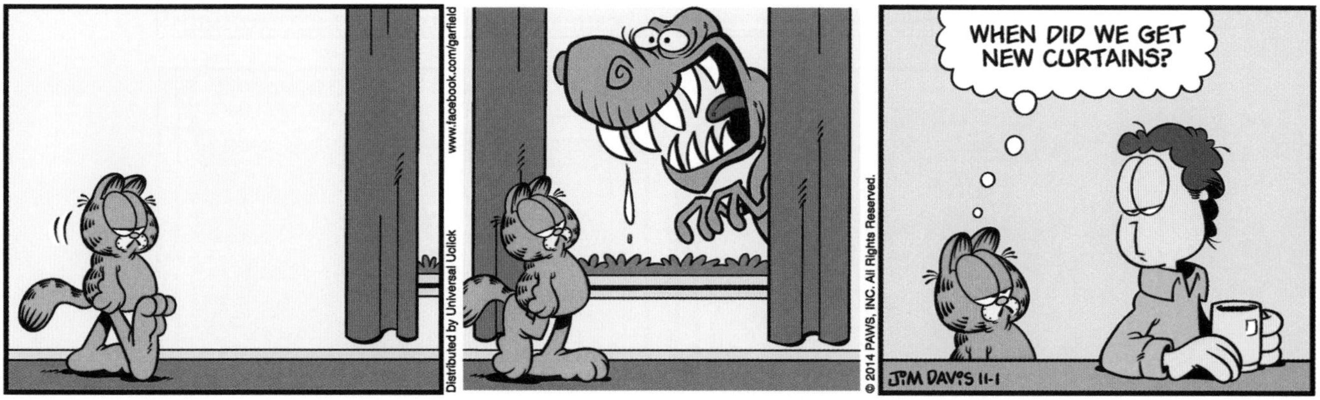
WHEN DID WE GET NEW CURTAINS?
JIM DAVIS 11-1
Distributed by Universal Uclick
www.facebook.com/garfield
© 2014 PAWS, INC. All Rights Reserved.

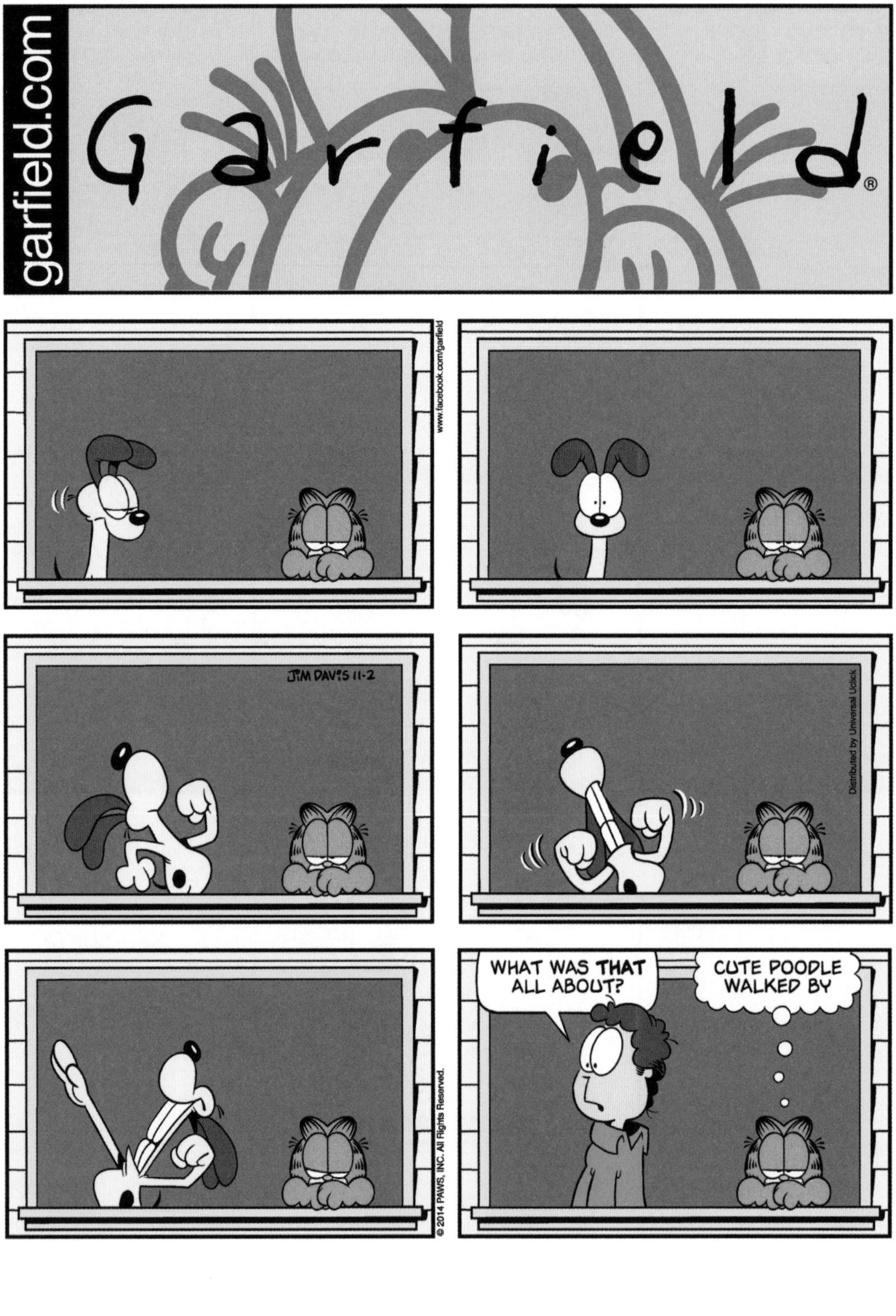
garfield.com
Garfield®
JIM DAVIS 11-2
WHAT WAS **THAT** ALL ABOUT?
CUTE POODLE WALKED BY

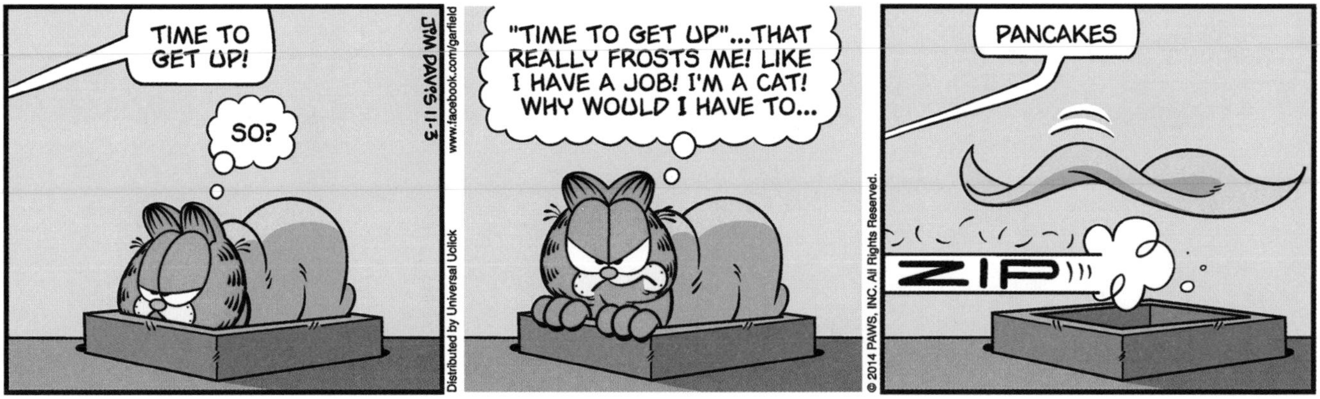
TIME TO GET UP!
SO?
JIM DAVIS 11-3
www.facebook.com/garfield
Distributed by Universal Uclick
"TIME TO GET UP"...THAT REALLY FROSTS ME! LIKE I HAVE A JOB! I'M A CAT! WHY WOULD I HAVE TO...
© 2014 PAWS, INC. All Rights Reserved.
PANCAKES
ZIP

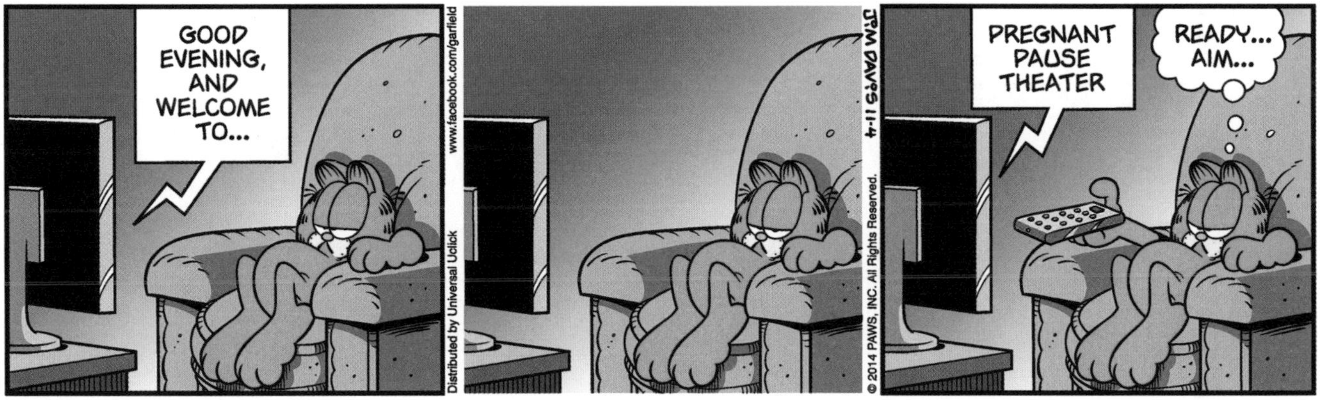
GOOD EVENING, AND WELCOME TO...
www.facebook.com/garfield
Distributed by Universal Uclick
JIM DAVIS 11-4
© 2014 PAWS, INC. All Rights Reserved.
PREGNANT PAUSE THEATER
READY... AIM...

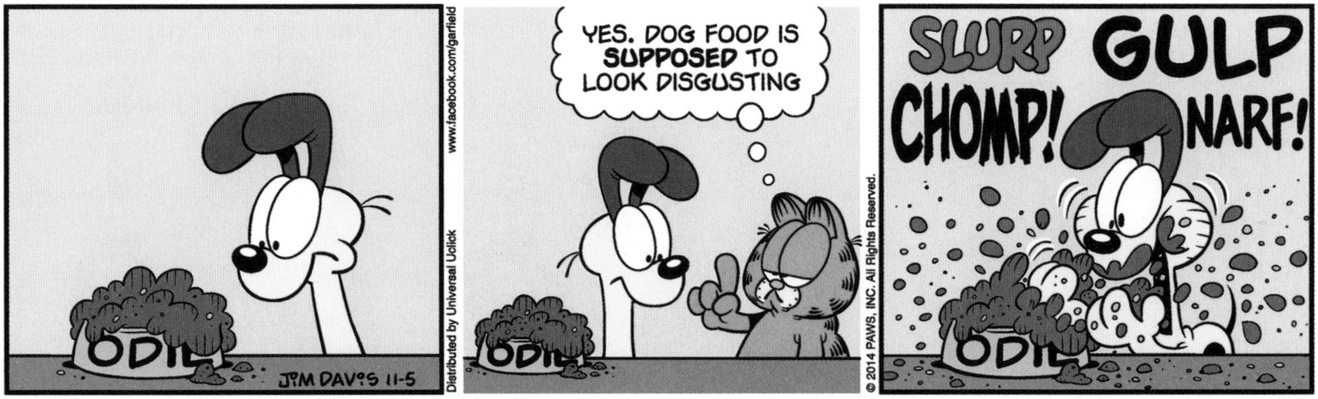
ODIE
JIM DAVIS 11-5
www.facebook.com/garfield
Distributed by Universal Uclick
YES. DOG FOOD IS **SUPPOSED** TO LOOK DISGUSTING
© 2014 PAWS, INC. All Rights Reserved.
SLURP
GULP
CHOMP!
NARF!

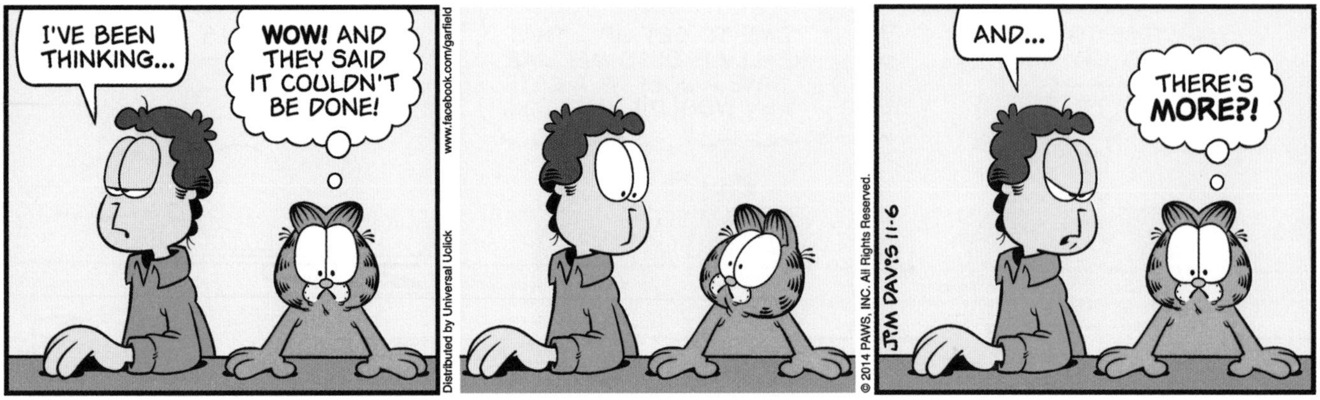
I'VE BEEN THINKING...
WOW! AND THEY SAID IT COULDN'T BE DONE!
www.facebook.com/garfield
Distributed by Universal Uclick
AND...
THERE'S MORE?!
JIM DAVIS 11-6
© 2014 PAWS, INC. All Rights Reserved.

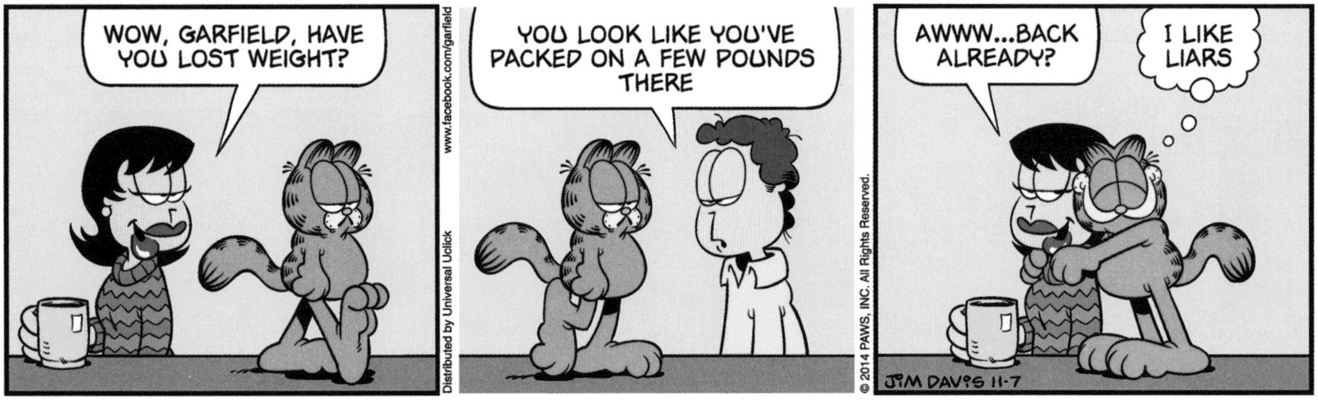
WOW, GARFIELD, HAVE YOU LOST WEIGHT?
www.facebook.com/garfield
Distributed by Universal Uclick
YOU LOOK LIKE YOU'VE PACKED ON A FEW POUNDS THERE
AWWW...BACK ALREADY?
I LIKE LIARS
JIM DAVIS 11-7
© 2014 PAWS, INC. All Rights Reserved.

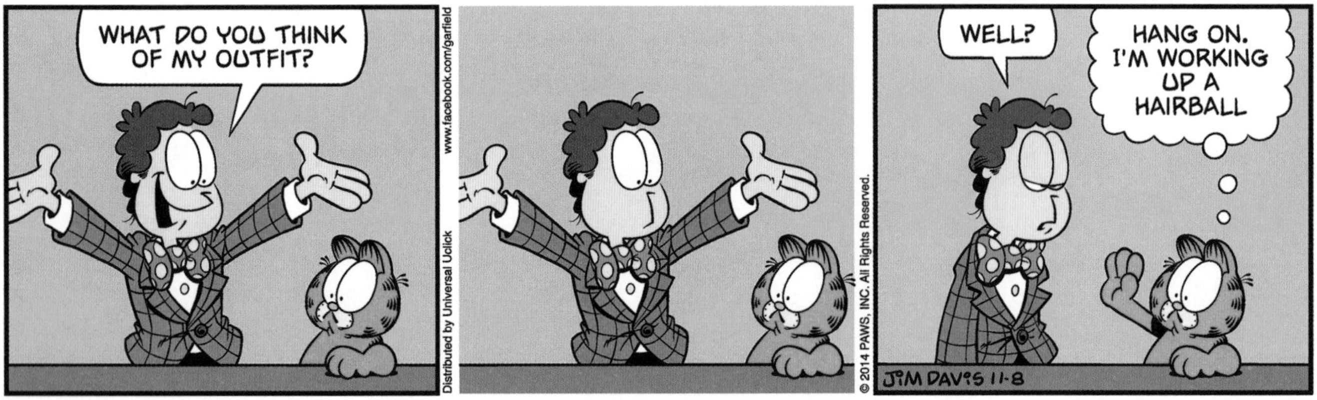
WHAT DO YOU THINK OF MY OUTFIT?
www.facebook.com/garfield
Distributed by Universal Uclick
WELL?
HANG ON. I'M WORKING UP A HAIRBALL
JIM DAVIS 11-8
© 2014 PAWS, INC. All Rights Reserved.

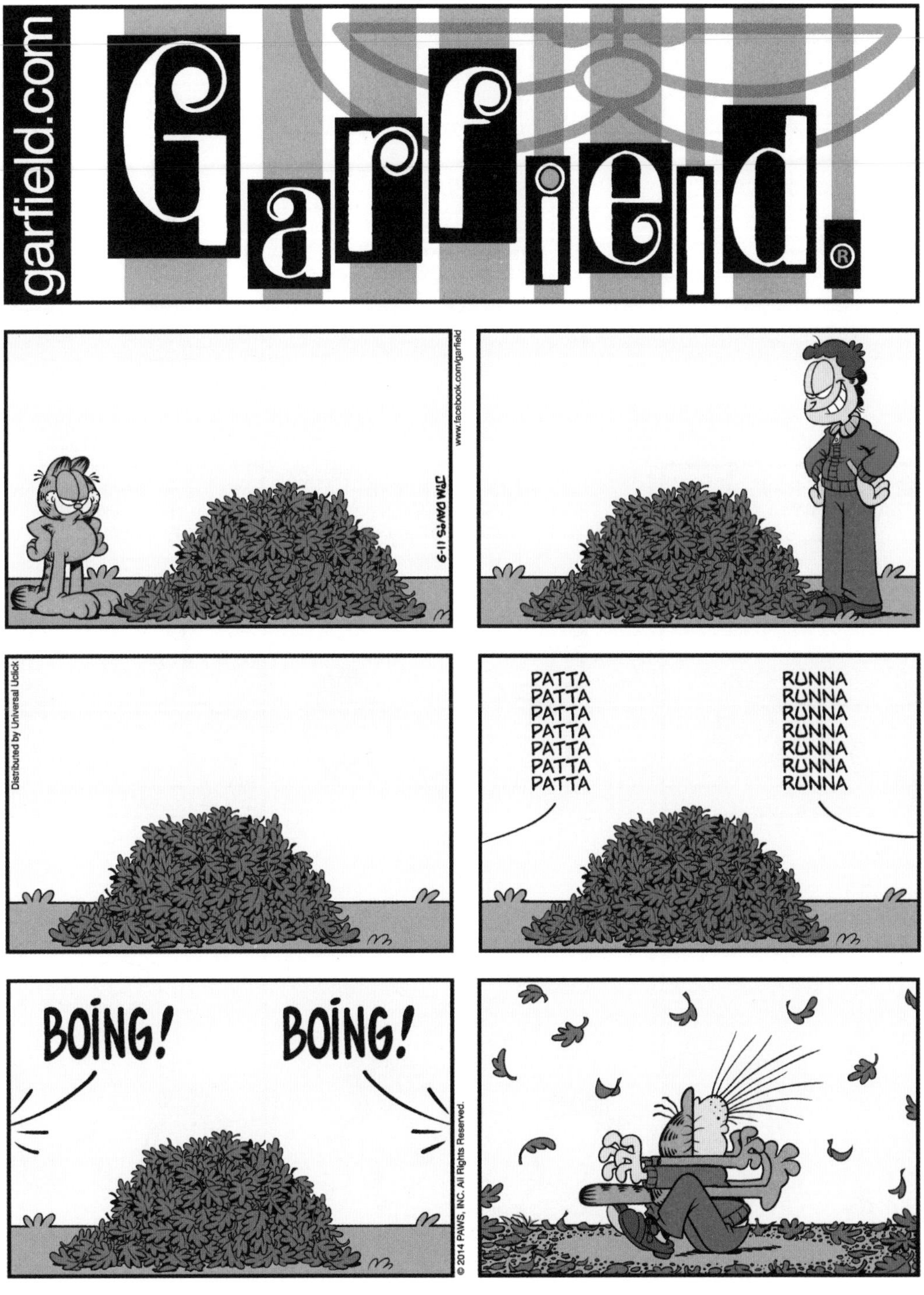
garfield.com
Garfield
JIM DAVIS 11-9
www.facebook.com/garfield
Distributed by Universal Uclick
PATTA PATTA PATTA PATTA PATTA PATTA PATTA
RUNNA RUNNA RUNNA RUNNA RUNNA RUNNA RUNNA
BOING!
BOING!
© 2014 PAWS, INC. All Rights Reserved.

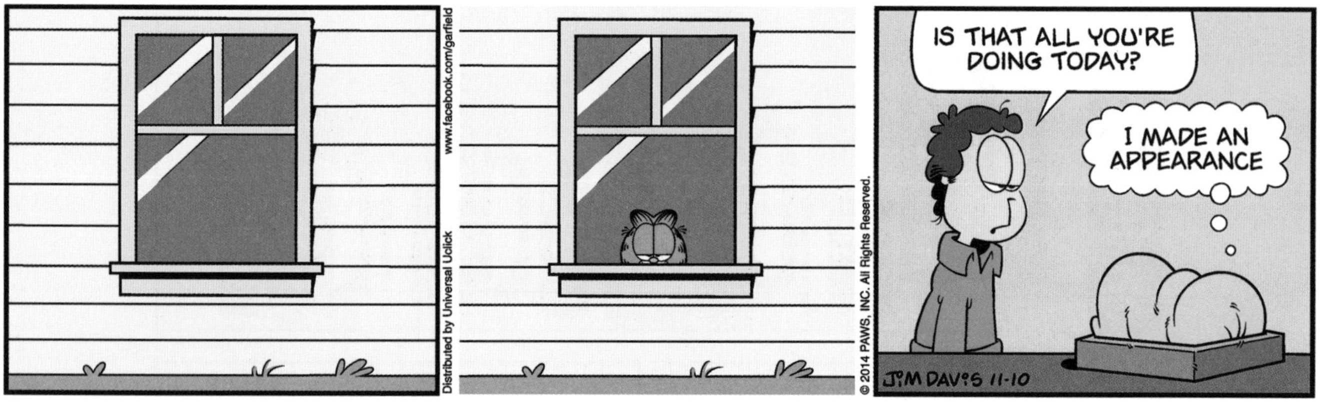
Distributed by Universal Uclick
www.facebook.com/garfield
© 2014 PAWS, INC. All Rights Reserved.
IS THAT ALL YOU'RE DOING TODAY?
I MADE AN APPEARANCE
JIM DAVIS 11-10

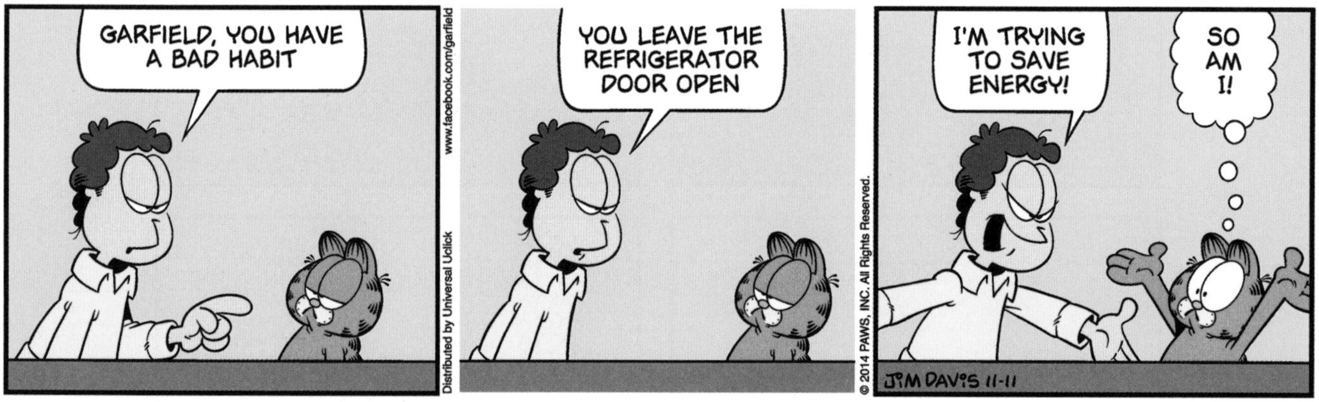
GARFIELD, YOU HAVE A BAD HABIT
Distributed by Universal Uclick
www.facebook.com/garfield
YOU LEAVE THE REFRIGERATOR DOOR OPEN
© 2014 PAWS, INC. All Rights Reserved.
I'M TRYING TO SAVE ENERGY!
SO AM I!
JIM DAVIS 11-11

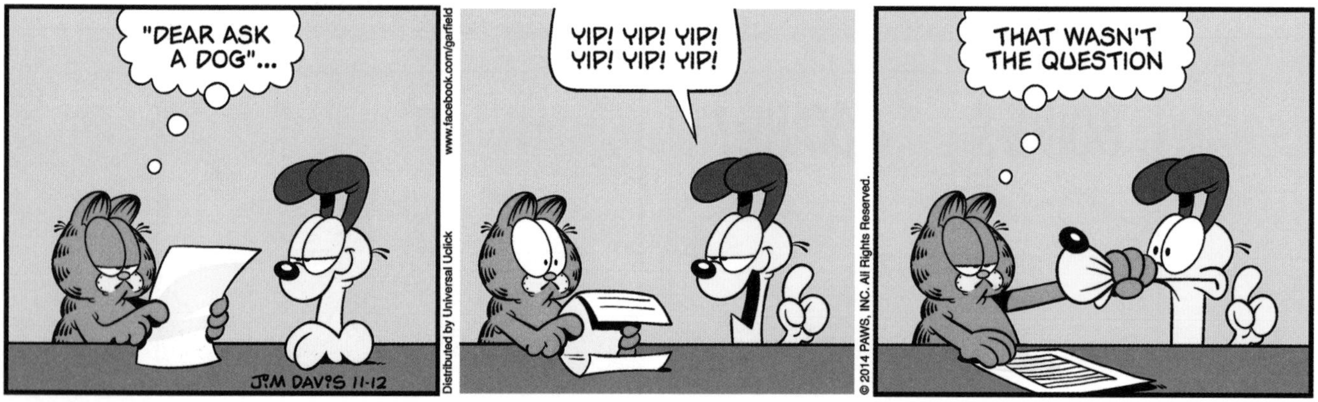
"DEAR ASK A DOG"...
JIM DAVIS 11-12
Distributed by Universal Uclick
www.facebook.com/garfield
YIP! YIP! YIP! YIP! YIP! YIP!
© 2014 PAWS, INC. All Rights Reserved.
THAT WASN'T THE QUESTION

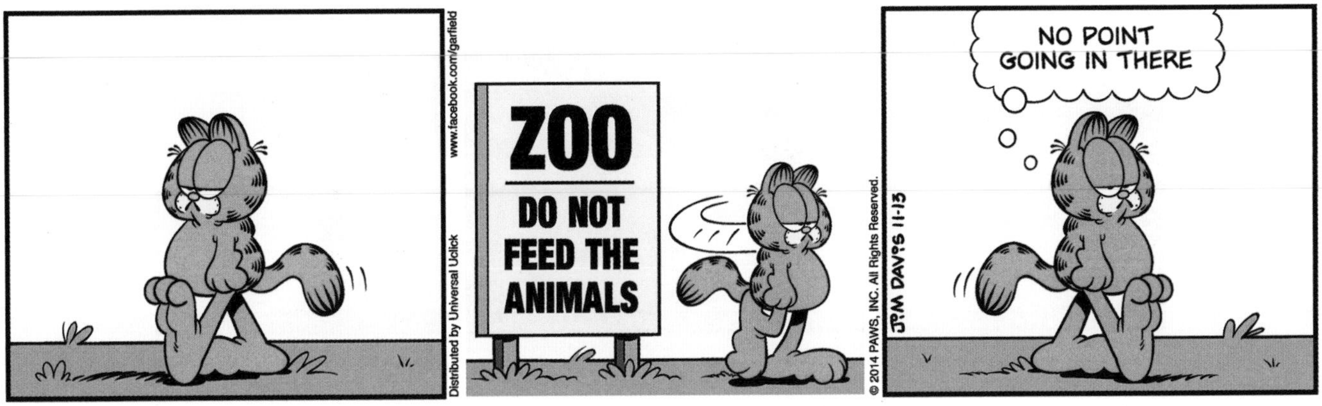
Distributed by Universal Uclick
www.facebook.com/garfield
ZOO
DO NOT FEED THE ANIMALS
© 2014 PAWS, INC. All Rights Reserved.
JIM DAVIS 11-13
NO POINT GOING IN THERE

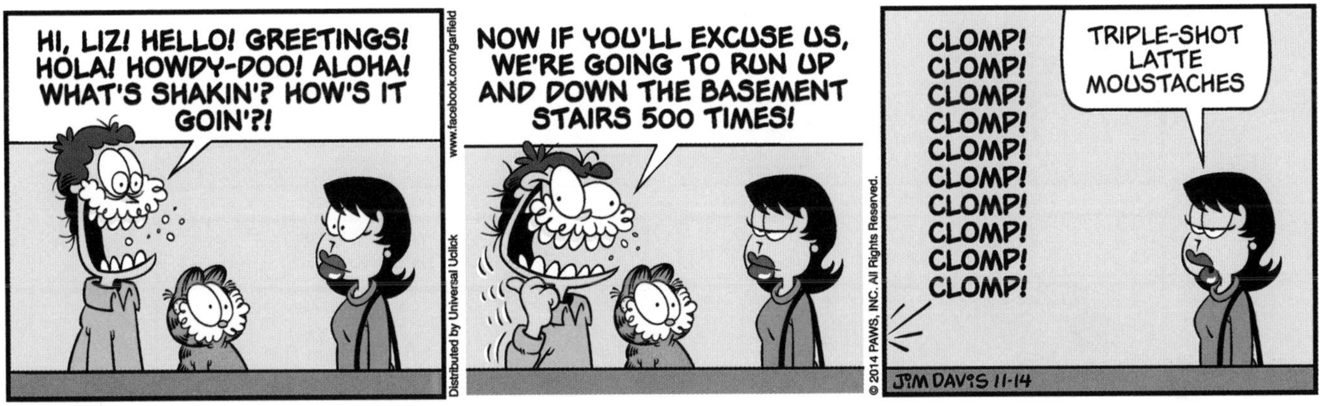
HI, LIZ! HELLO! GREETINGS! HOLA! HOWDY-DOO! ALOHA! WHAT'S SHAKIN'? HOW'S IT GOIN'?!
Distributed by Universal Uclick
www.facebook.com/garfield
NOW IF YOU'LL EXCUSE US, WE'RE GOING TO RUN UP AND DOWN THE BASEMENT STAIRS 500 TIMES!
© 2014 PAWS, INC. All Rights Reserved.
CLOMP! CLOMP! CLOMP! CLOMP! CLOMP! CLOMP! CLOMP! CLOMP! CLOMP! CLOMP!
TRIPLE-SHOT LATTE MOUSTACHES
JIM DAVIS 11-14

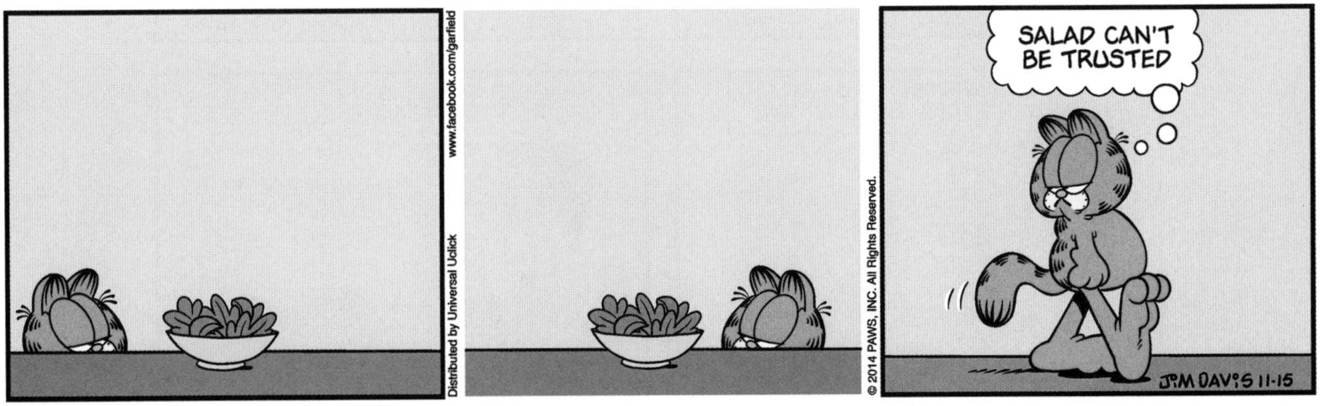
Distributed by Universal Uclick
www.facebook.com/garfield
© 2014 PAWS, INC. All Rights Reserved.
SALAD CAN'T BE TRUSTED
JIM DAVIS 11-15

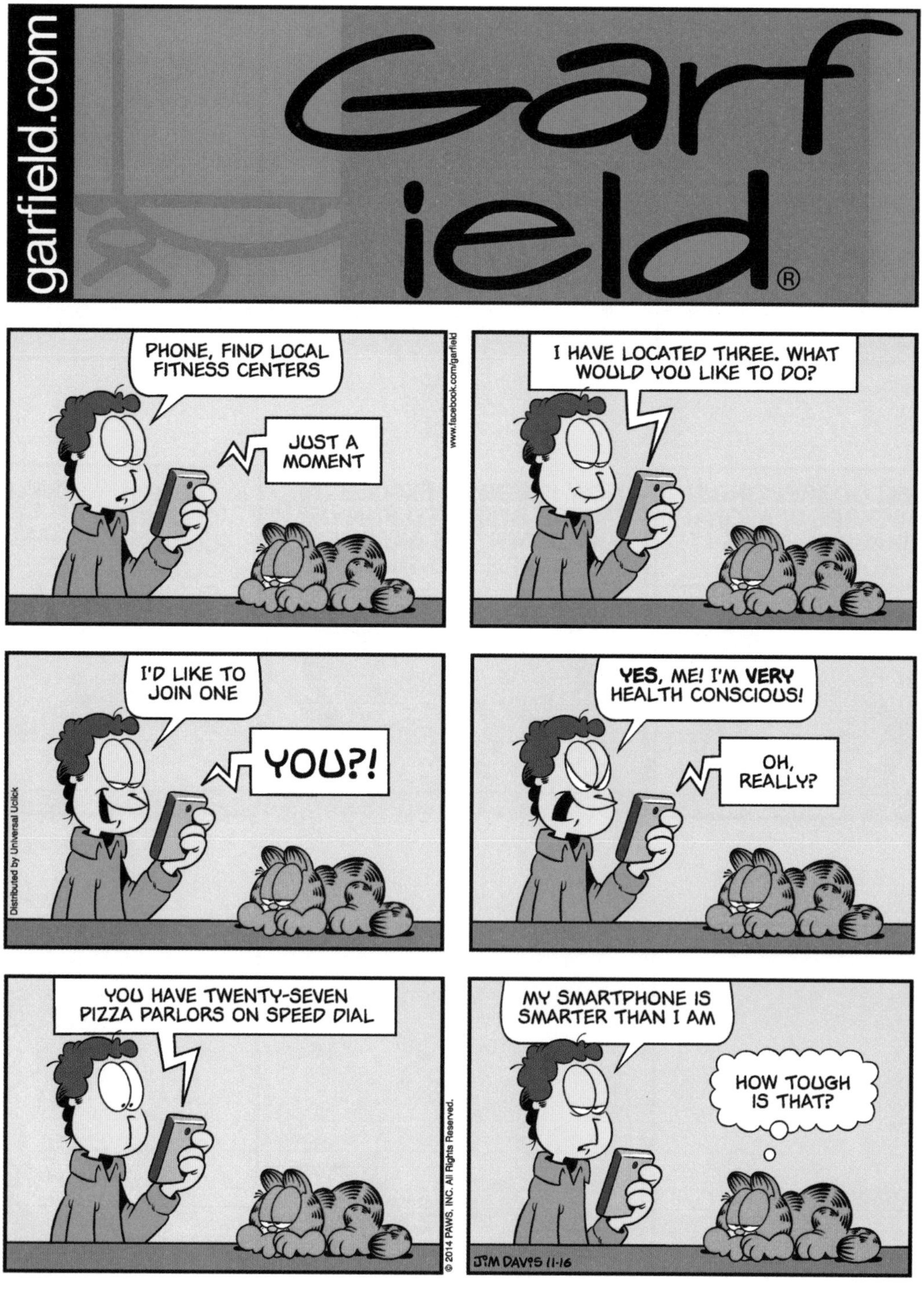
garfield.com
Garfield®
PHONE, FIND LOCAL FITNESS CENTERS
JUST A MOMENT
www.facebook.com/garfield
I HAVE LOCATED THREE. WHAT WOULD YOU LIKE TO DO?
I'D LIKE TO JOIN ONE
YOU?!
Distributed by Universal Uclick
YES, ME! I'M VERY HEALTH CONSCIOUS!
OH, REALLY?
YOU HAVE TWENTY-SEVEN PIZZA PARLORS ON SPEED DIAL
© 2014 PAWS, INC. All Rights Reserved.
MY SMARTPHONE IS SMARTER THAN I AM
HOW TOUGH IS THAT?
JIM DAVIS 11-16

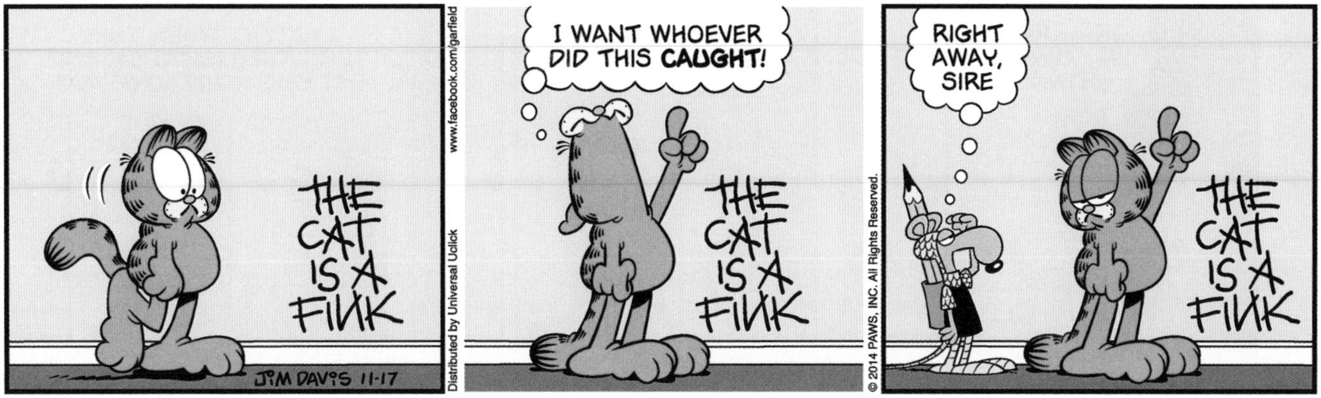
THE CAT IS A FINK
JIM DAVIS 11-17
Distributed by Universal Uclick www.facebook.com/garfield
I WANT WHOEVER DID THIS CAUGHT!
THE CAT IS A FINK
© 2014 PAWS, INC. All Rights Reserved.
RIGHT AWAY, SIRE
THE CAT IS A FINK

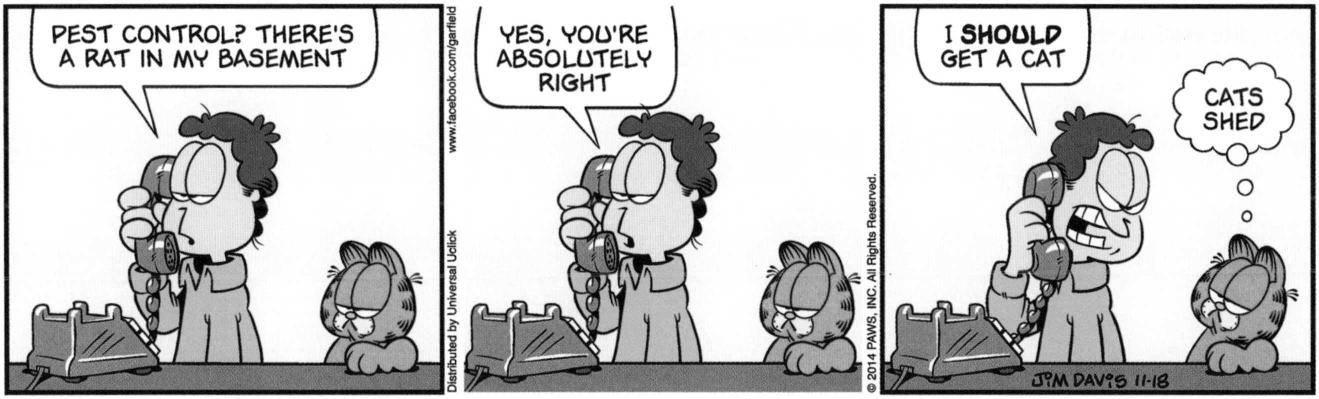
PEST CONTROL? THERE'S A RAT IN MY BASEMENT
Distributed by Universal Uclick www.facebook.com/garfield
YES, YOU'RE ABSOLUTELY RIGHT
© 2014 PAWS, INC. All Rights Reserved.
I SHOULD GET A CAT
CATS SHED
JIM DAVIS 11-18

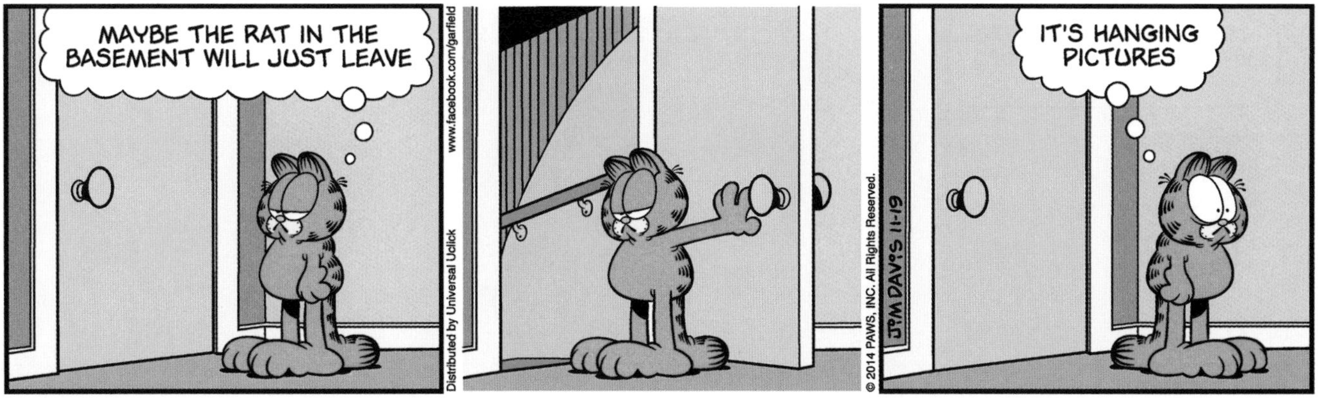
MAYBE THE RAT IN THE BASEMENT WILL JUST LEAVE
Distributed by Universal Uclick www.facebook.com/garfield
© 2014 PAWS, INC. All Rights Reserved.
JIM DAVIS 11-19
IT'S HANGING PICTURES

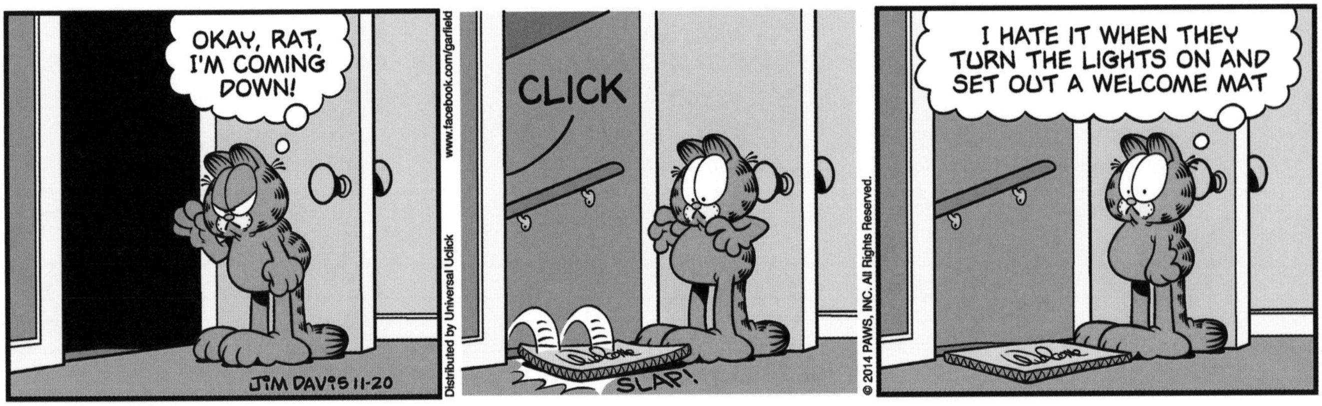
OKAY, RAT, I'M COMING DOWN!
JIM DAVIS 11-20
Distributed by Universal Uclick
www.facebook.com/garfield
CLICK
SLAP!
© 2014 PAWS, INC. All Rights Reserved.
I HATE IT WHEN THEY TURN THE LIGHTS ON AND SET OUT A WELCOME MAT

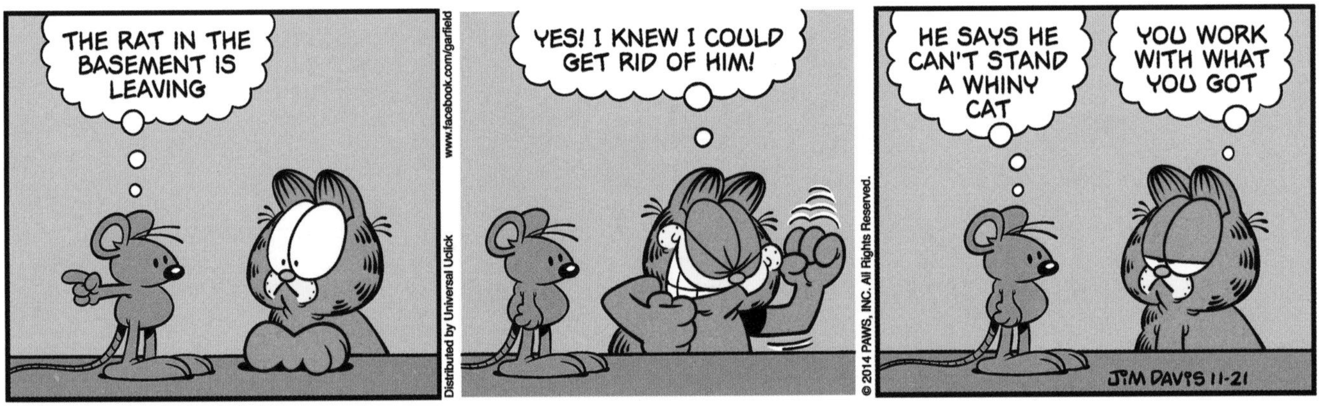
THE RAT IN THE BASEMENT IS LEAVING
Distributed by Universal Uclick
www.facebook.com/garfield
YES! I KNEW I COULD GET RID OF HIM!
© 2014 PAWS, INC. All Rights Reserved.
HE SAYS HE CAN'T STAND A WHINY CAT
YOU WORK WITH WHAT YOU GOT
JIM DAVIS 11-21

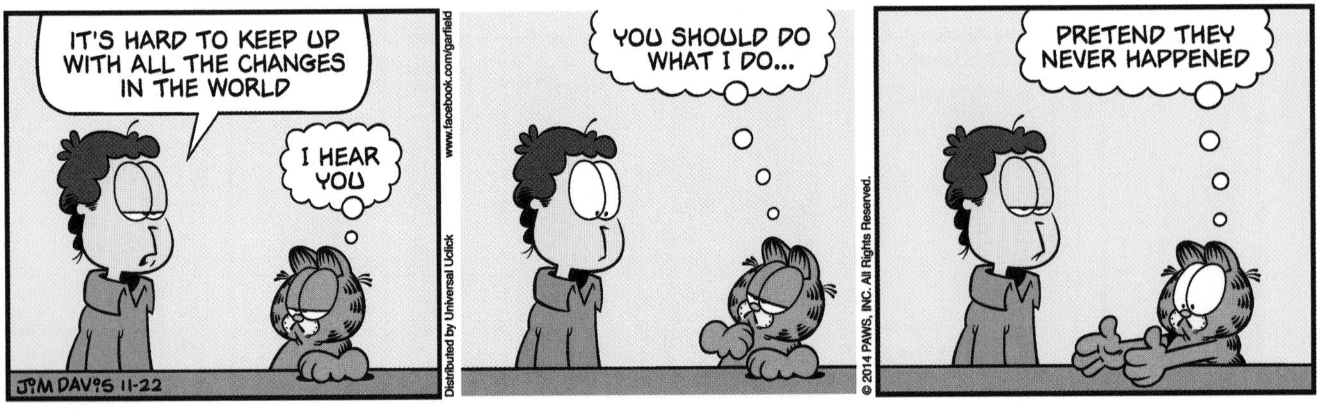
IT'S HARD TO KEEP UP WITH ALL THE CHANGES IN THE WORLD
I HEAR YOU
JIM DAVIS 11-22
Distributed by Universal Uclick
www.facebook.com/garfield
YOU SHOULD DO WHAT I DO...
© 2014 PAWS, INC. All Rights Reserved.
PRETEND THEY NEVER HAPPENED

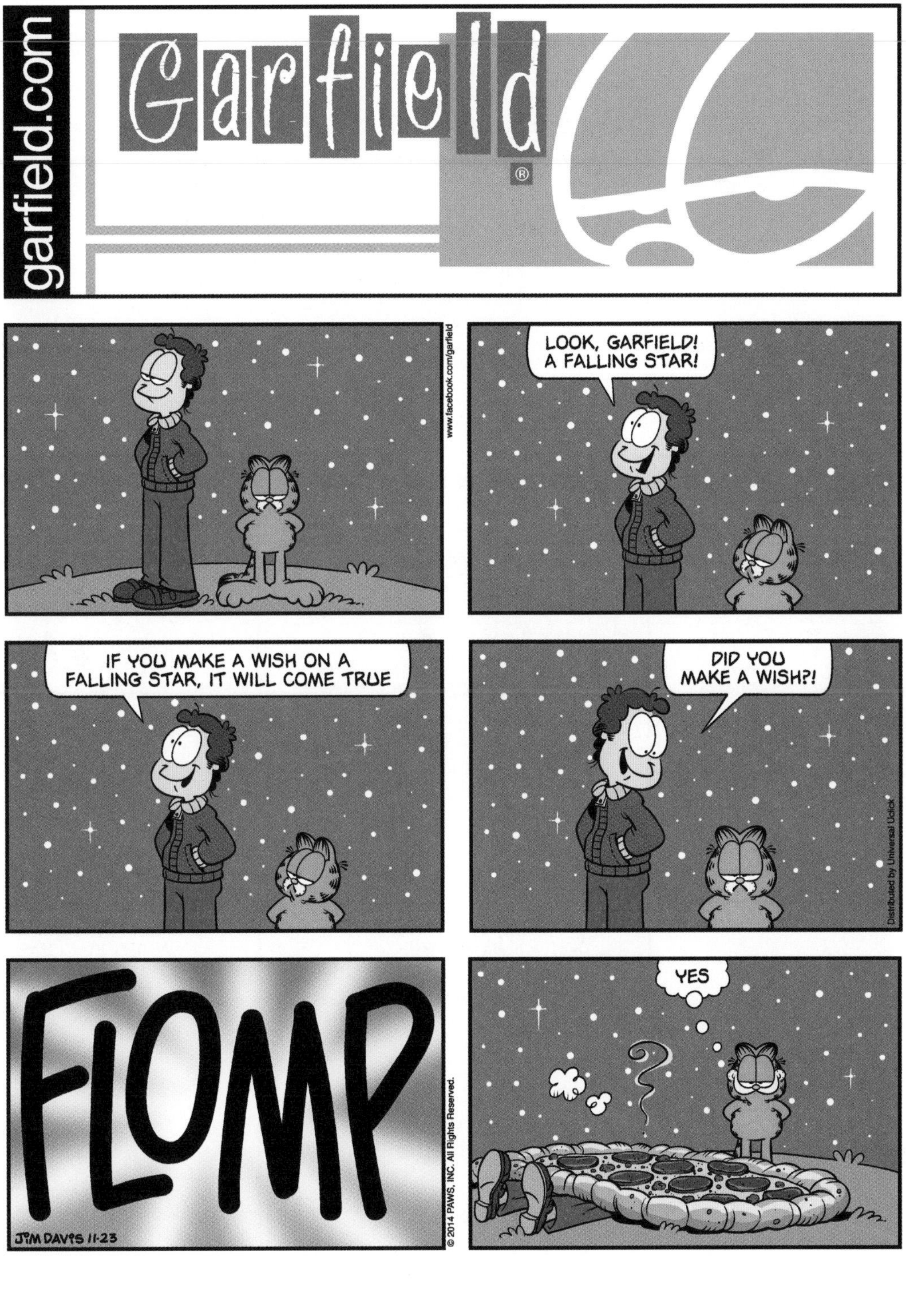
garfield.com
Garfield
www.facebook.com/garfield
LOOK, GARFIELD! A FALLING STAR!
IF YOU MAKE A WISH ON A FALLING STAR, IT WILL COME TRUE
DID YOU MAKE A WISH?!
Distributed by Universal Uclick
FLOMP
JIM DAVIS 11-23
© 2014 PAWS, INC. All Rights Reserved.
YES

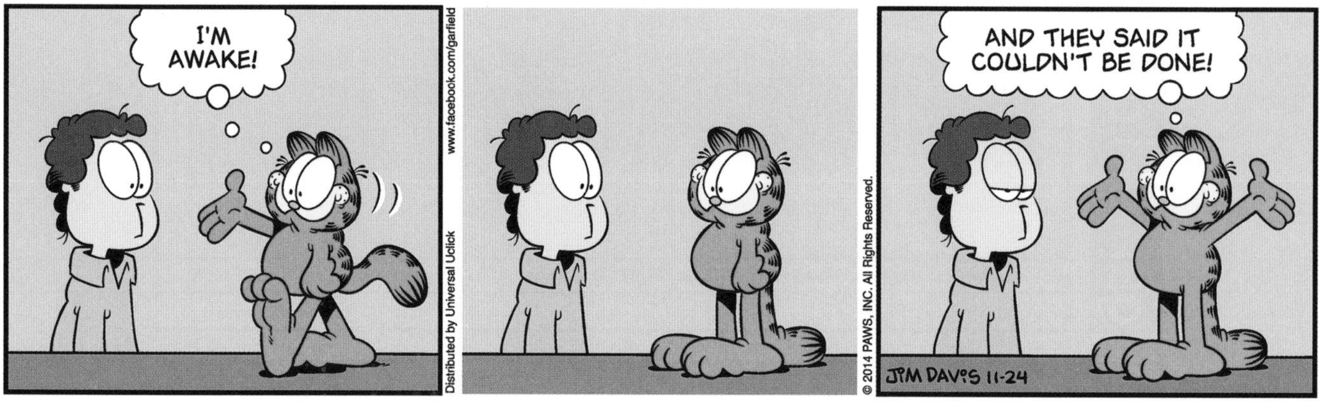
I'M AWAKE!
Distributed by Universal Uclick www.facebook.com/garfield
AND THEY SAID IT COULDN'T BE DONE!
© 2014 PAWS, INC. All Rights Reserved.
JIM DAVIS 11-24

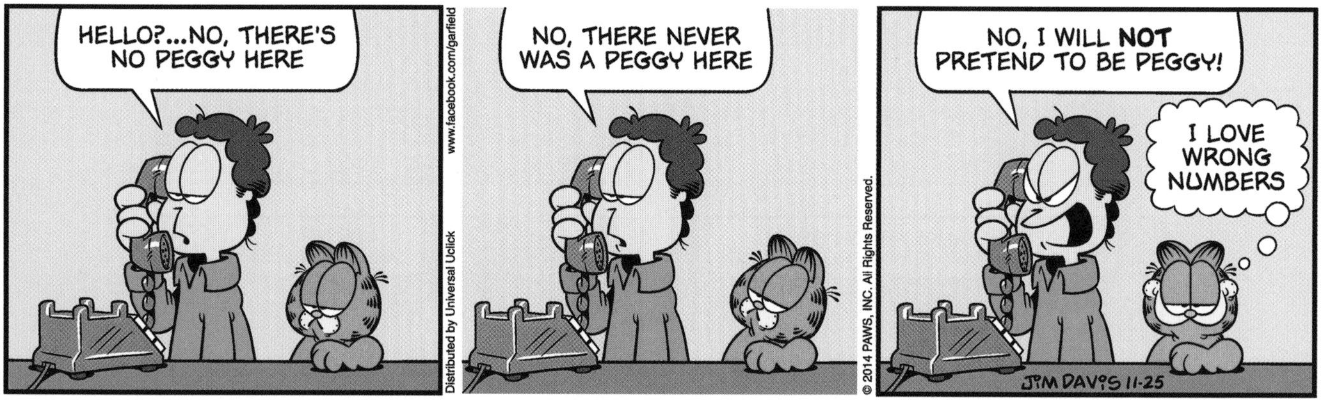
HELLO?...NO, THERE'S NO PEGGY HERE
Distributed by Universal Uclick www.facebook.com/garfield
NO, THERE NEVER WAS A PEGGY HERE
© 2014 PAWS, INC. All Rights Reserved.
NO, I WILL **NOT** PRETEND TO BE PEGGY!
I LOVE WRONG NUMBERS
JIM DAVIS 11-25

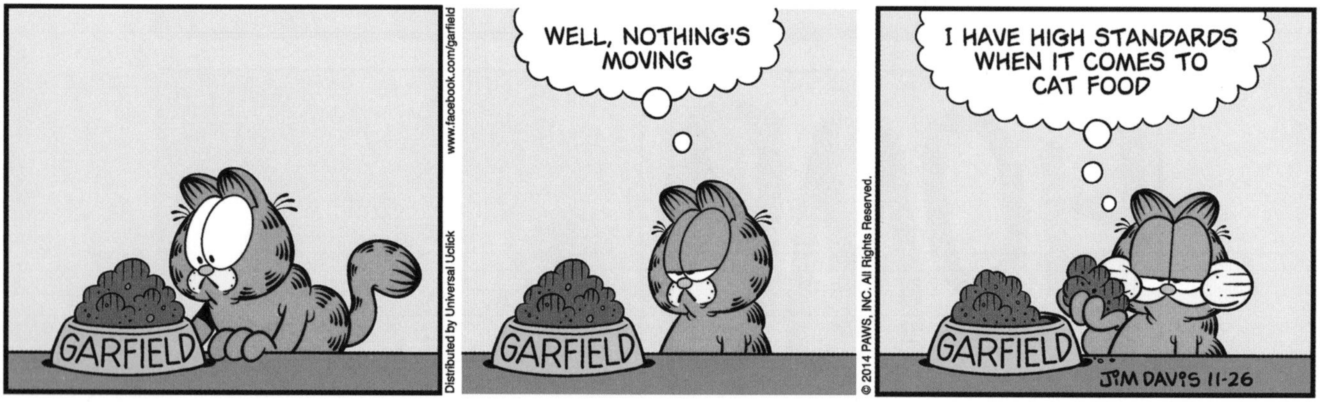
GARFIELD
Distributed by Universal Uclick www.facebook.com/garfield
WELL, NOTHING'S MOVING
GARFIELD
© 2014 PAWS, INC. All Rights Reserved.
I HAVE HIGH STANDARDS WHEN IT COMES TO CAT FOOD
GARFIELD
JIM DAVIS 11-26

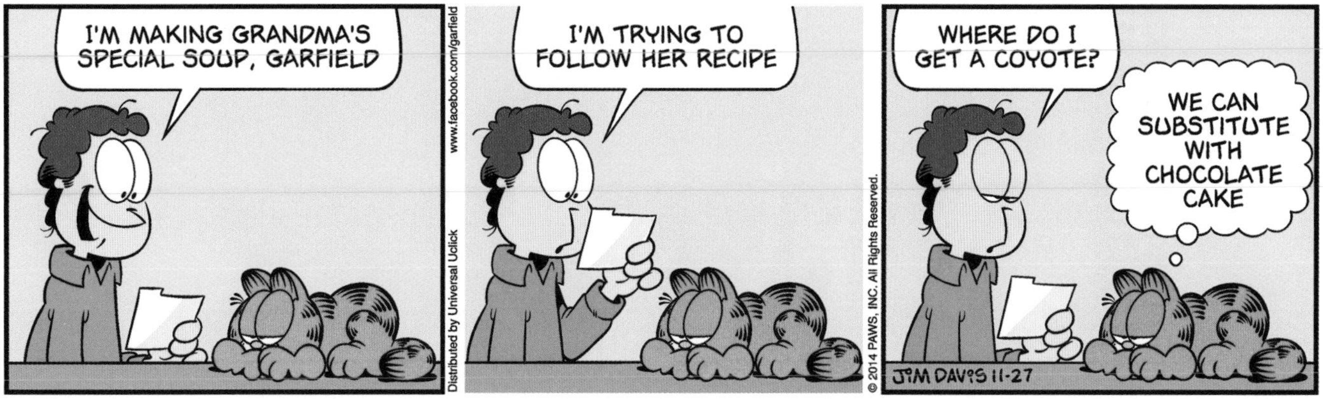
I'M MAKING GRANDMA'S SPECIAL SOUP, GARFIELD
I'M TRYING TO FOLLOW HER RECIPE
WHERE DO I GET A COYOTE?
WE CAN SUBSTITUTE WITH CHOCOLATE CAKE
JIM DAVIS 11-27
Distributed by Universal Uclick www.facebook.com/garfield
© 2014 PAWS, INC. All Rights Reserved.

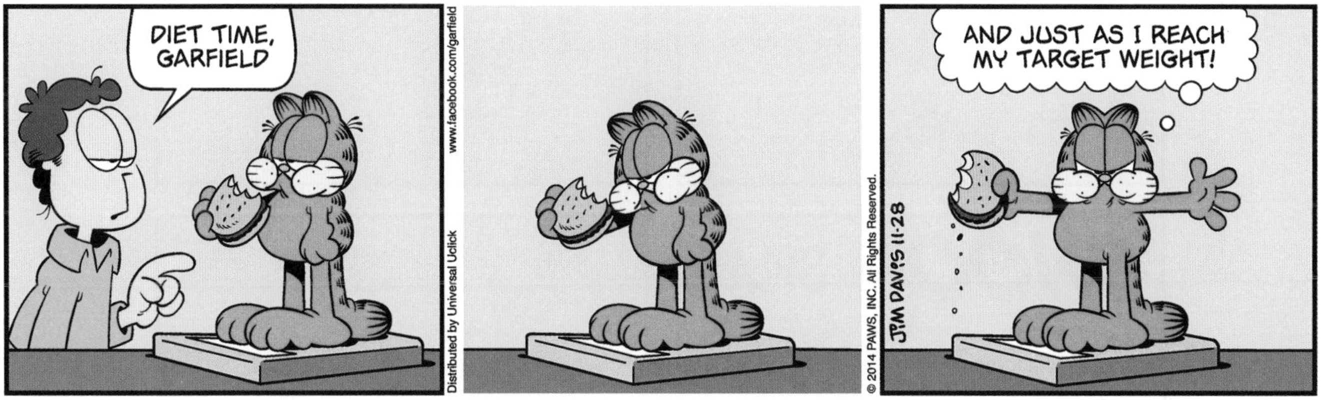
DIET TIME, GARFIELD
AND JUST AS I REACH MY TARGET WEIGHT!
JIM DAVIS 11-28
Distributed by Universal Uclick www.facebook.com/garfield
© 2014 PAWS, INC. All Rights Reserved.

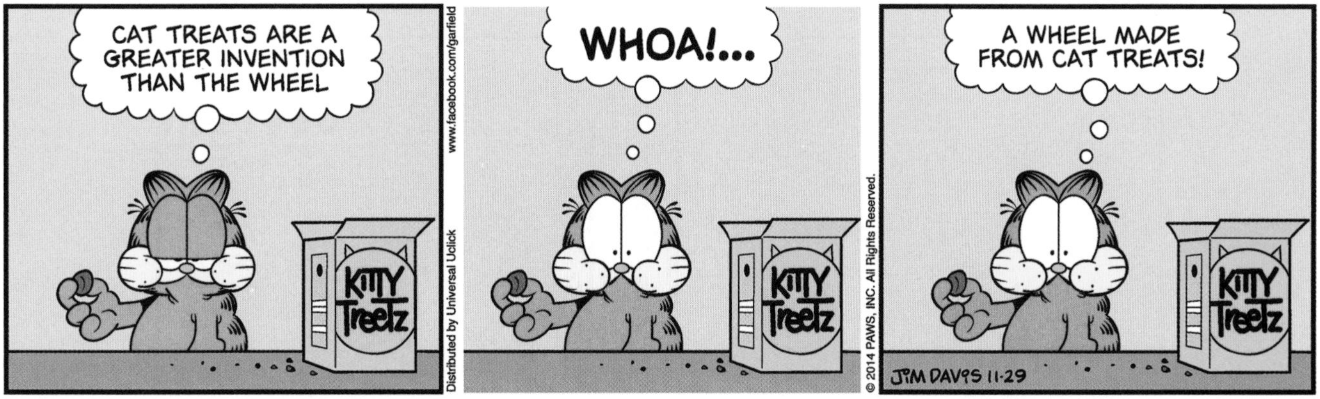
CAT TREATS ARE A GREATER INVENTION THAN THE WHEEL
KITTY Treetz
WHOA!...
A WHEEL MADE FROM CAT TREATS!
JIM DAVIS 11-29
Distributed by Universal Uclick www.facebook.com/garfield
© 2014 PAWS, INC. All Rights Reserved.

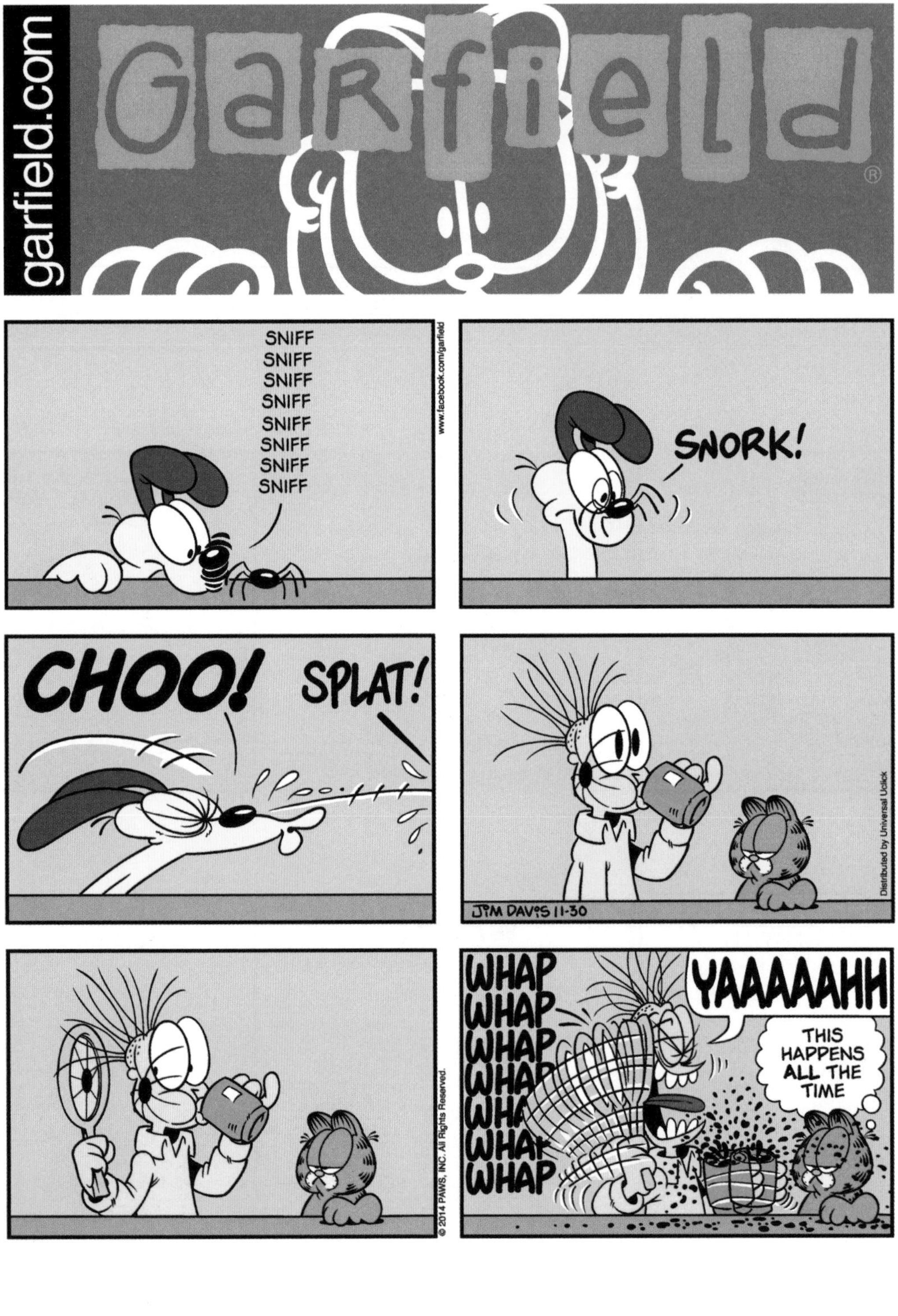
garfield.com
Garfield
SNIFF SNIFF SNIFF SNIFF SNIFF SNIFF SNIFF SNIFF
SNORK!
CHOO!
SPLAT!
JIM DAVIS 11-30
WHAP WHAP WHAP WHAP WHAP WHAP WHAP WHAP
YAAAAAHH
THIS HAPPENS **ALL** THE TIME
www.facebook.com/garfield
Distributed by Universal Uclick
© 2014 PAWS, INC. All Rights Reserved.

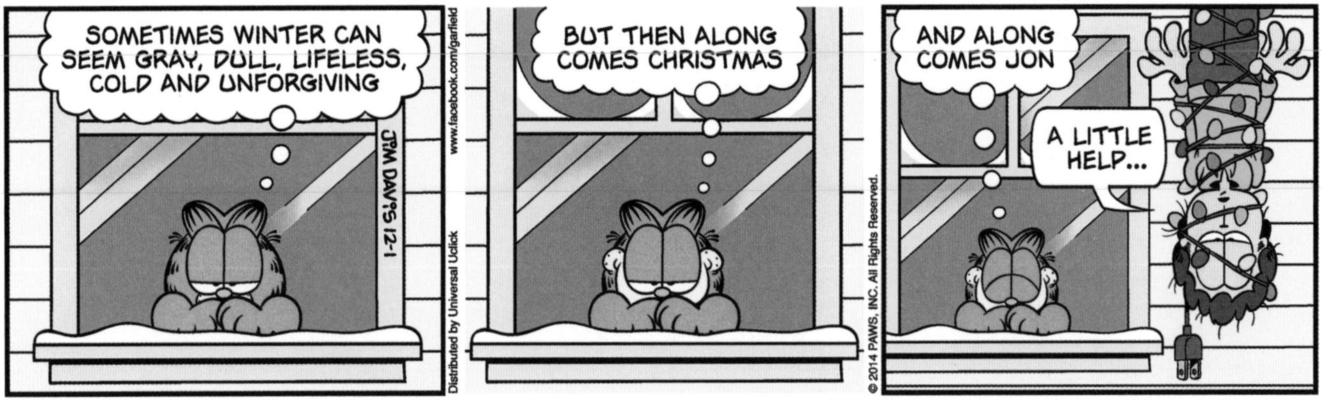
SOMETIMES WINTER CAN SEEM GRAY, DULL, LIFELESS, COLD AND UNFORGIVING
JIM DAVIS 12-1
Distributed by Universal Uclick www.facebook.com/garfield
BUT THEN ALONG COMES CHRISTMAS
© 2014 PAWS, INC. All Rights Reserved.
AND ALONG COMES JON
A LITTLE HELP...

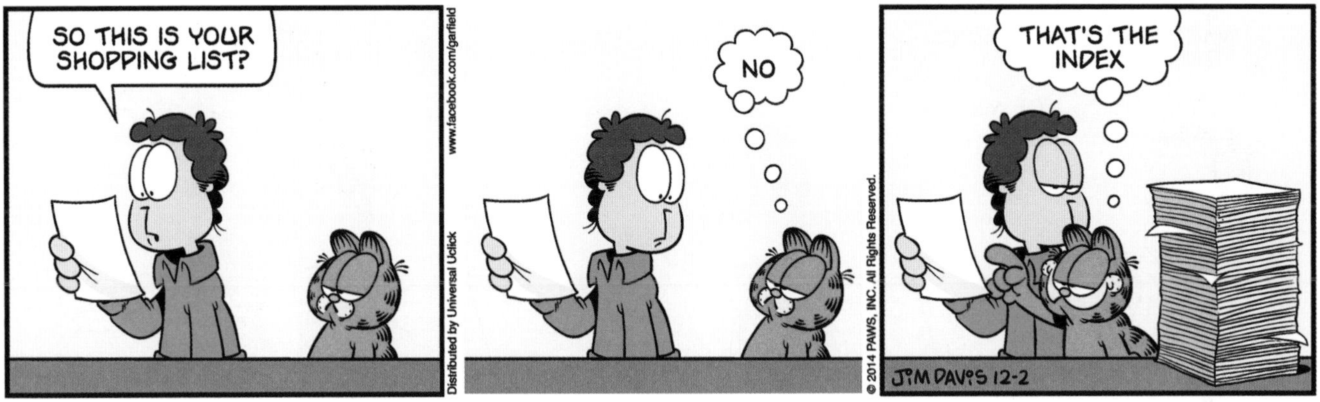
SO THIS IS YOUR SHOPPING LIST?
Distributed by Universal Uclick www.facebook.com/garfield
NO
© 2014 PAWS, INC. All Rights Reserved.
THAT'S THE INDEX
JIM DAVIS 12-2

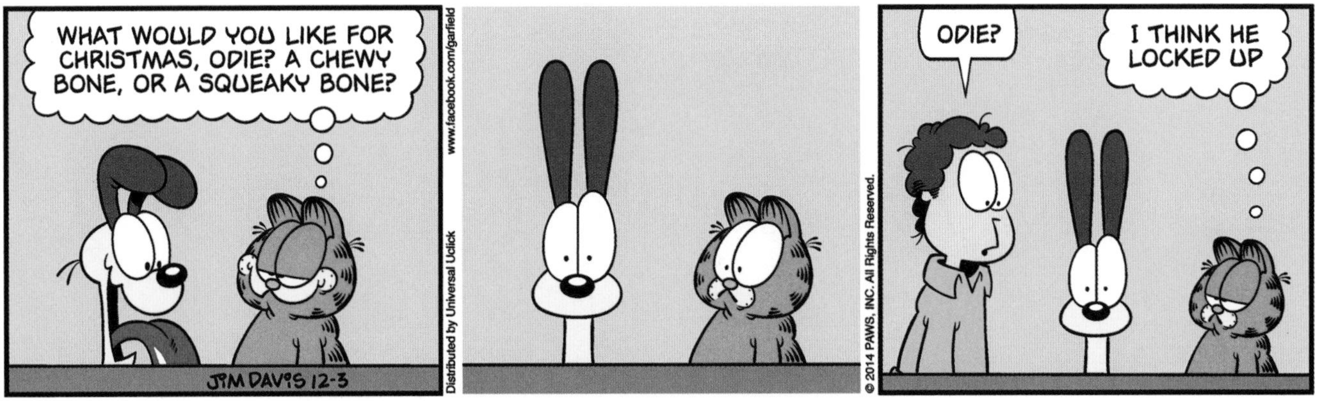
WHAT WOULD YOU LIKE FOR CHRISTMAS, ODIE? A CHEWY BONE, OR A SQUEAKY BONE?
JIM DAVIS 12-3
Distributed by Universal Uclick www.facebook.com/garfield
© 2014 PAWS, INC. All Rights Reserved.
ODIE?
I THINK HE LOCKED UP

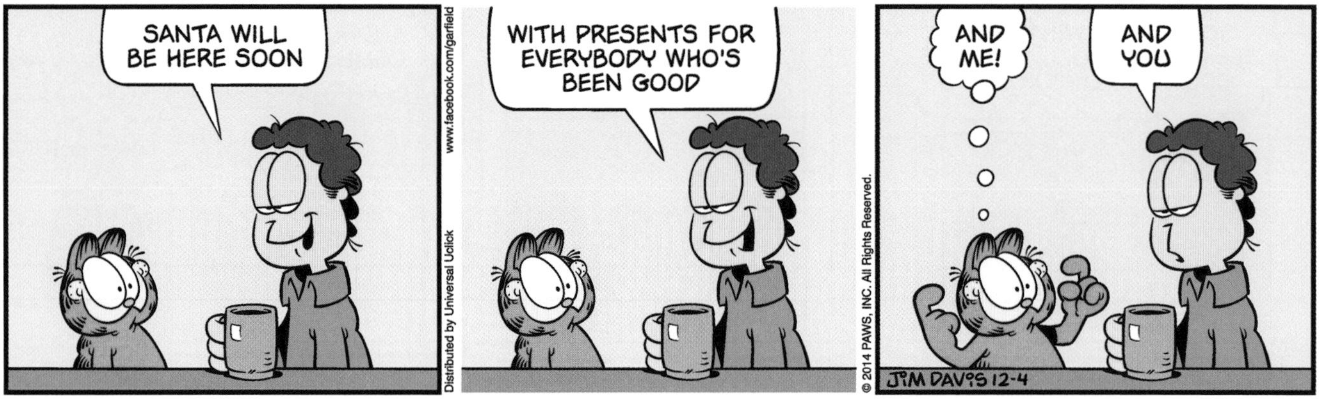
SANTA WILL BE HERE SOON
WITH PRESENTS FOR EVERYBODY WHO'S BEEN GOOD
AND YOU
AND ME!
JIM DAVIS 12-4
www.facebook.com/garfield
Distributed by Universal Uclick
© 2014 PAWS, INC. All Rights Reserved.

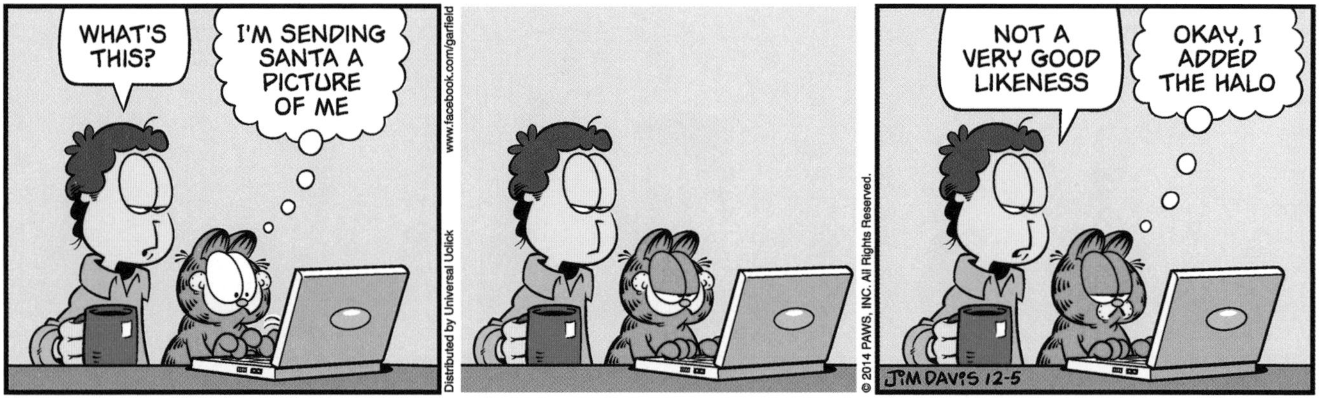
WHAT'S THIS?
I'M SENDING SANTA A PICTURE OF ME
NOT A VERY GOOD LIKENESS
OKAY, I ADDED THE HALO
JIM DAVIS 12-5
www.facebook.com/garfield
Distributed by Universal Uclick
© 2014 PAWS, INC. All Rights Reserved.

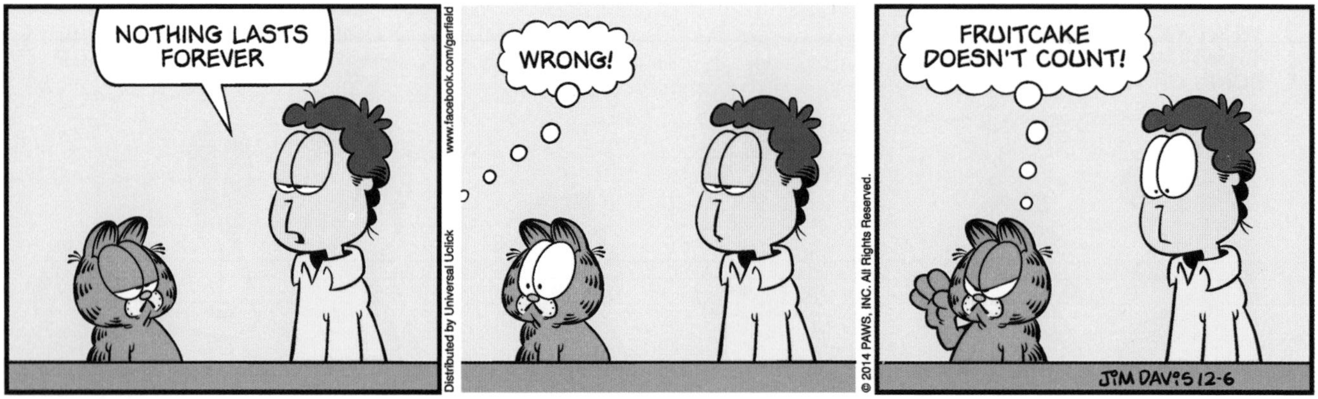
NOTHING LASTS FOREVER
WRONG!
FRUITCAKE DOESN'T COUNT!
JIM DAVIS 12-6
www.facebook.com/garfield
Distributed by Universal Uclick
© 2014 PAWS, INC. All Rights Reserved.

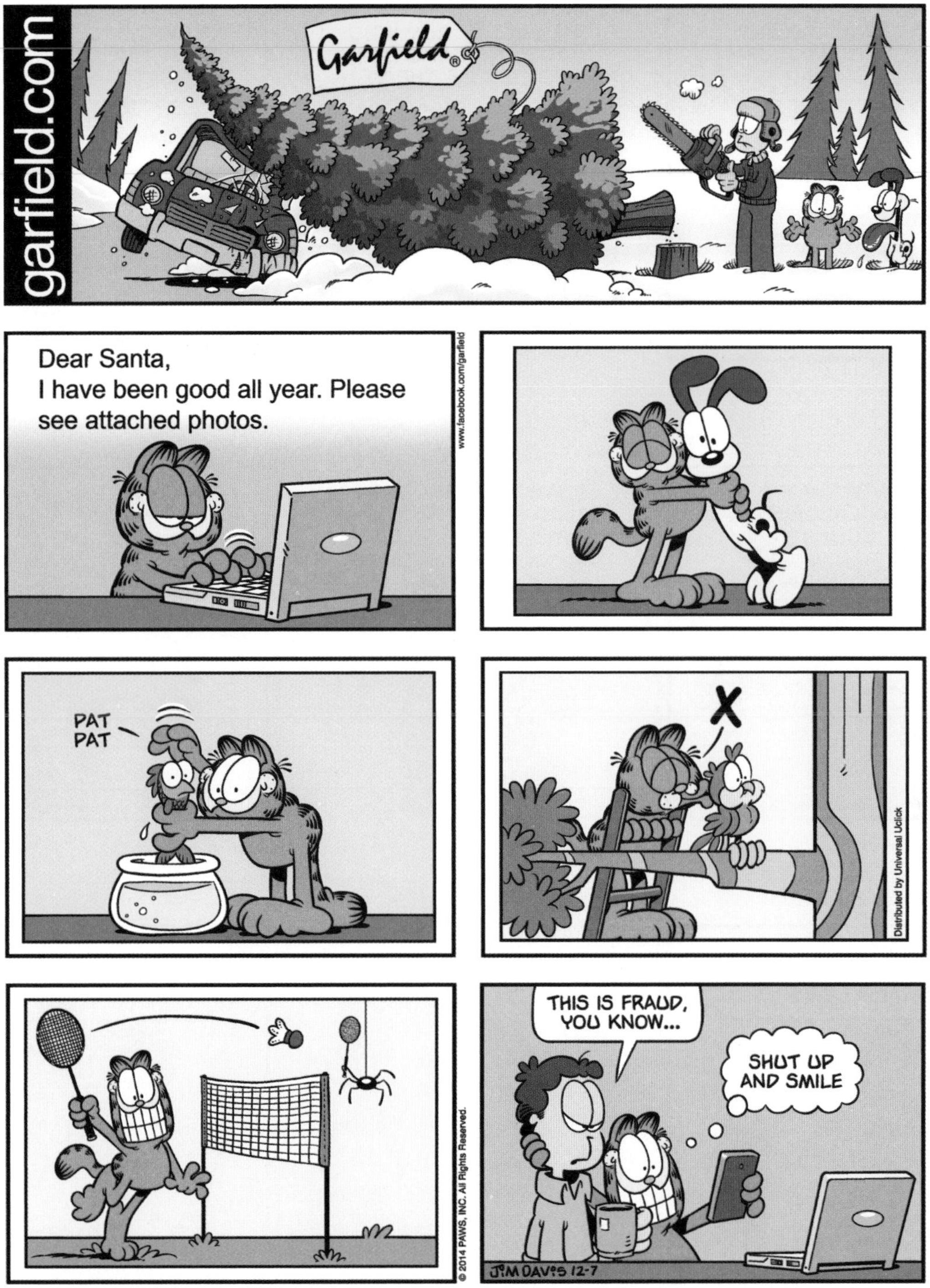
garfield.com
Garfield®
Dear Santa,
I have been good all year. Please see attached photos.
www.facebook.com/garfield
PAT PAT
X
Distributed by Universal Uclick
© 2014 PAWS, INC. All Rights Reserved.
THIS IS FRAUD, YOU KNOW...
SHUT UP AND SMILE
JIM DAVIS 12-7

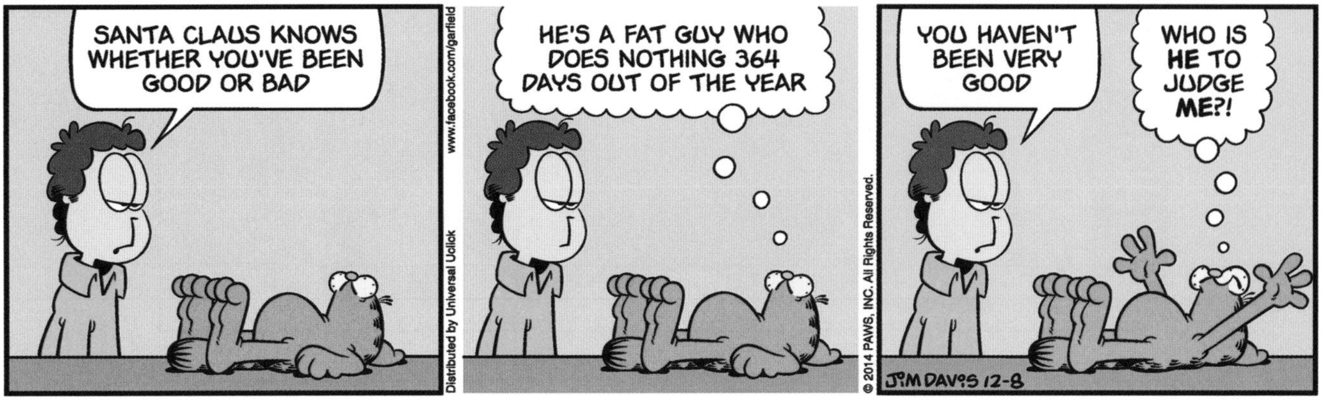
SANTA CLAUS KNOWS WHETHER YOU'VE BEEN GOOD OR BAD
HE'S A FAT GUY WHO DOES NOTHING 364 DAYS OUT OF THE YEAR
YOU HAVEN'T BEEN VERY GOOD
WHO IS **HE** TO JUDGE **ME**?!
JIM DAVIS 12-8
www.facebook.com/garfield
Distributed by Universal Uclick
© 2014 PAWS, INC. All Rights Reserved.

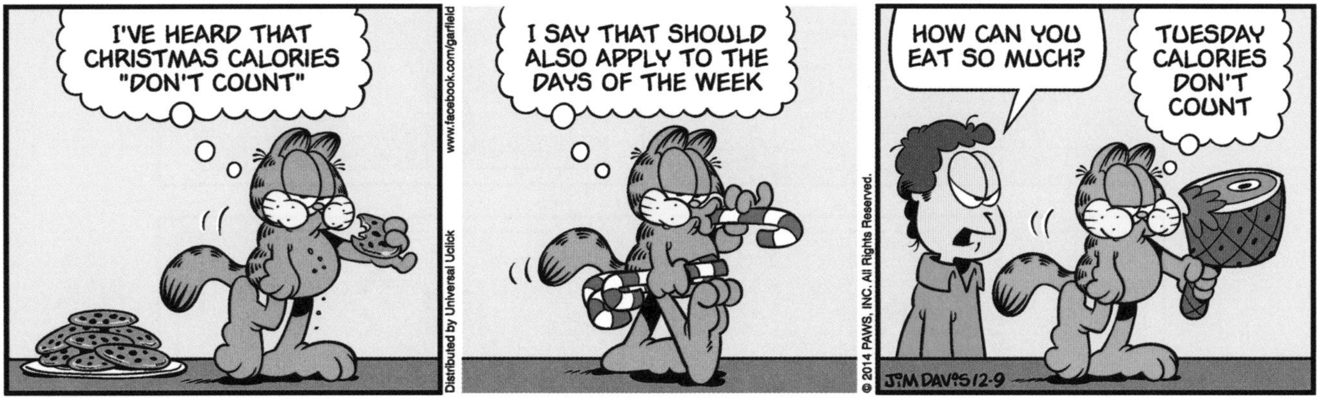
I'VE HEARD THAT CHRISTMAS CALORIES "DON'T COUNT"
I SAY THAT SHOULD ALSO APPLY TO THE DAYS OF THE WEEK
HOW CAN YOU EAT SO MUCH?
TUESDAY CALORIES DON'T COUNT
JIM DAVIS 12-9
www.facebook.com/garfield
Distributed by Universal Uclick
© 2014 PAWS, INC. All Rights Reserved.

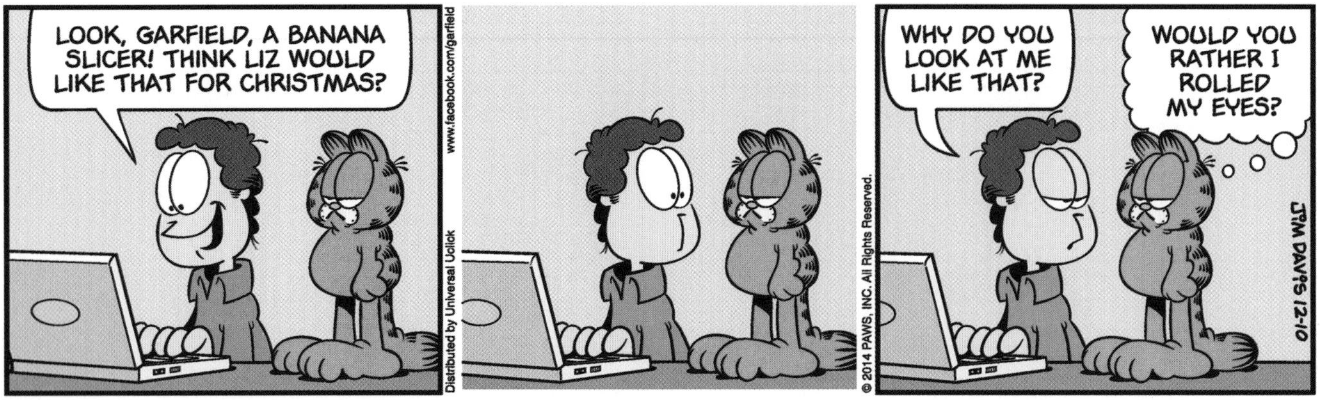
LOOK, GARFIELD, A BANANA SLICER! THINK LIZ WOULD LIKE THAT FOR CHRISTMAS?
WHY DO YOU LOOK AT ME LIKE THAT?
WOULD YOU RATHER I ROLLED MY EYES?
JIM DAVIS 12-10
www.facebook.com/garfield
Distributed by Universal Uclick
© 2014 PAWS, INC. All Rights Reserved.

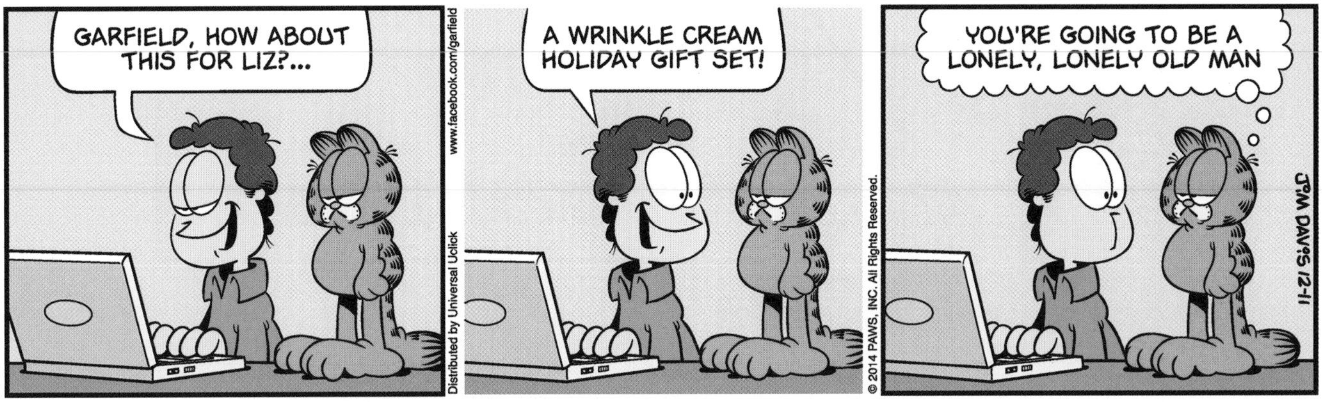
GARFIELD, HOW ABOUT THIS FOR LIZ?...
A WRINKLE CREAM HOLIDAY GIFT SET!
YOU'RE GOING TO BE A LONELY, LONELY OLD MAN
JIM DAVIS 12-11
Distributed by Universal Uclick www.facebook.com/garfield
© 2014 PAWS, INC. All Rights Reserved.

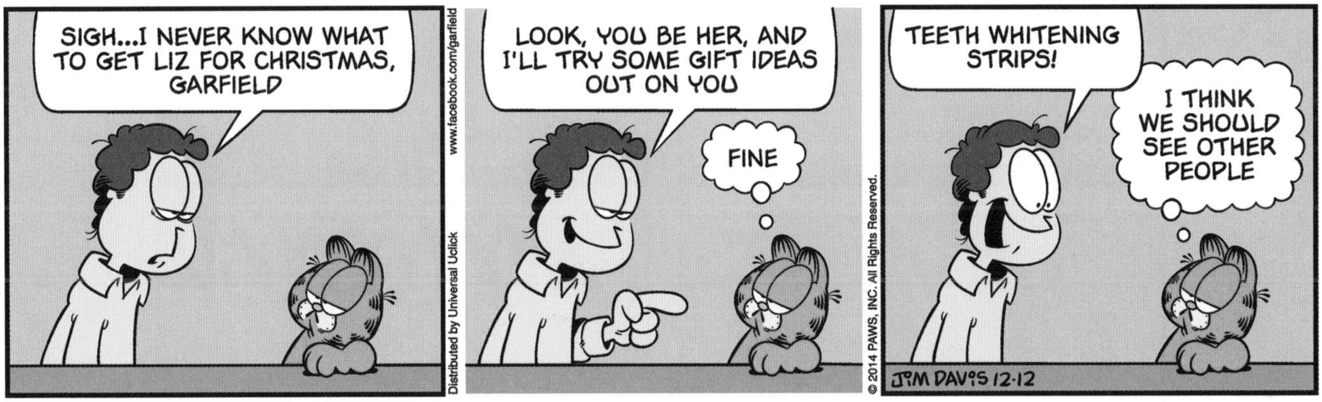
SIGH...I NEVER KNOW WHAT TO GET LIZ FOR CHRISTMAS, GARFIELD
LOOK, YOU BE HER, AND I'LL TRY SOME GIFT IDEAS OUT ON YOU
FINE
TEETH WHITENING STRIPS!
I THINK WE SHOULD SEE OTHER PEOPLE
JIM DAVIS 12-12
Distributed by Universal Uclick www.facebook.com/garfield
© 2014 PAWS, INC. All Rights Reserved.

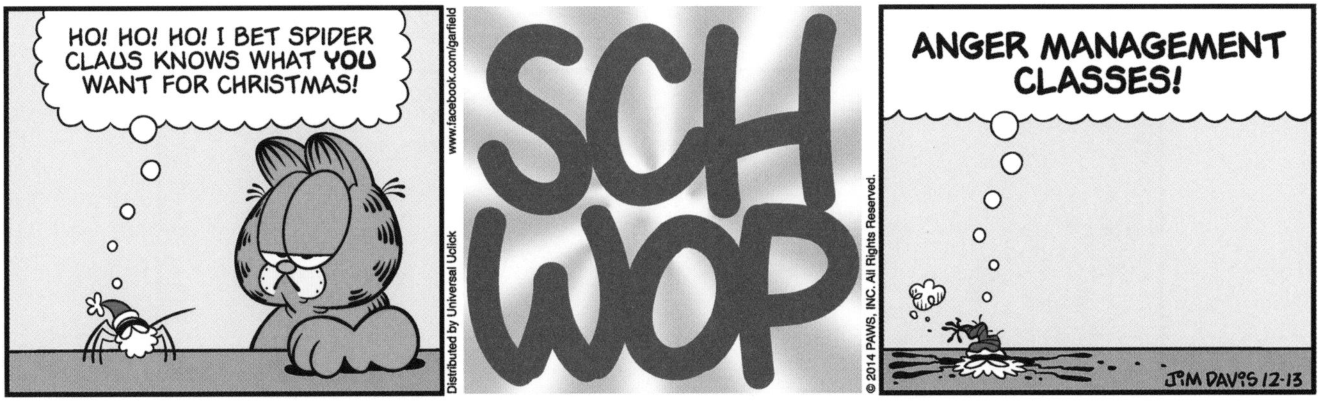
HO! HO! HO! I BET SPIDER CLAUS KNOWS WHAT **YOU** WANT FOR CHRISTMAS!
SCH WOP
ANGER MANAGEMENT CLASSES!
JIM DAVIS 12-13
Distributed by Universal Uclick www.facebook.com/garfield
© 2014 PAWS, INC. All Rights Reserved.

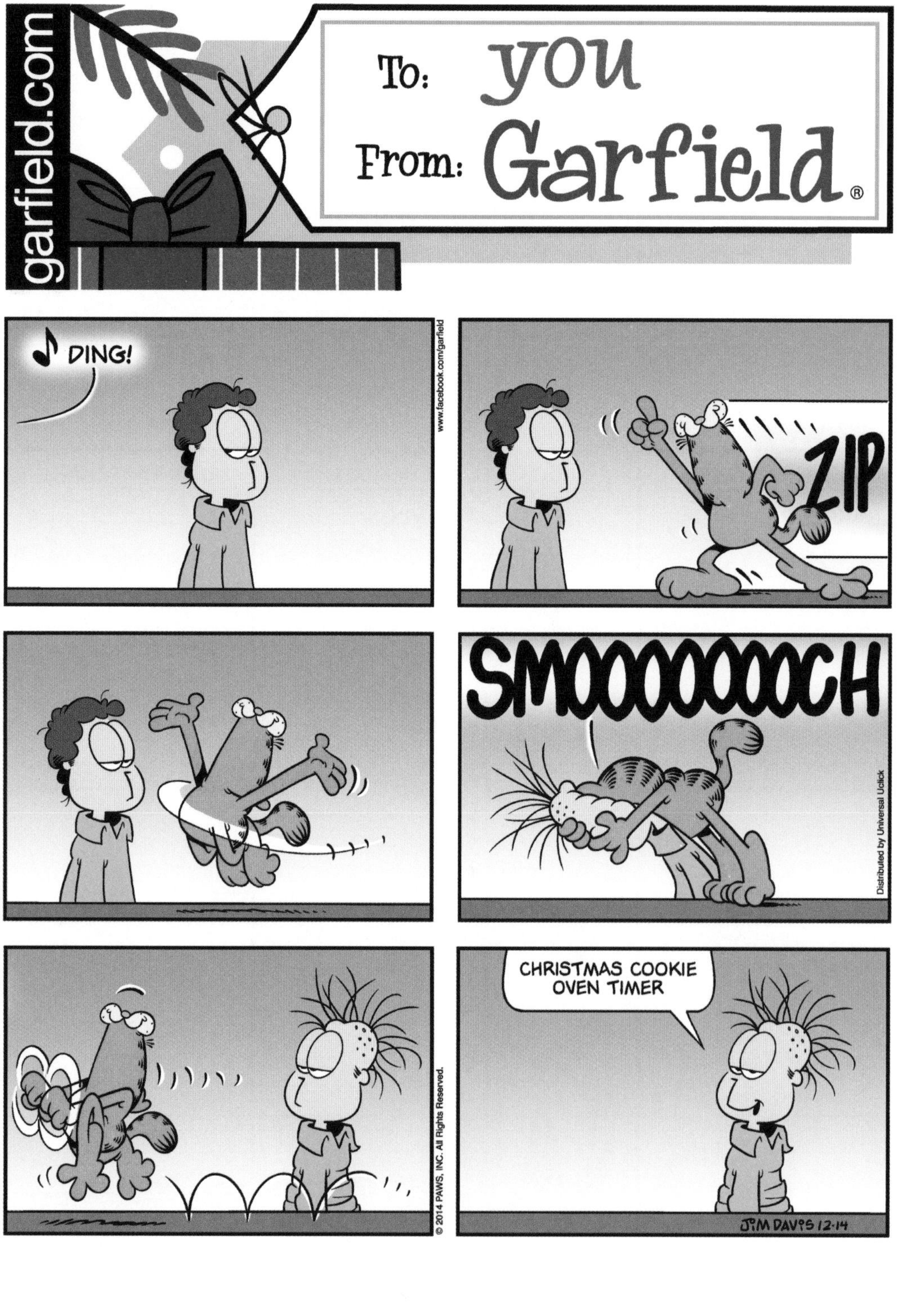
garfield.com
To: you
From: Garfield®
DING!
ZIP
SMOOOOOOOCH
CHRISTMAS COOKIE OVEN TIMER
JIM DAVIS 12-14
www.facebook.com/garfield
Distributed by Universal Uclick
© 2014 PAWS, INC. All Rights Reserved.

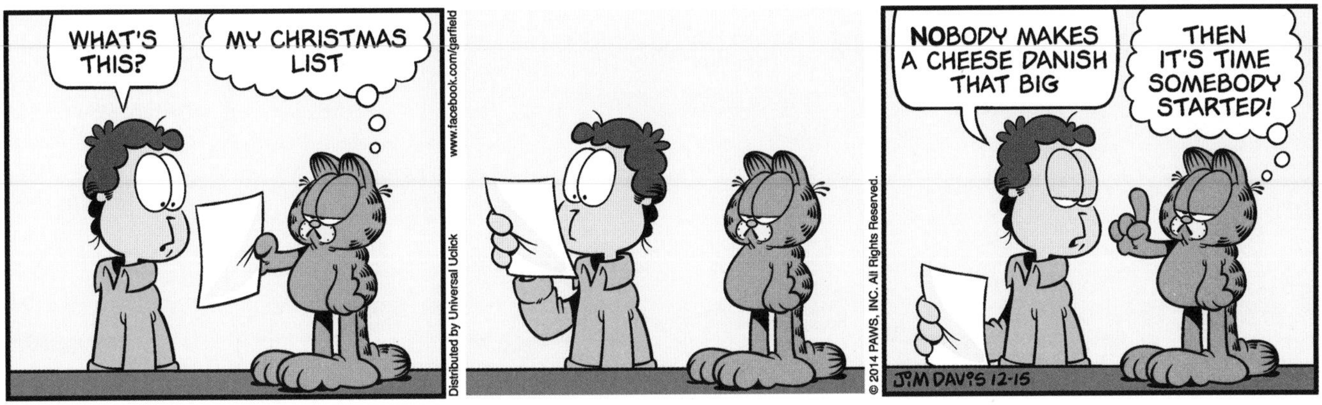
WHAT'S THIS?
MY CHRISTMAS LIST
NOBODY MAKES A CHEESE DANISH THAT BIG
THEN IT'S TIME SOMEBODY STARTED!
JIM DAVIS 12-15

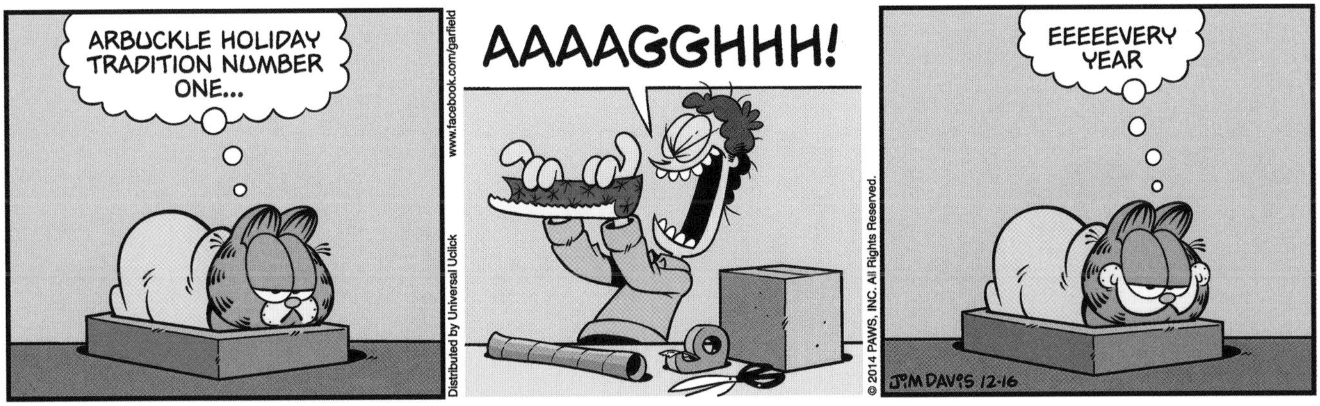
ARBUCKLE HOLIDAY TRADITION NUMBER ONE...
AAAAGGHHH!
EEEEEVERY YEAR
JIM DAVIS 12-16

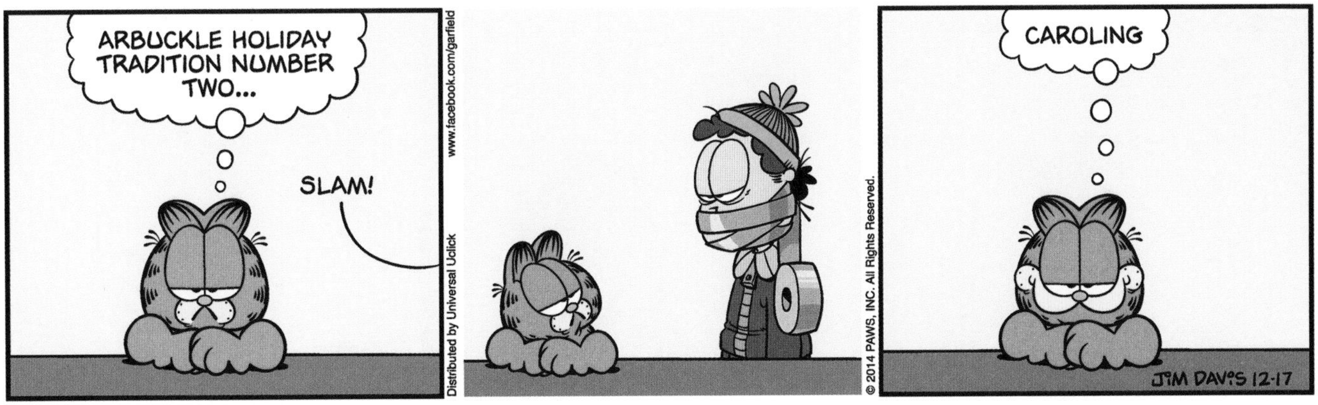
ARBUCKLE HOLIDAY TRADITION NUMBER TWO...
SLAM!
CAROLING
JIM DAVIS 12-17

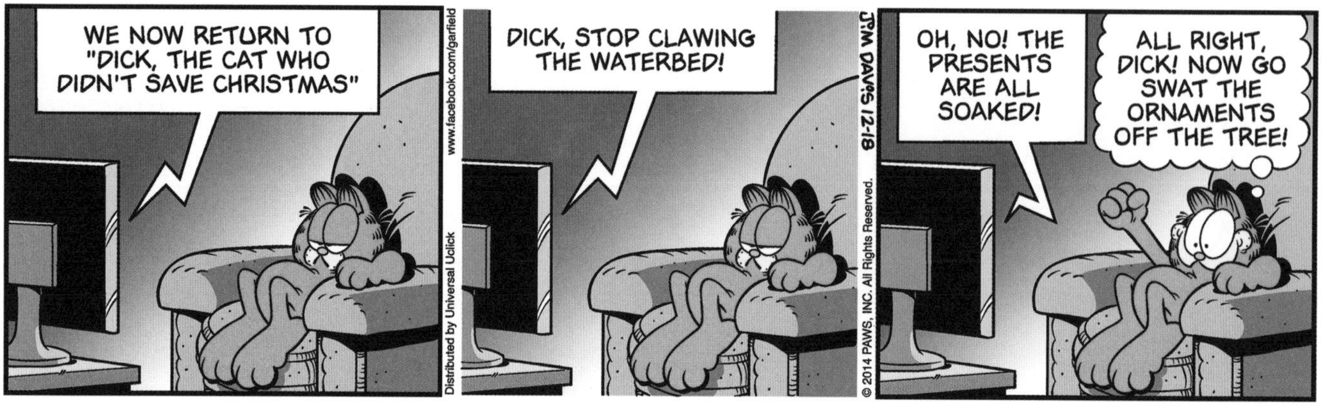

WE NOW RETURN TO "DICK, THE CAT WHO DIDN'T SAVE CHRISTMAS"
DICK, STOP CLAWING THE WATERBED!
OH, NO! THE PRESENTS ARE ALL SOAKED!
ALL RIGHT, DICK! NOW GO SWAT THE ORNAMENTS OFF THE TREE!
JIM DAVIS 12-18
Distributed by Universal Uclick www.facebook.com/garfield
© 2014 PAWS, INC. All Rights Reserved.

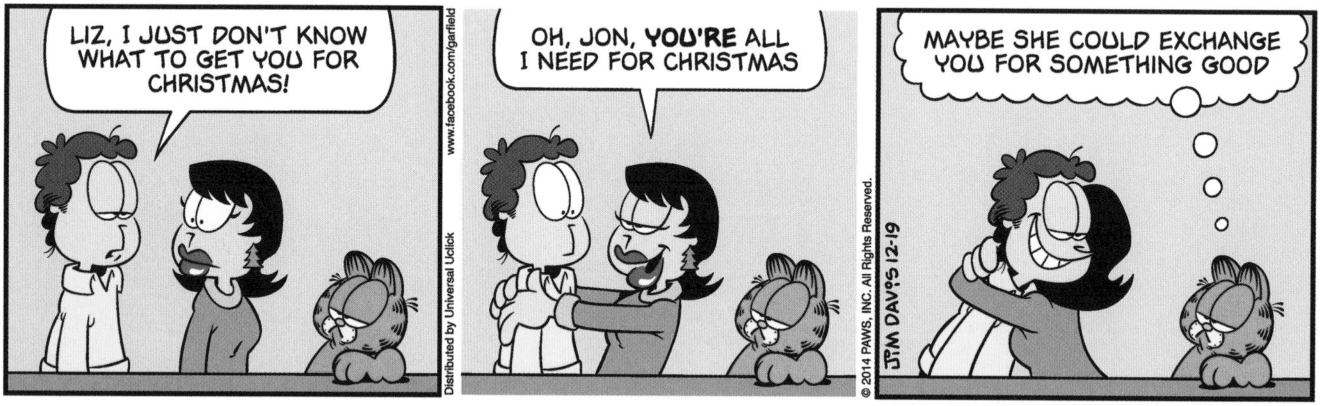

LIZ, I JUST DON'T KNOW WHAT TO GET YOU FOR CHRISTMAS!
OH, JON, **YOU'RE** ALL I NEED FOR CHRISTMAS
MAYBE SHE COULD EXCHANGE YOU FOR SOMETHING GOOD
JIM DAVIS 12-19
Distributed by Universal Uclick www.facebook.com/garfield
© 2014 PAWS, INC. All Rights Reserved.

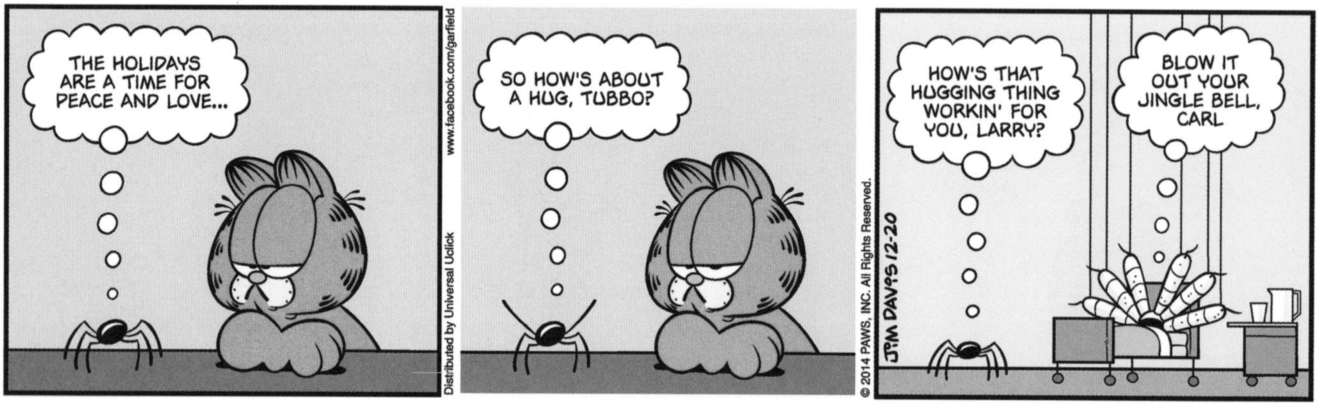

THE HOLIDAYS ARE A TIME FOR PEACE AND LOVE...
SO HOW'S ABOUT A HUG, TUBBO?
HOW'S THAT HUGGING THING WORKIN' FOR YOU, LARRY?
BLOW IT OUT YOUR JINGLE BELL, CARL
JIM DAVIS 12-20
Distributed by Universal Uclick www.facebook.com/garfield
© 2014 PAWS, INC. All Rights Reserved.

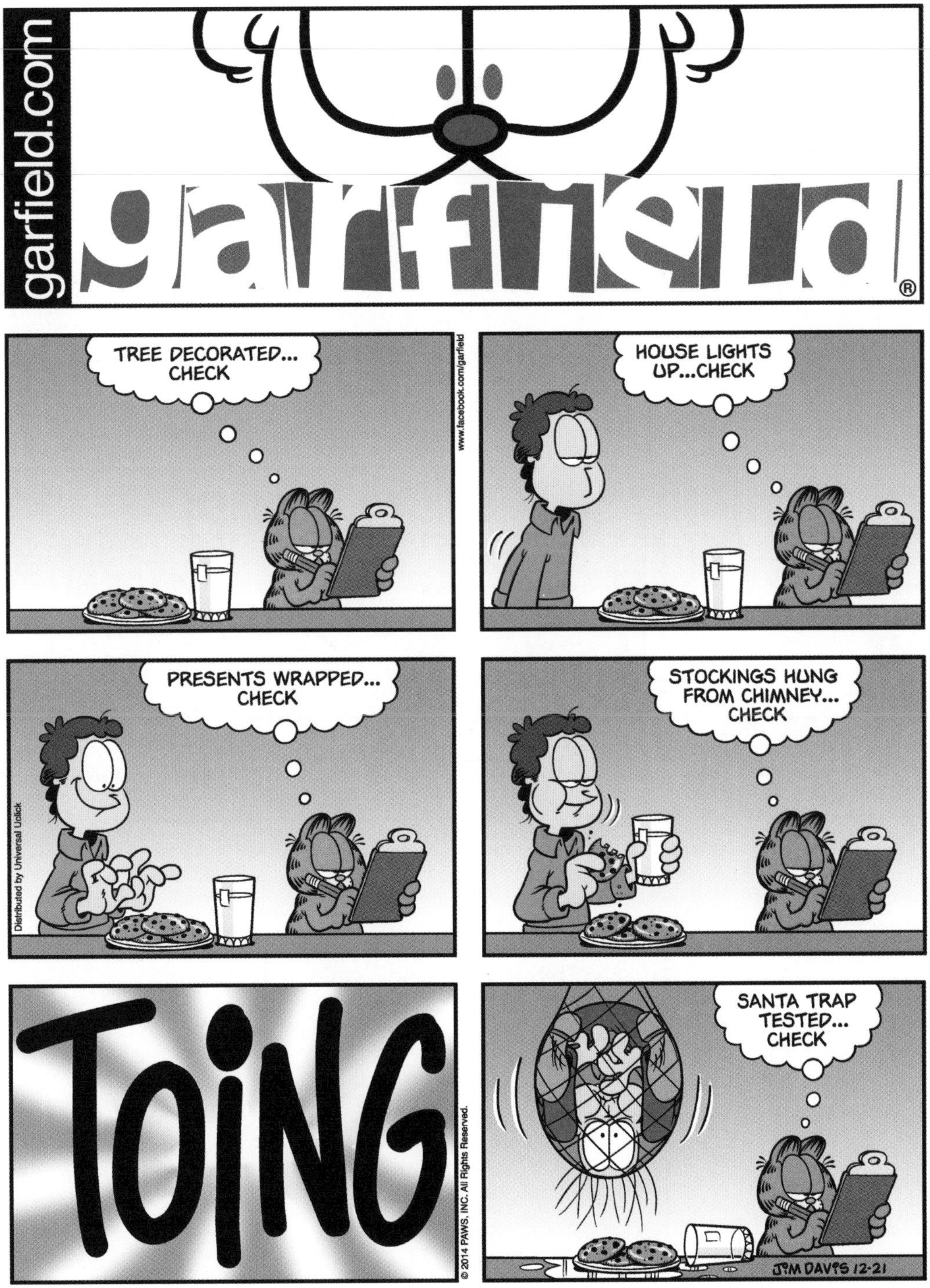
garfield.com
garfield
TREE DECORATED... CHECK
www.facebook.com/garfield
HOUSE LIGHTS UP...CHECK
PRESENTS WRAPPED... CHECK
Distributed by Universal Uclick
STOCKINGS HUNG FROM CHIMNEY... CHECK
TOING
© 2014 PAWS, INC. All Rights Reserved.
SANTA TRAP TESTED... CHECK
JIM DAVIS 12-21

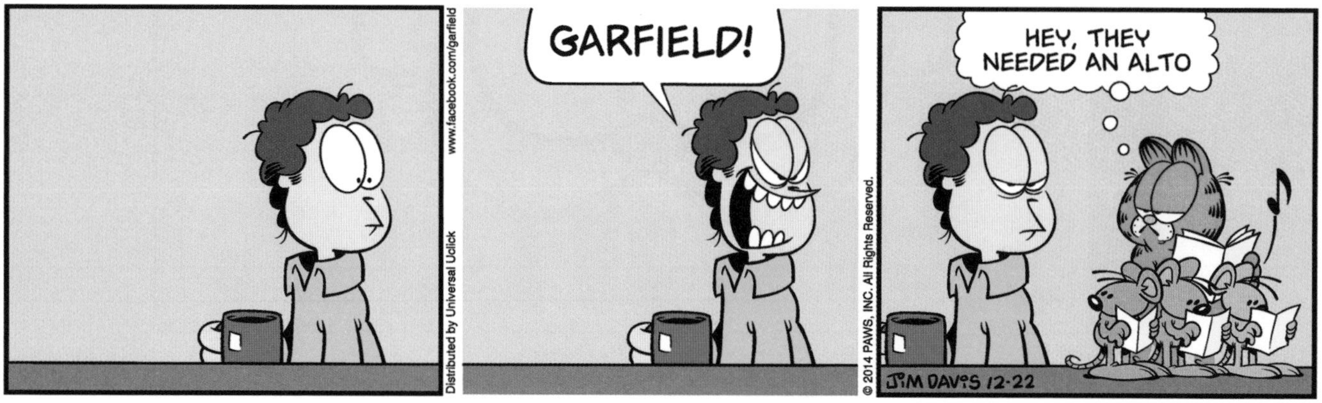
GARFIELD!
HEY, THEY NEEDED AN ALTO
JIM DAVIS 12-22
Distributed by Universal Uclick www.facebook.com/garfield
© 2014 PAWS, INC. All Rights Reserved.

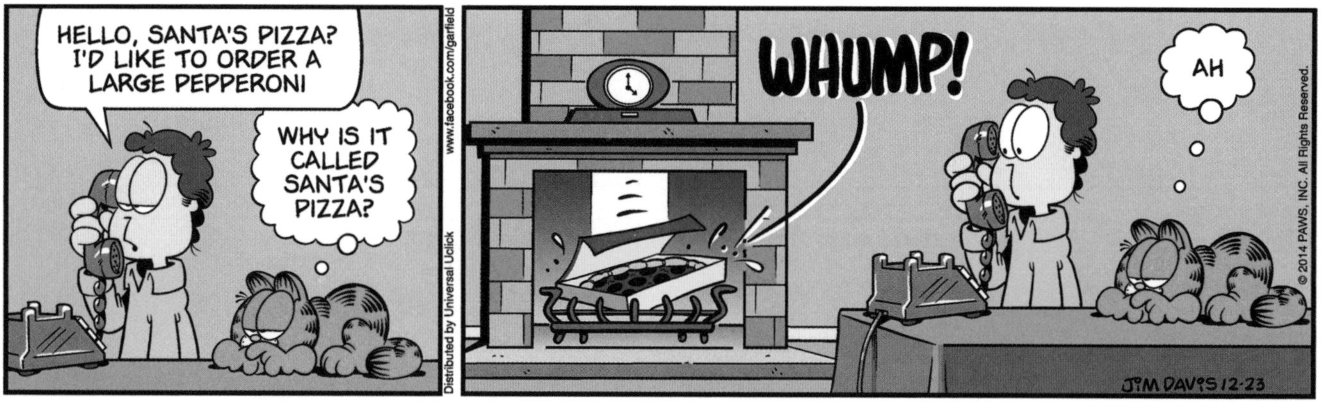
HELLO, SANTA'S PIZZA? I'D LIKE TO ORDER A LARGE PEPPERONI
WHY IS IT CALLED SANTA'S PIZZA?
WHUMP!
AH
JIM DAVIS 12-23
Distributed by Universal Uclick www.facebook.com/garfield
© 2014 PAWS, INC. All Rights Reserved.

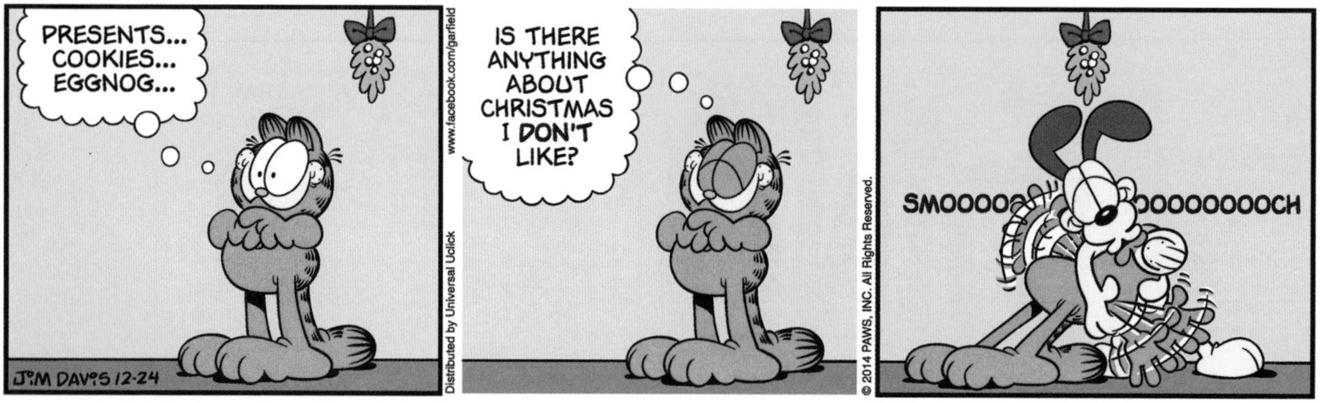
PRESENTS... COOKIES... EGGNOG...
IS THERE ANYTHING ABOUT CHRISTMAS I **DON'T** LIKE?
SMOOOO
OOOOOOOOCH
JIM DAVIS 12-24
Distributed by Universal Uclick www.facebook.com/garfield
© 2014 PAWS, INC. All Rights Reserved.

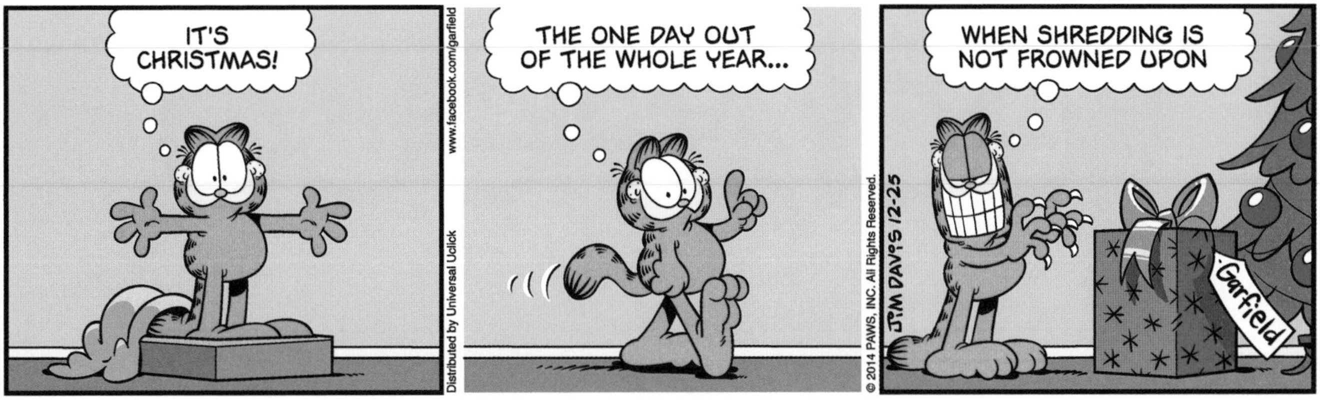
IT'S CHRISTMAS!
THE ONE DAY OUT OF THE WHOLE YEAR...
WHEN SHREDDING IS NOT FROWNED UPON
Garfield
JIM DAVIS 12-25
Distributed by Universal Uclick www.facebook.com/garfield
© 2014 PAWS, INC. All Rights Reserved.

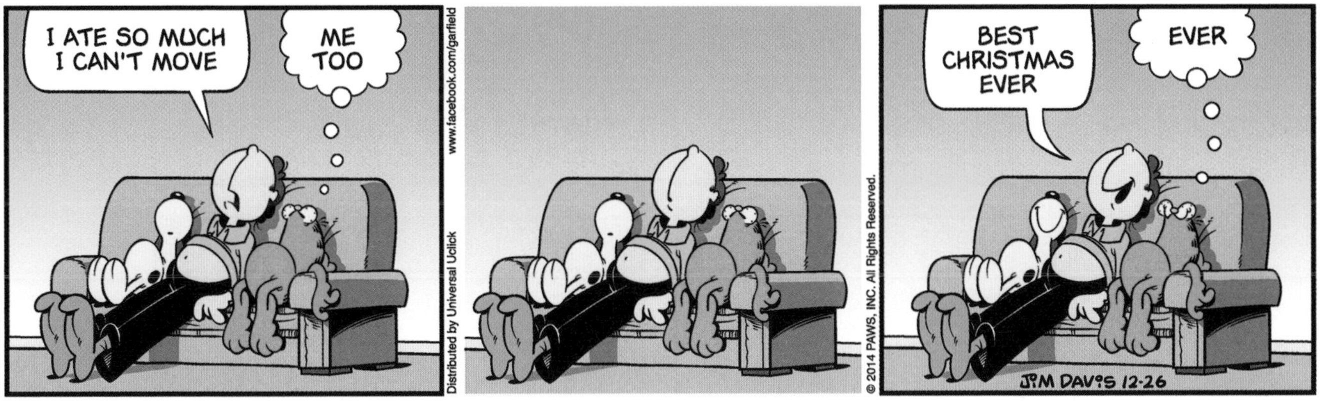
I ATE SO MUCH I CAN'T MOVE
ME TOO
BEST CHRISTMAS EVER
EVER
JIM DAVIS 12-26
Distributed by Universal Uclick www.facebook.com/garfield
© 2014 PAWS, INC. All Rights Reserved.

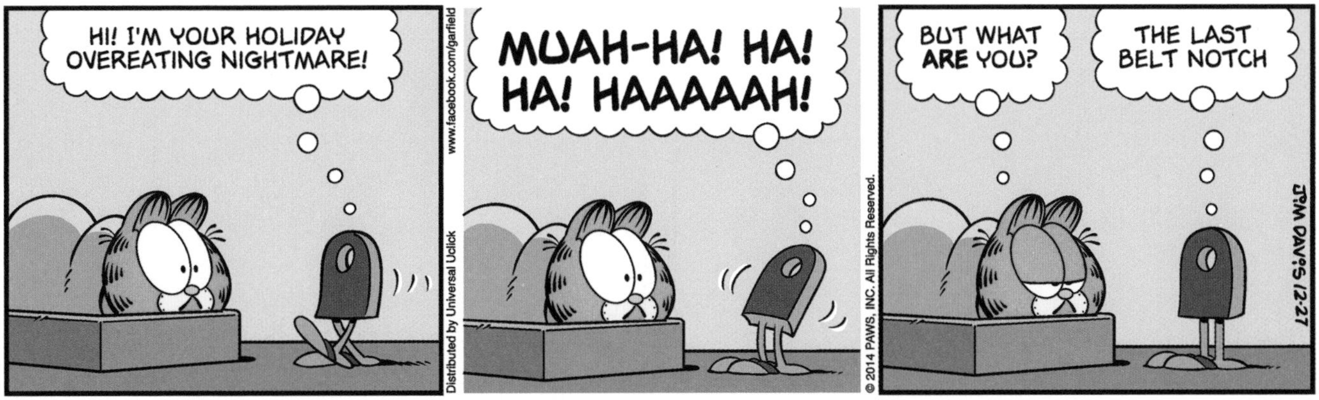
HI! I'M YOUR HOLIDAY OVEREATING NIGHTMARE!
MUAH-HA! HA! HA! HAAAAAH!
BUT WHAT ARE YOU?
THE LAST BELT NOTCH
JIM DAVIS 12-27
Distributed by Universal Uclick www.facebook.com/garfield
© 2014 PAWS, INC. All Rights Reserved.

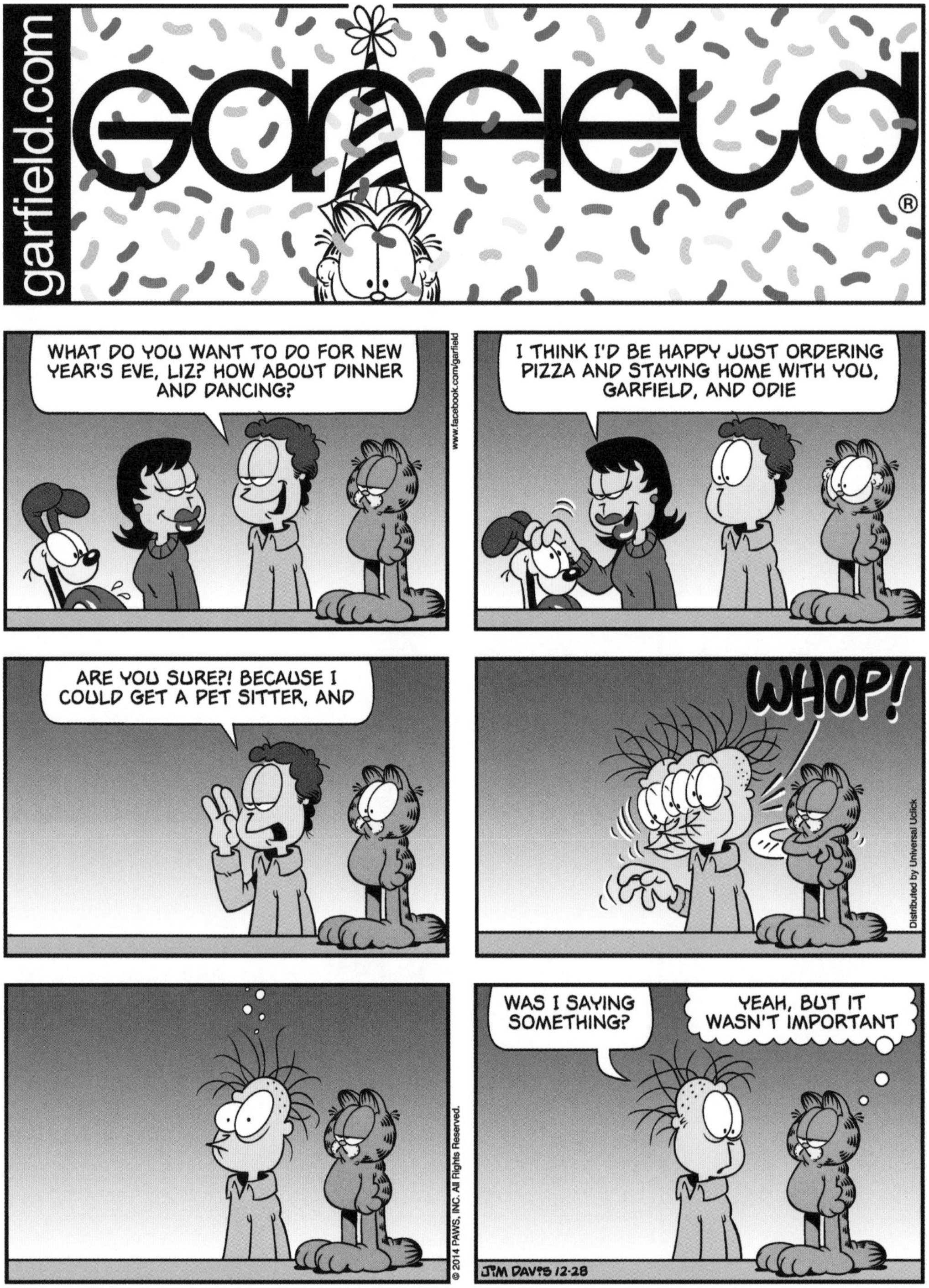
garfield.com
GARFIELD
WHAT DO YOU WANT TO DO FOR NEW YEAR'S EVE, LIZ? HOW ABOUT DINNER AND DANCING?
www.facebook.com/garfield
I THINK I'D BE HAPPY JUST ORDERING PIZZA AND STAYING HOME WITH YOU, GARFIELD, AND ODIE
ARE YOU SURE?! BECAUSE I COULD GET A PET SITTER, AND
WHOP!
Distributed by Universal Uclick
© 2014 PAWS, INC. All Rights Reserved.
WAS I SAYING SOMETHING?
YEAH, BUT IT WASN'T IMPORTANT
JIM DAVIS 12-28

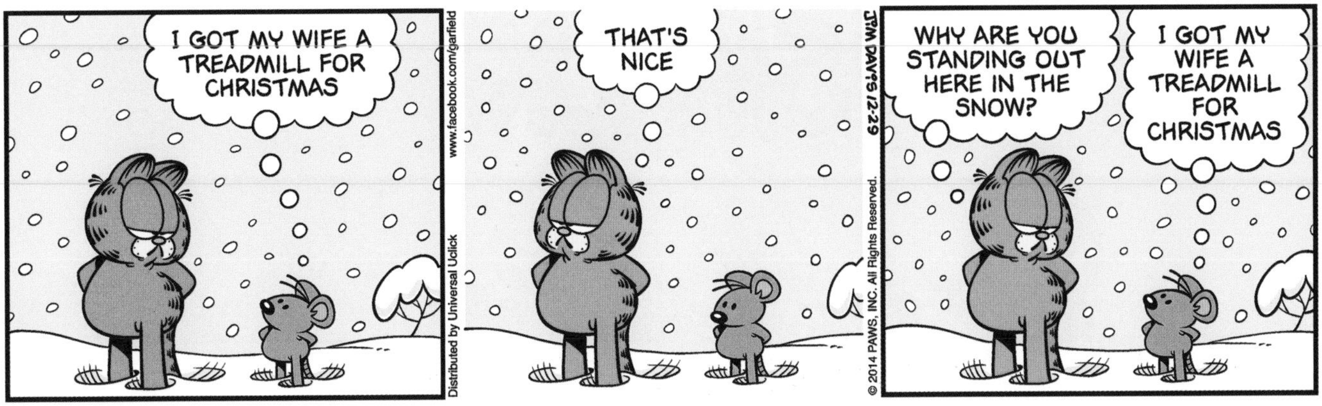
I GOT MY WIFE A TREADMILL FOR CHRISTMAS
THAT'S NICE
JIM DAVIS 12-29
WHY ARE YOU STANDING OUT HERE IN THE SNOW?
I GOT MY WIFE A TREADMILL FOR CHRISTMAS
www.facebook.com/garfield
Distributed by Universal Uclick
© 2014 PAWS, INC. All Rights Reserved.

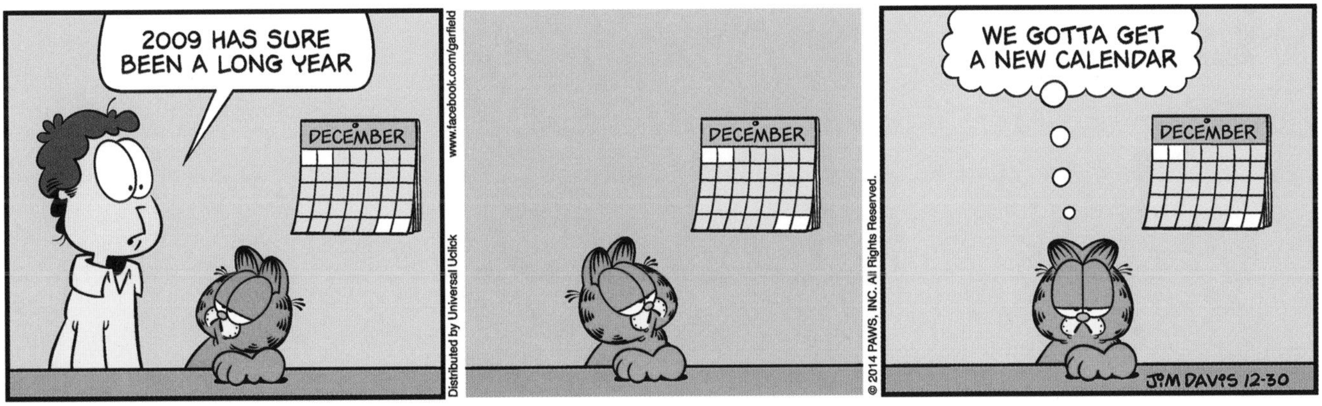
2009 HAS SURE BEEN A LONG YEAR
DECEMBER
DECEMBER
WE GOTTA GET A NEW CALENDAR
DECEMBER
JIM DAVIS 12-30
www.facebook.com/garfield
Distributed by Universal Uclick
© 2014 PAWS, INC. All Rights Reserved.

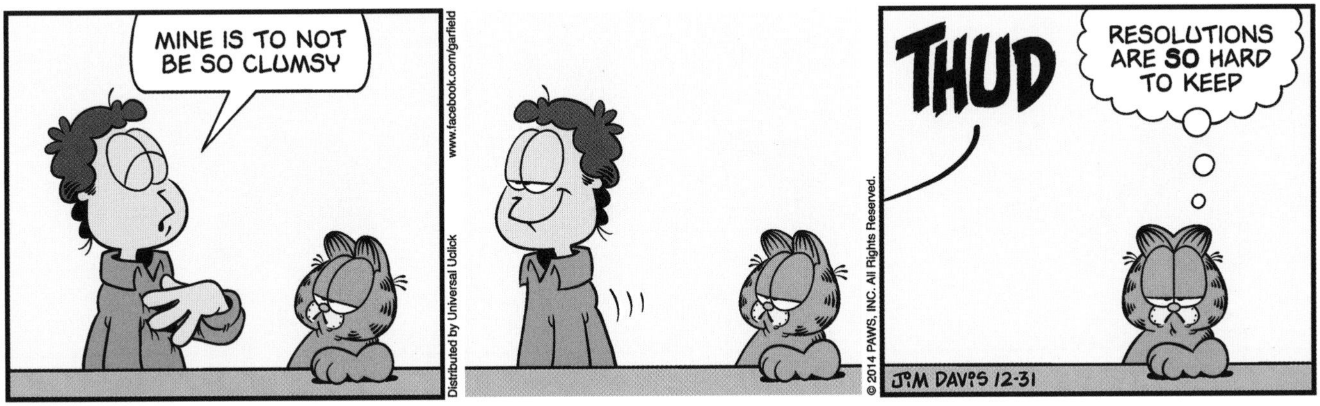
MINE IS TO NOT BE SO CLUMSY
THUD
RESOLUTIONS ARE **SO** HARD TO KEEP
JIM DAVIS 12-31
www.facebook.com/garfield
Distributed by Universal Uclick
© 2014 PAWS, INC. All Rights Reserved.

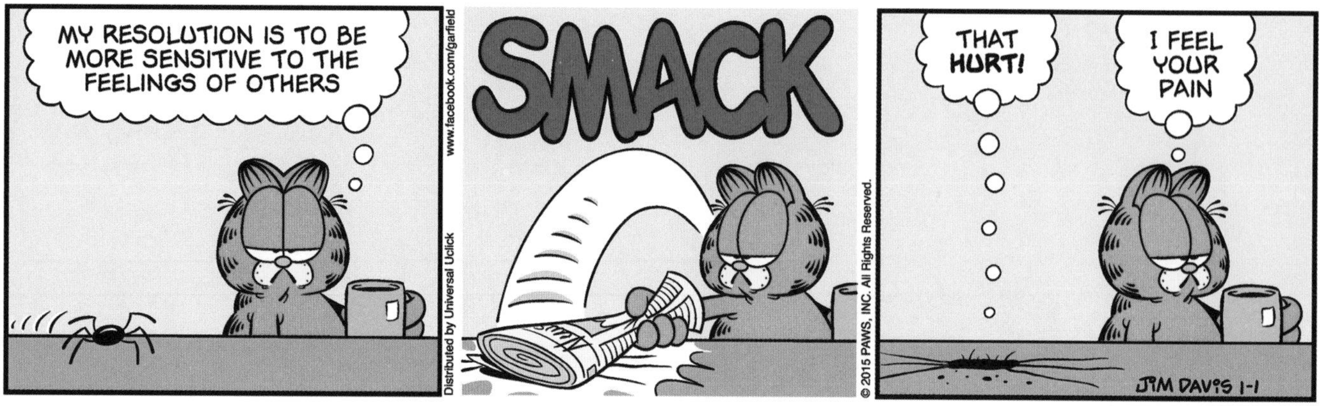
MY RESOLUTION IS TO BE MORE SENSITIVE TO THE FEELINGS OF OTHERS
www.facebook.com/garfield
Distributed by Universal Uclick
SMACK
© 2015 PAWS, INC. All Rights Reserved.
THAT HURT!
I FEEL YOUR PAIN
JIM DAVIS 1-1

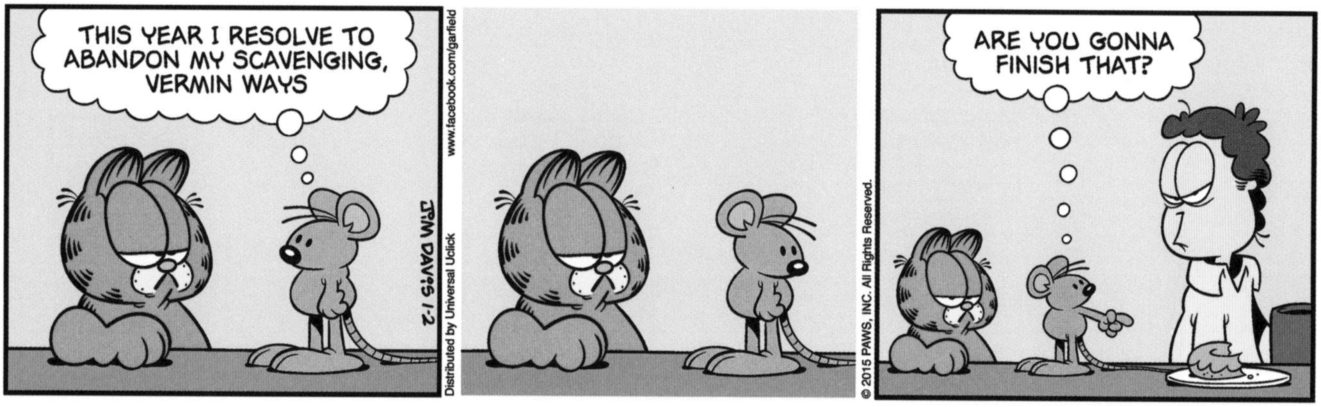
THIS YEAR I RESOLVE TO ABANDON MY SCAVENGING, VERMIN WAYS
JIM DAVIS 1-2
www.facebook.com/garfield
Distributed by Universal Uclick
© 2015 PAWS, INC. All Rights Reserved.
ARE YOU GONNA FINISH THAT?

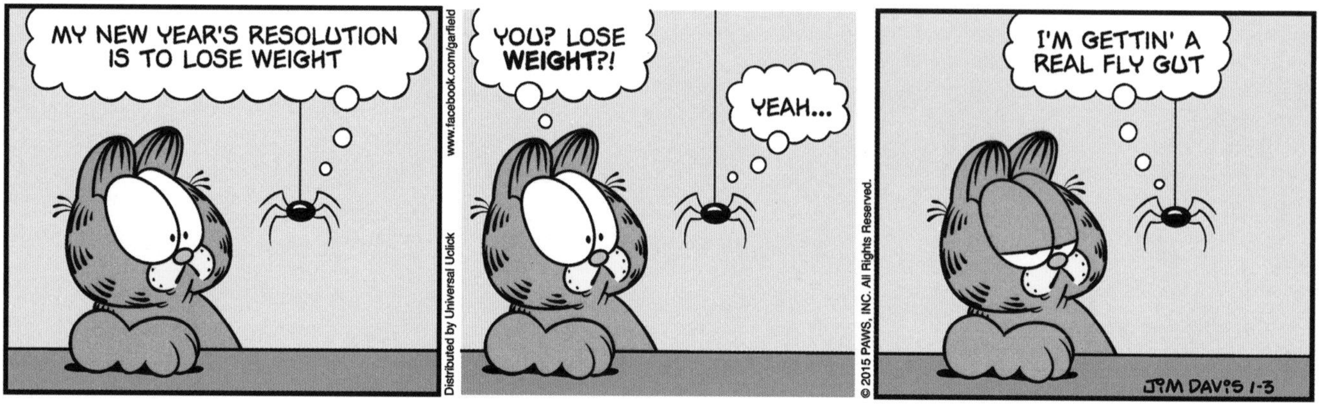
MY NEW YEAR'S RESOLUTION IS TO LOSE WEIGHT
www.facebook.com/garfield
Distributed by Universal Uclick
YOU? LOSE WEIGHT?!
YEAH...
© 2015 PAWS, INC. All Rights Reserved.
I'M GETTIN' A REAL FLY GUT
JIM DAVIS 1-3

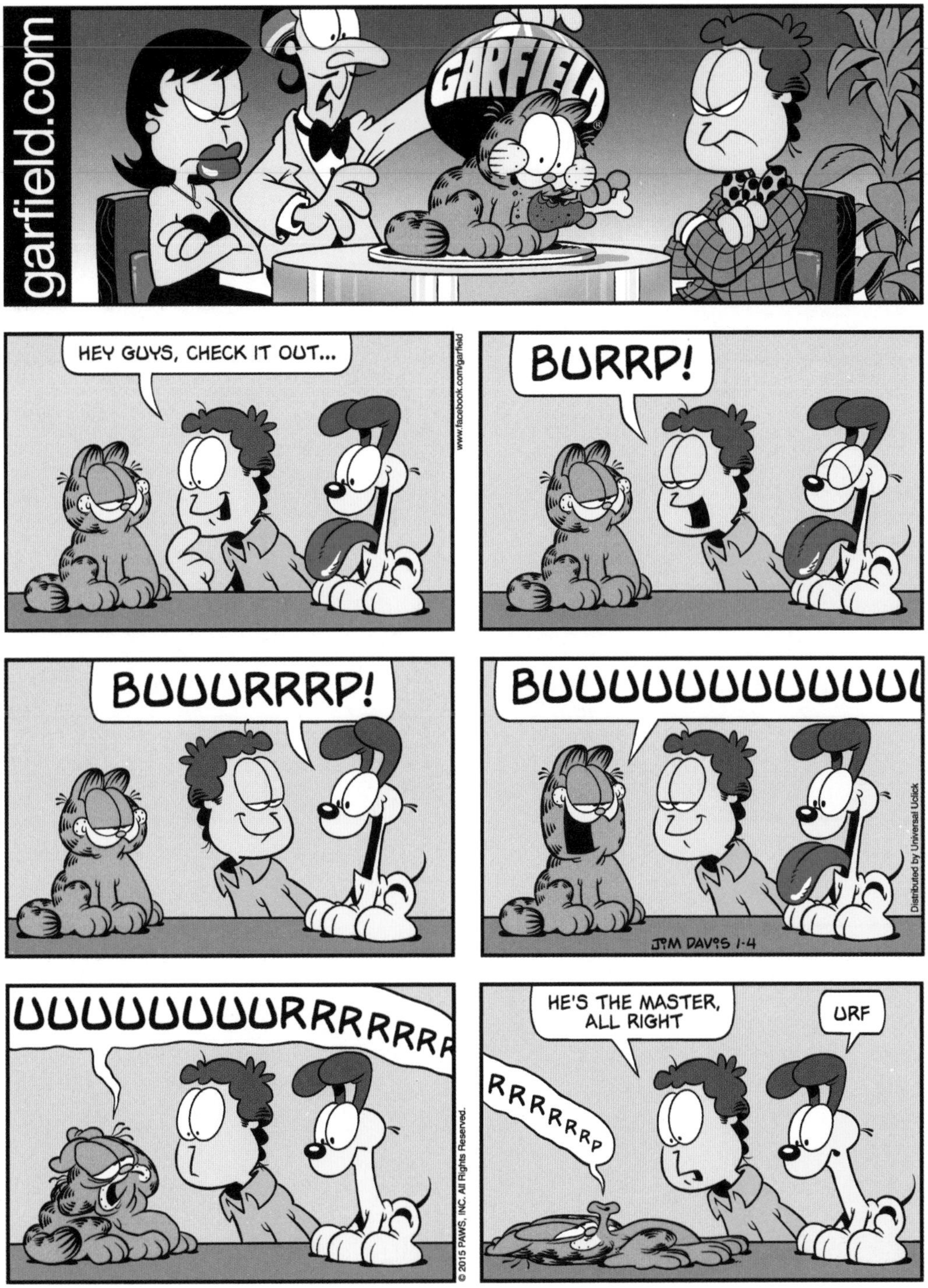
garfield.com
GARFIELD
HEY GUYS, CHECK IT OUT...
www.facebook.com/garfield
BURRP!
BUUURRRP!
BUUUUUUUUUUUUU
JIM DAVIS 1-4
Distributed by Universal Uclick
UUUUUUUUURRRRRR
© 2015 PAWS, INC. All Rights Reserved.
RRRRRRRP
HE'S THE MASTER, ALL RIGHT
URF

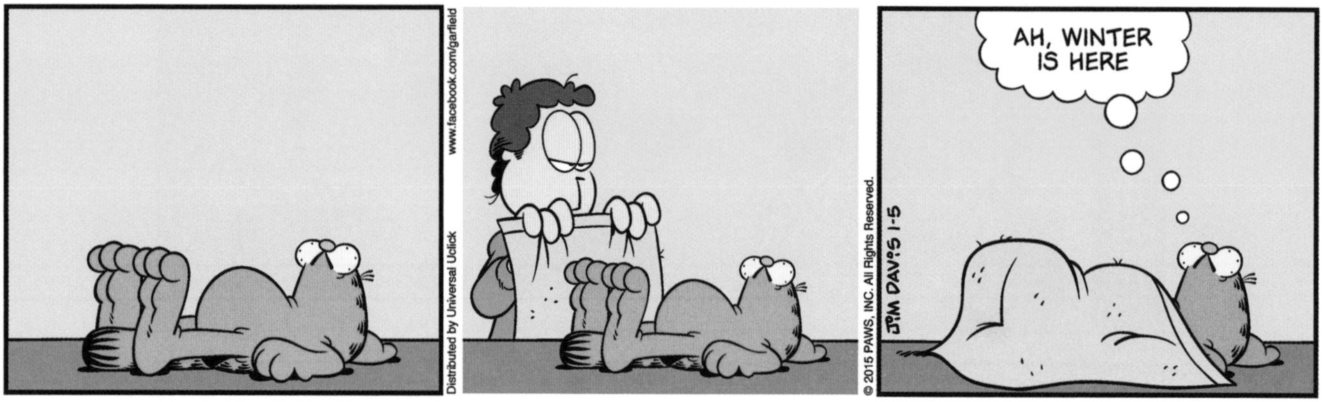
AH, WINTER IS HERE
JIM DAVIS 1-5
Distributed by Universal Uclick www.facebook.com/garfield
© 2015 PAWS, INC. All Rights Reserved.

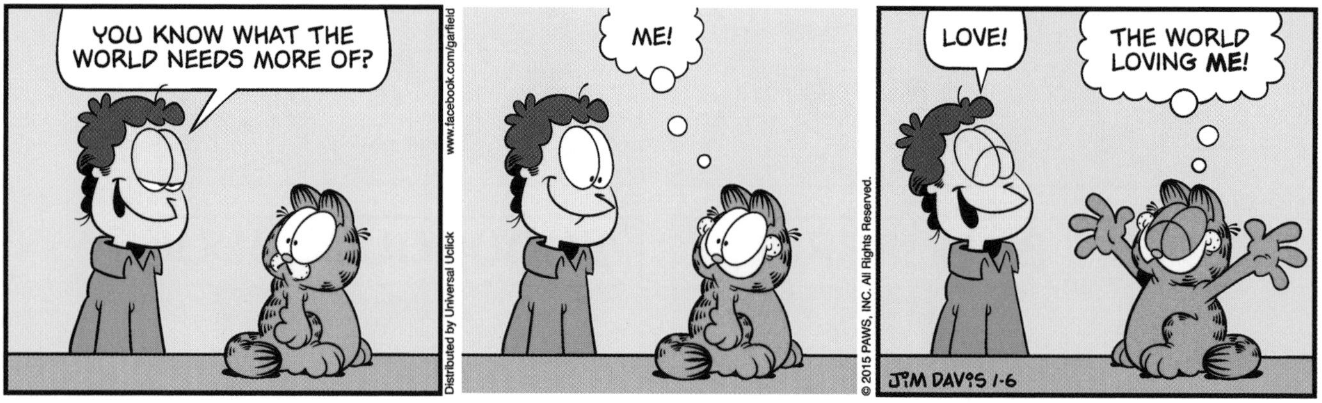
YOU KNOW WHAT THE WORLD NEEDS MORE OF?
ME!
LOVE!
THE WORLD LOVING **ME**!
JIM DAVIS 1-6
Distributed by Universal Uclick www.facebook.com/garfield
© 2015 PAWS, INC. All Rights Reserved.

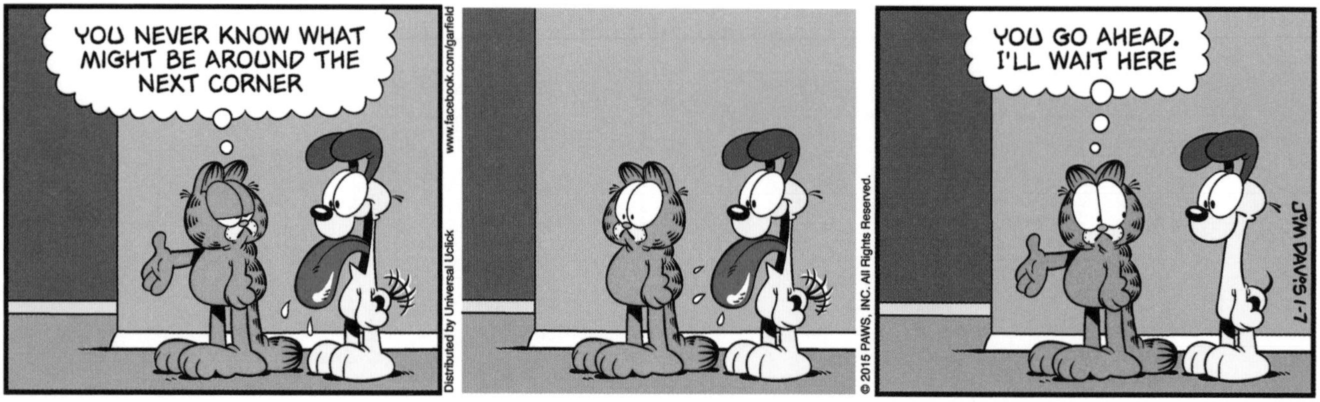
YOU NEVER KNOW WHAT MIGHT BE AROUND THE NEXT CORNER
YOU GO AHEAD. I'LL WAIT HERE
JIM DAVIS 1-7
Distributed by Universal Uclick www.facebook.com/garfield
© 2015 PAWS, INC. All Rights Reserved.

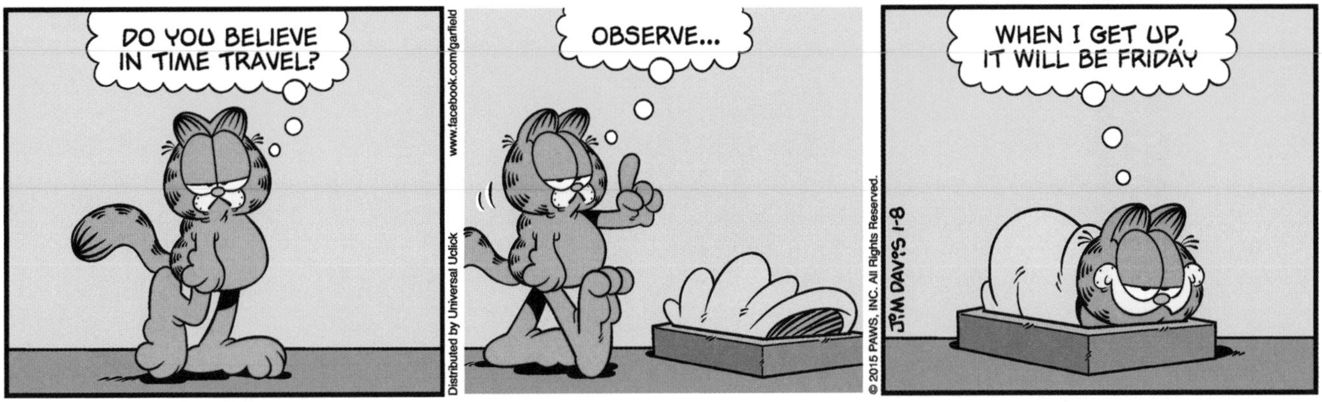
DO YOU BELIEVE IN TIME TRAVEL?
OBSERVE...
WHEN I GET UP, IT WILL BE FRIDAY
JIM DAVIS 1-8
Distributed by Universal Uclick www.facebook.com/garfield
© 2015 PAWS, INC. All Rights Reserved.

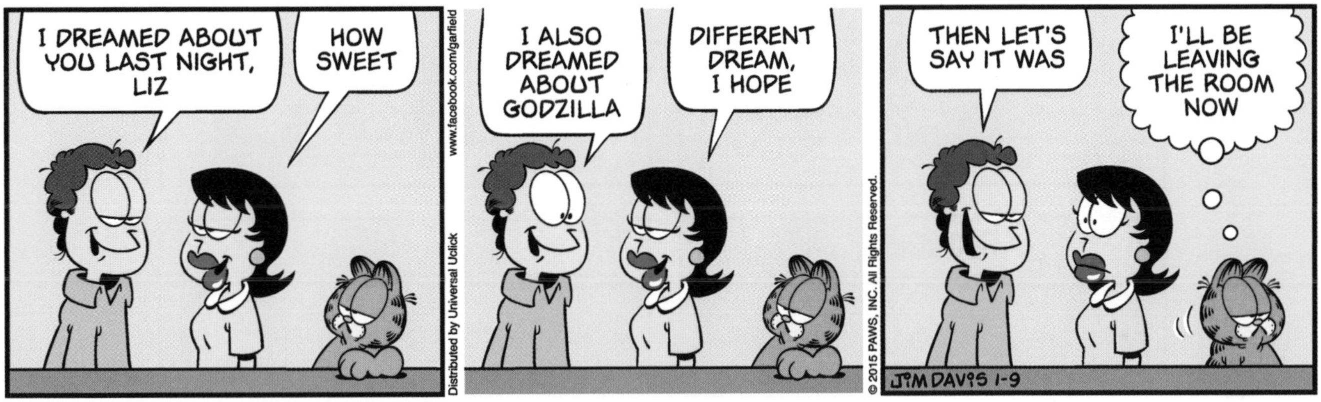
I DREAMED ABOUT YOU LAST NIGHT, LIZ
HOW SWEET
I ALSO DREAMED ABOUT GODZILLA
DIFFERENT DREAM, I HOPE
THEN LET'S SAY IT WAS
I'LL BE LEAVING THE ROOM NOW
JIM DAVIS 1-9
Distributed by Universal Uclick www.facebook.com/garfield
© 2015 PAWS, INC. All Rights Reserved.

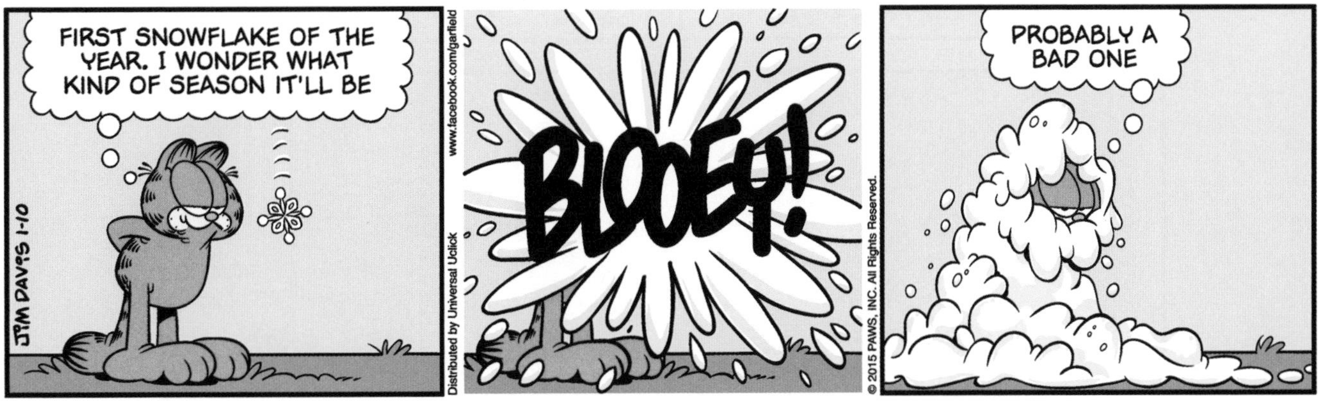
FIRST SNOWFLAKE OF THE YEAR. I WONDER WHAT KIND OF SEASON IT'LL BE
JIM DAVIS 1-10
BLOOEY!
PROBABLY A BAD ONE
Distributed by Universal Uclick www.facebook.com/garfield
© 2015 PAWS, INC. All Rights Reserved.

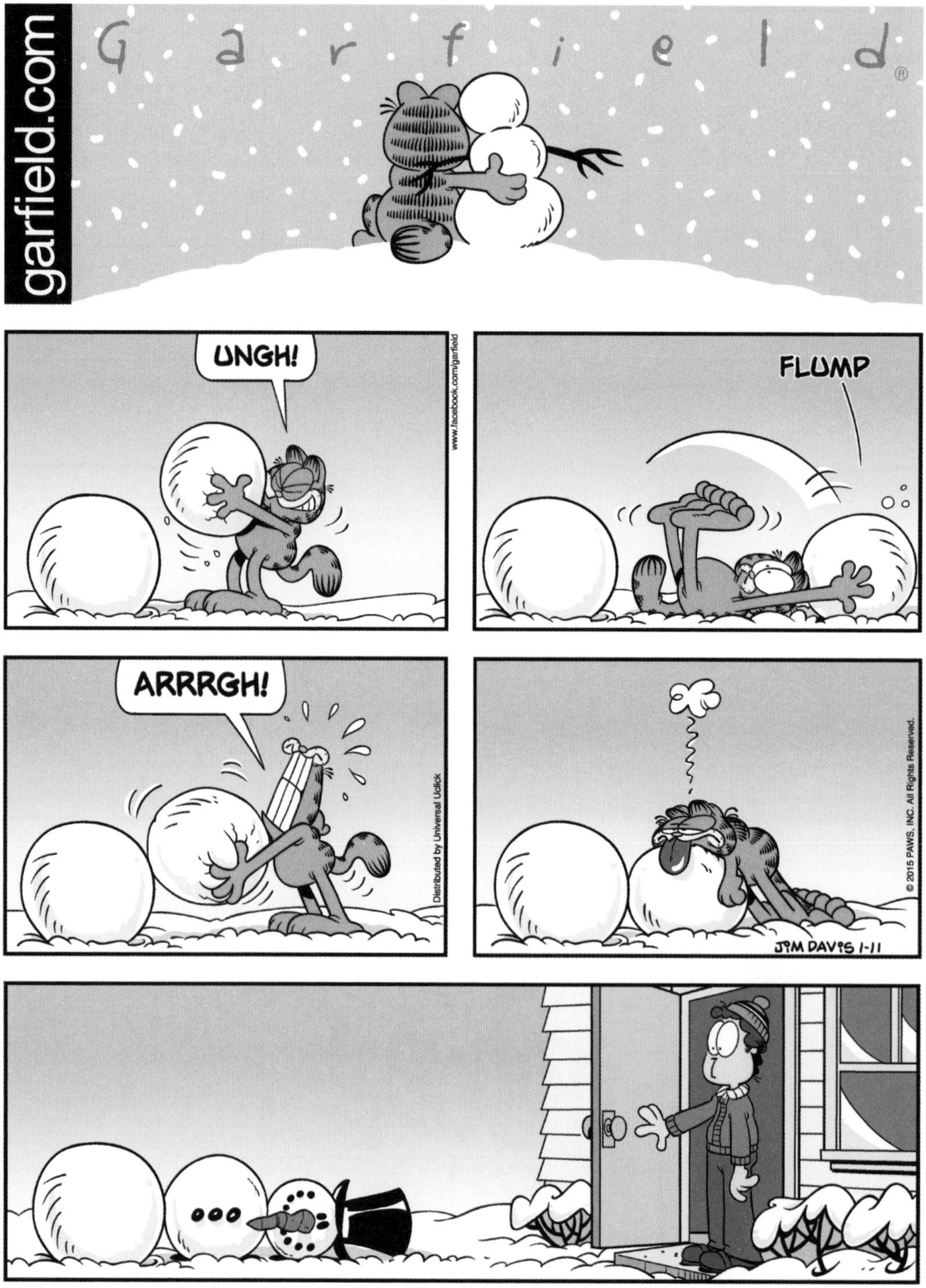
garfield.com
Garfield®
www.facebook.com/garfield
UNGH!
FLUMP
ARRRGH!
Distributed by Universal Uclick
© 2015 PAWS, INC. All Rights Reserved.
JIM DAVIS 1-11

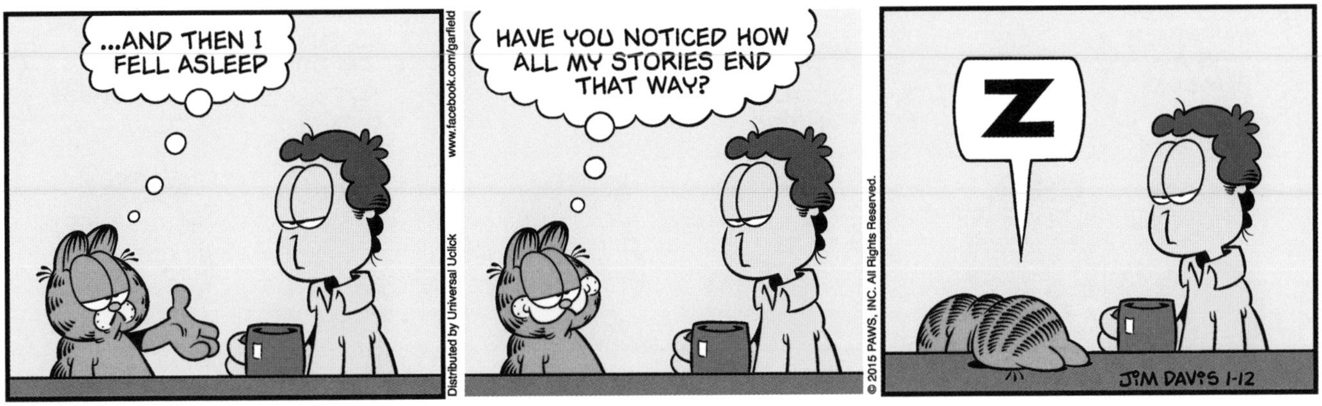
...AND THEN I FELL ASLEEP
HAVE YOU NOTICED HOW ALL MY STORIES END THAT WAY?
Z
JIM DAVIS 1-12
Distributed by Universal Uclick www.facebook.com/garfield
© 2015 PAWS, INC. All Rights Reserved.

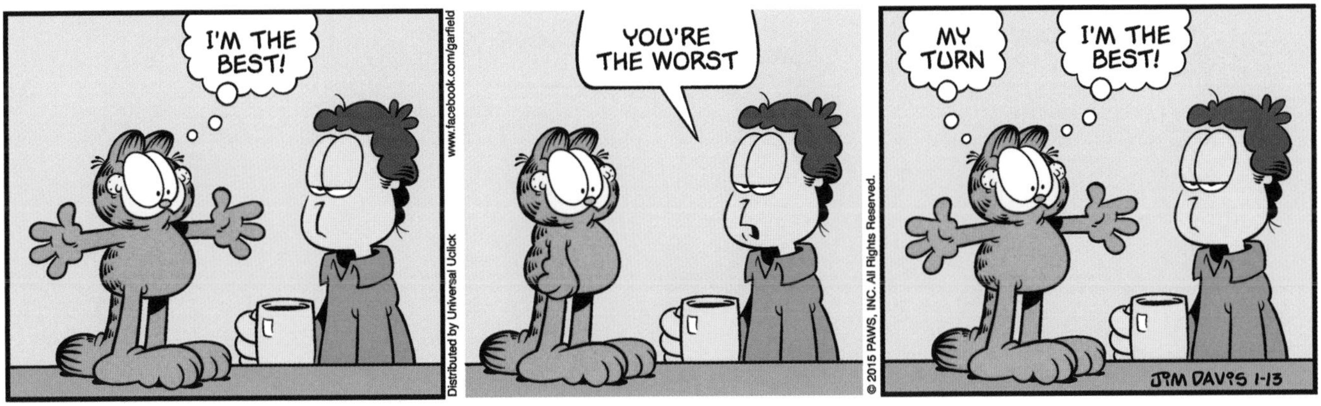
I'M THE BEST!
YOU'RE THE WORST
MY TURN
I'M THE BEST!
JIM DAVIS 1-13
Distributed by Universal Uclick www.facebook.com/garfield
© 2015 PAWS, INC. All Rights Reserved.

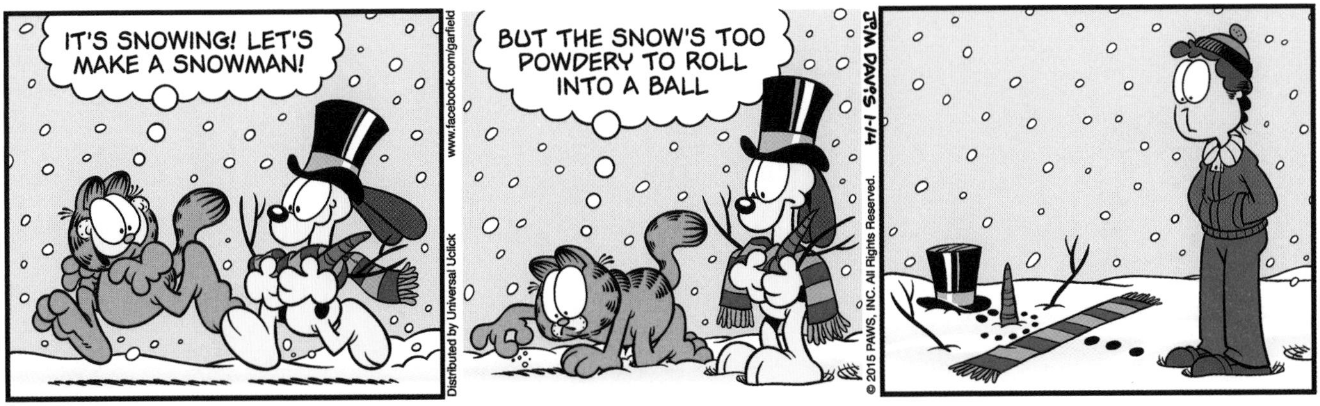
IT'S SNOWING! LET'S MAKE A SNOWMAN!
BUT THE SNOW'S TOO POWDERY TO ROLL INTO A BALL
JIM DAVIS 1-14
Distributed by Universal Uclick www.facebook.com/garfield
© 2015 PAWS, INC. All Rights Reserved.

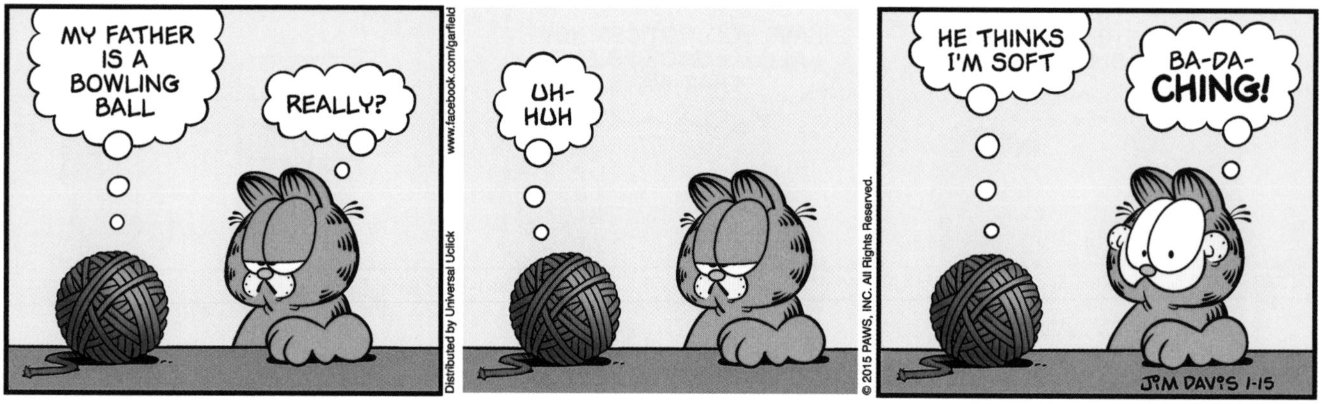
MY FATHER IS A BOWLING BALL
REALLY?
UH-HUH
HE THINKS I'M SOFT
BA-DA-CHING!
JIM DAVIS 1-15
www.facebook.com/garfield
Distributed by Universal Uclick
© 2015 PAWS, INC. All Rights Reserved.

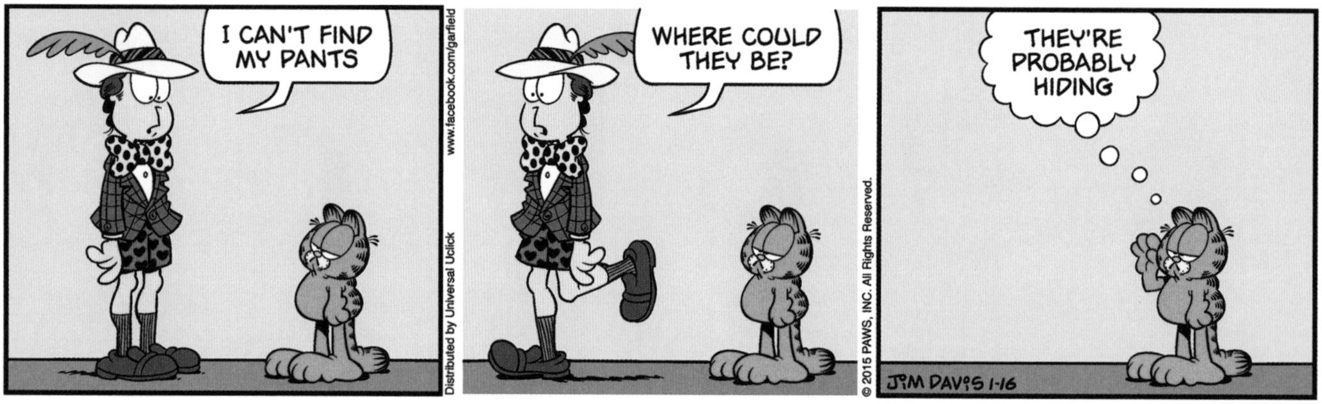
I CAN'T FIND MY PANTS
WHERE COULD THEY BE?
THEY'RE PROBABLY HIDING
JIM DAVIS 1-16
www.facebook.com/garfield
Distributed by Universal Uclick
© 2015 PAWS, INC. All Rights Reserved.

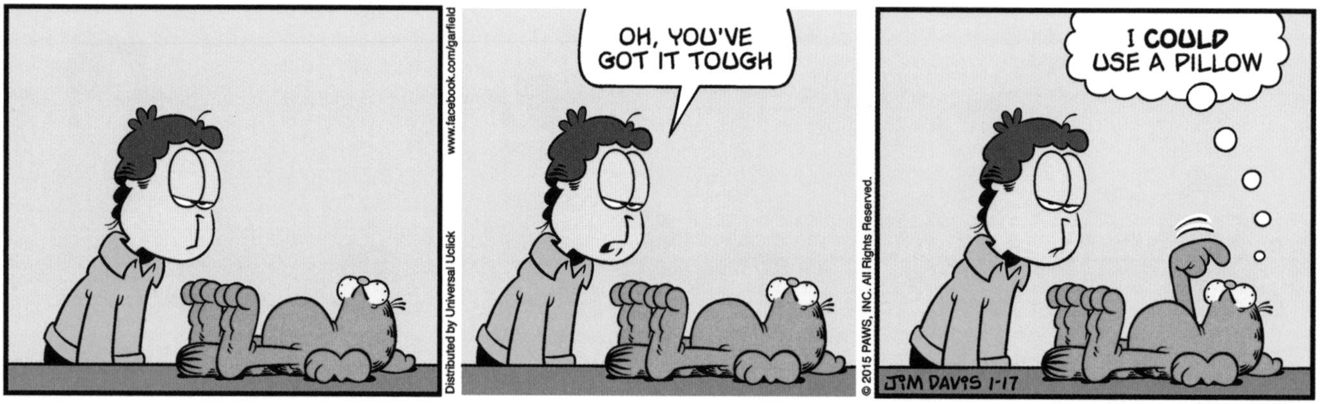
OH, YOU'VE GOT IT TOUGH
I COULD USE A PILLOW
JIM DAVIS 1-17
www.facebook.com/garfield
Distributed by Universal Uclick
© 2015 PAWS, INC. All Rights Reserved.

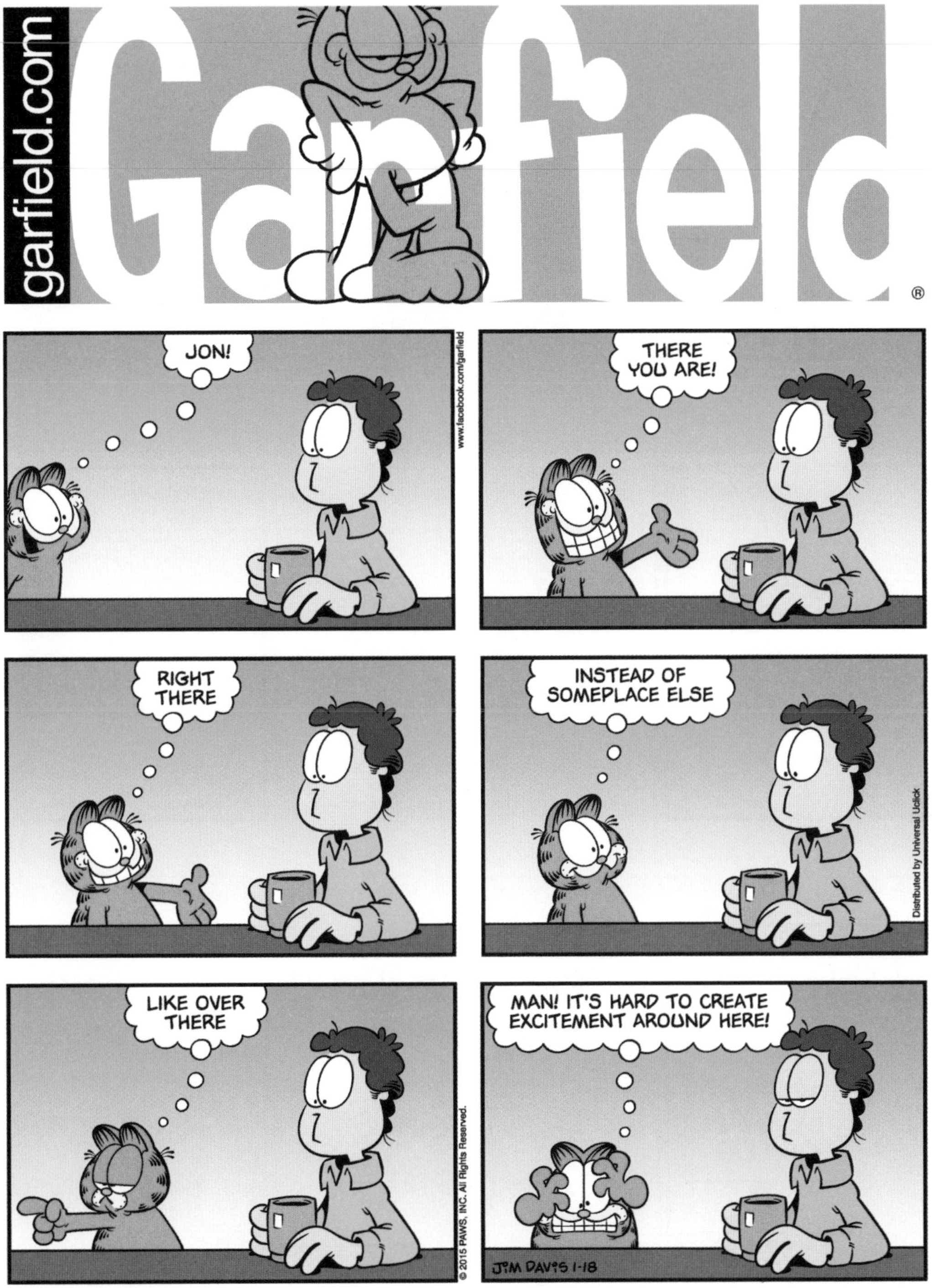
garfield.com
Garfield®
www.facebook.com/garfield
JON!
THERE YOU ARE!
RIGHT THERE
INSTEAD OF SOMEPLACE ELSE
Distributed by Universal Uclick
LIKE OVER THERE
MAN! IT'S HARD TO CREATE EXCITEMENT AROUND HERE!
© 2015 PAWS, INC. All Rights Reserved.
JIM DAVIS 1-18

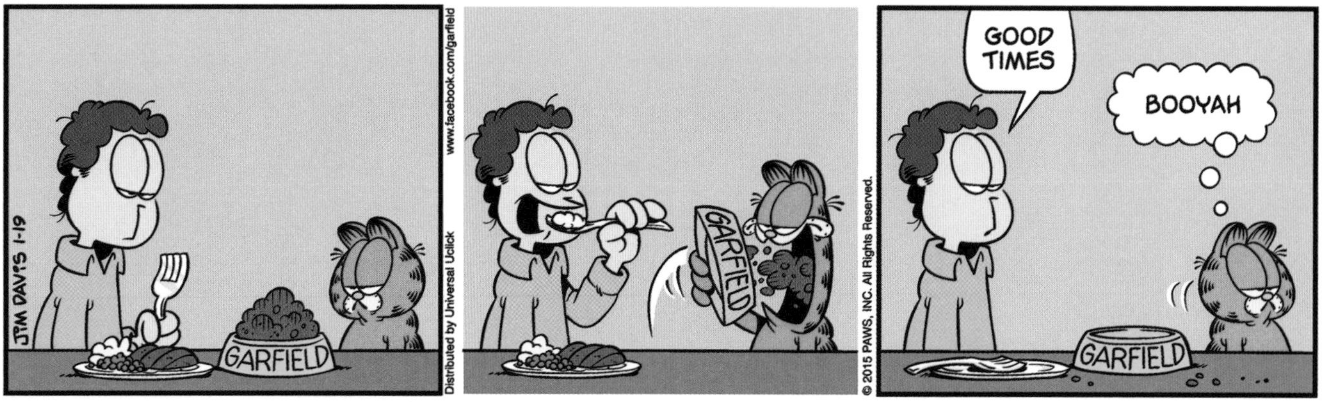
JIM DAVIS 1-19
GARFIELD
Distributed by Universal Uclick
www.facebook.com/garfield
GARFIELD
© 2015 PAWS, INC. All Rights Reserved.
GOOD TIMES
BOOYAH
GARFIELD

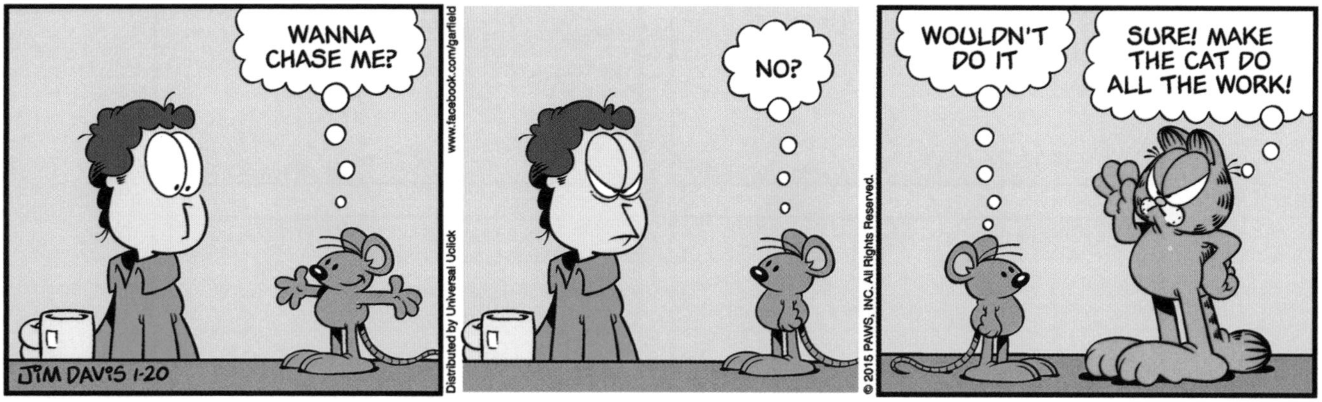
WANNA CHASE ME?
JIM DAVIS 1-20
Distributed by Universal Uclick
www.facebook.com/garfield
NO?
© 2015 PAWS, INC. All Rights Reserved.
WOULDN'T DO IT
SURE! MAKE THE CAT DO ALL THE WORK!

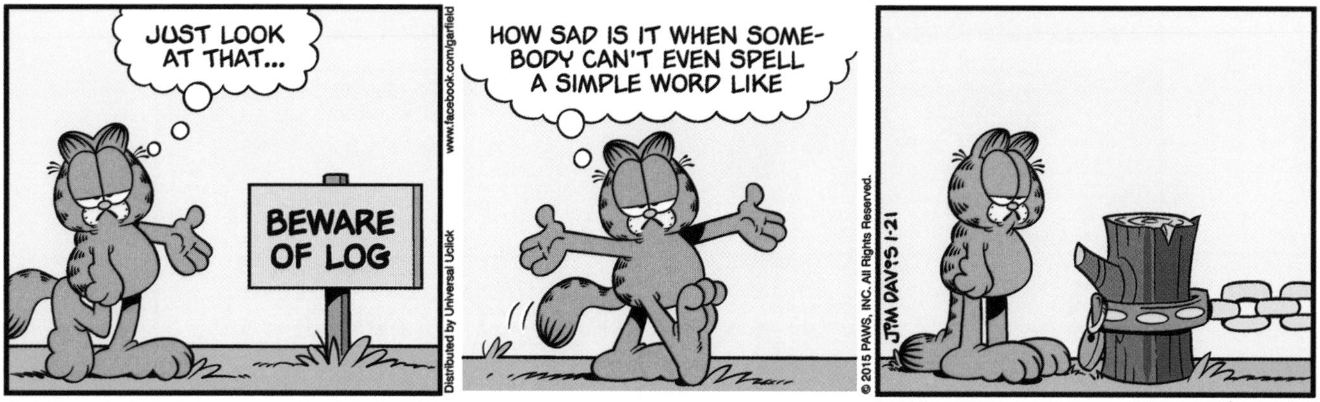
JUST LOOK AT THAT...
BEWARE OF LOG
Distributed by Universal Uclick
www.facebook.com/garfield
HOW SAD IS IT WHEN SOMEBODY CAN'T EVEN SPELL A SIMPLE WORD LIKE
© 2015 PAWS, INC. All Rights Reserved.
JIM DAVIS 1-21

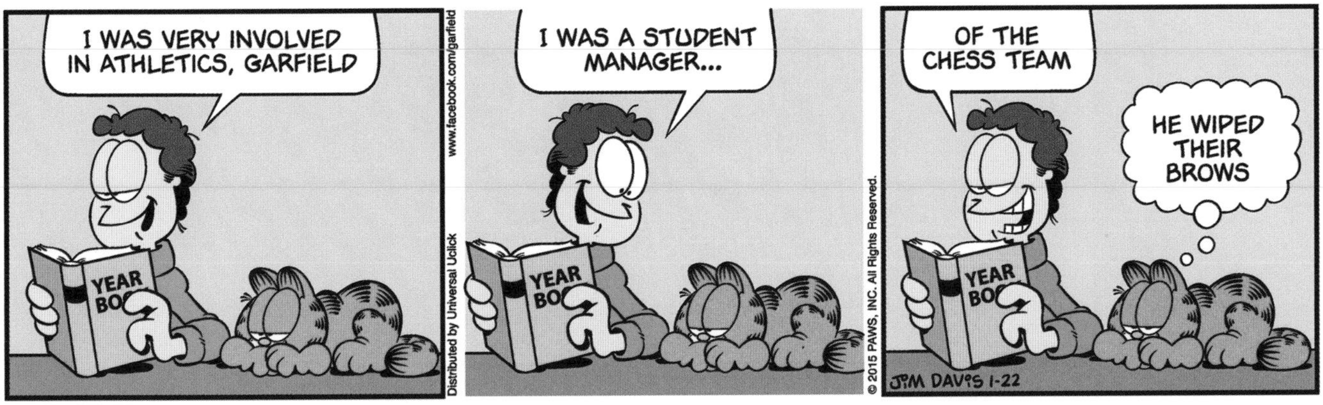
I WAS VERY INVOLVED IN ATHLETICS, GARFIELD
I WAS A STUDENT MANAGER...
OF THE CHESS TEAM
HE WIPED THEIR BROWS
YEAR BOOK
JIM DAVIS 1-22
Distributed by Universal Uclick www.facebook.com/garfield
© 2015 PAWS, INC. All Rights Reserved.

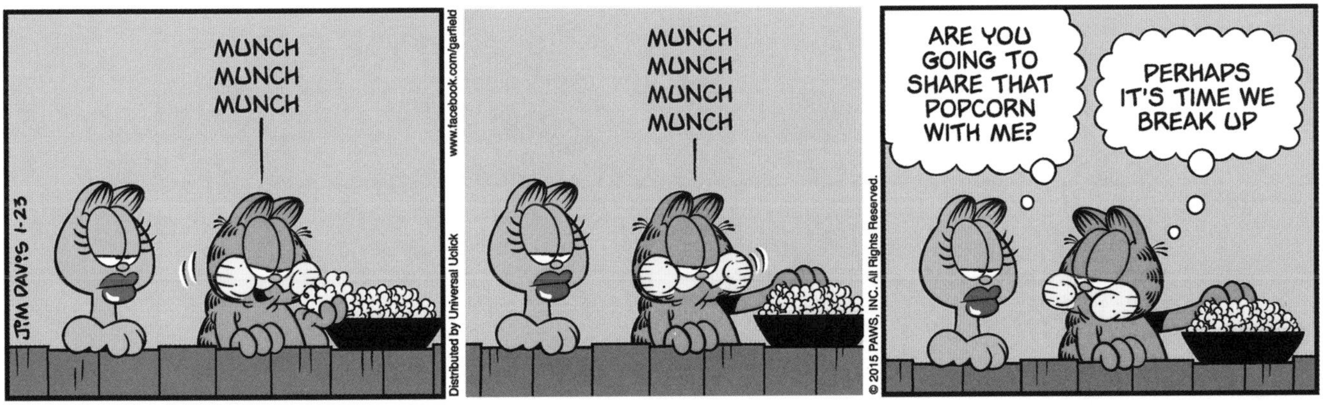
MUNCH MUNCH MUNCH
MUNCH MUNCH MUNCH MUNCH
ARE YOU GOING TO SHARE THAT POPCORN WITH ME?
PERHAPS IT'S TIME WE BREAK UP
JIM DAVIS 1-23
Distributed by Universal Uclick www.facebook.com/garfield
© 2015 PAWS, INC. All Rights Reserved.

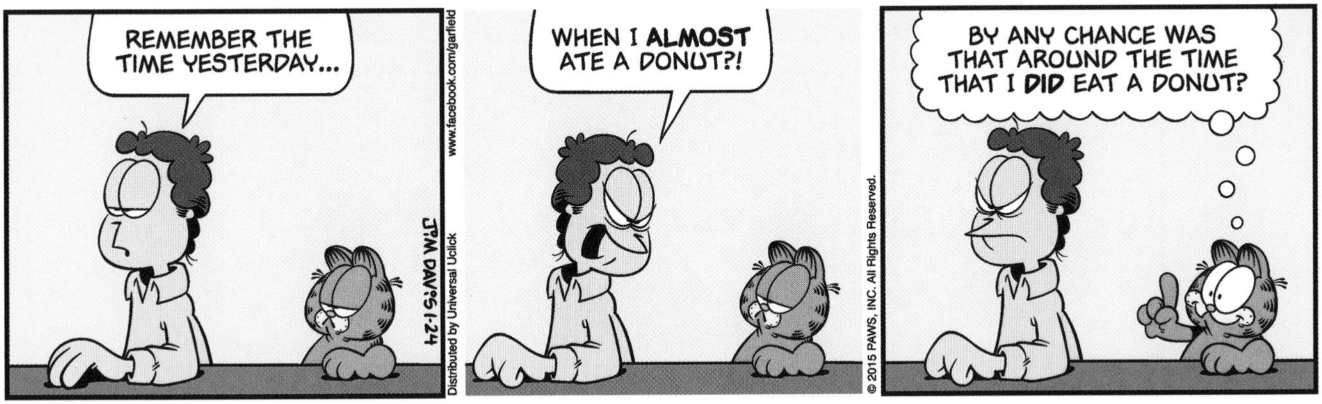
REMEMBER THE TIME YESTERDAY...
WHEN I **ALMOST** ATE A DONUT?!
BY ANY CHANCE WAS THAT AROUND THE TIME THAT I **DID** EAT A DONUT?
JIM DAVIS 1-24
Distributed by Universal Uclick www.facebook.com/garfield
© 2015 PAWS, INC. All Rights Reserved.

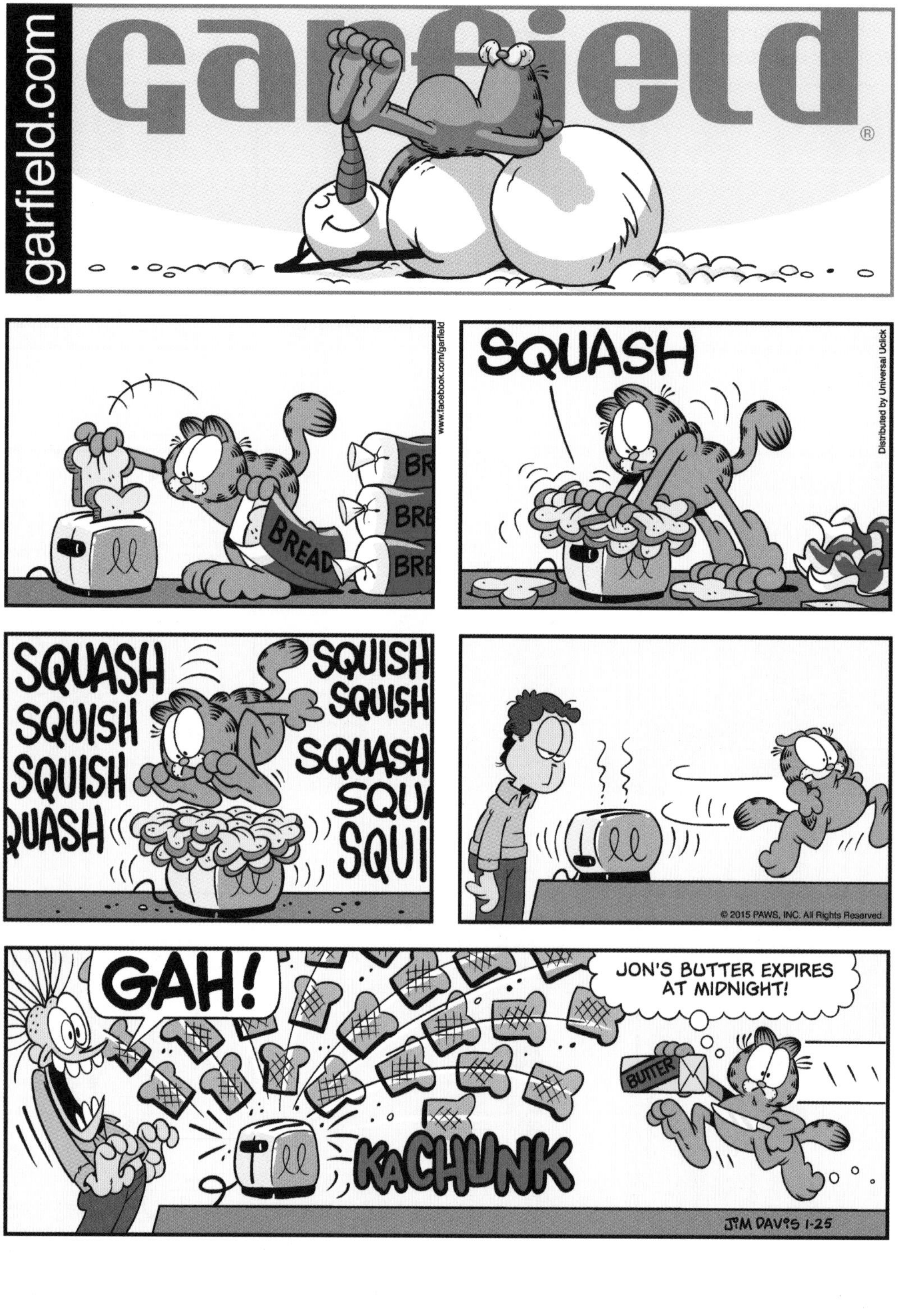
garfield.com
garfield
www.facebook.com/garfield
BREAD
BR
BRE
BRE
SQUASH
Distributed by Universal Uclick
SQUASH
SQUISH
SQUISH
QUASH
SQUISH
SQUISH
SQUASH
SQU
SQUI
© 2015 PAWS, INC. All Rights Reserved.
GAH!
JON'S BUTTER EXPIRES AT MIDNIGHT!
BUTTER
KACHUNK
JIM DAVIS 1-25

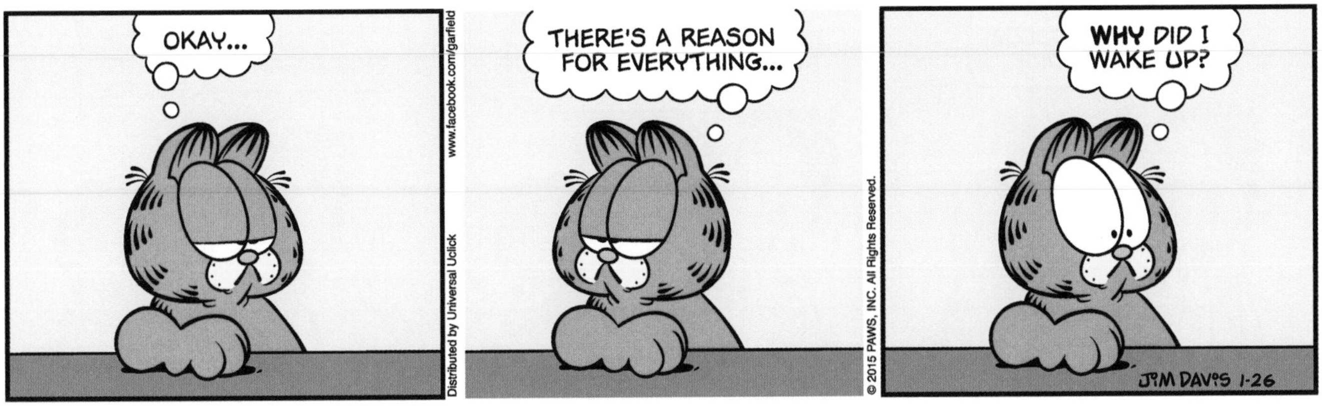
OKAY...
THERE'S A REASON FOR EVERYTHING...
WHY DID I WAKE UP?
JIM DAVIS 1-26
www.facebook.com/garfield
Distributed by Universal Uclick
© 2015 PAWS, INC. All Rights Reserved.

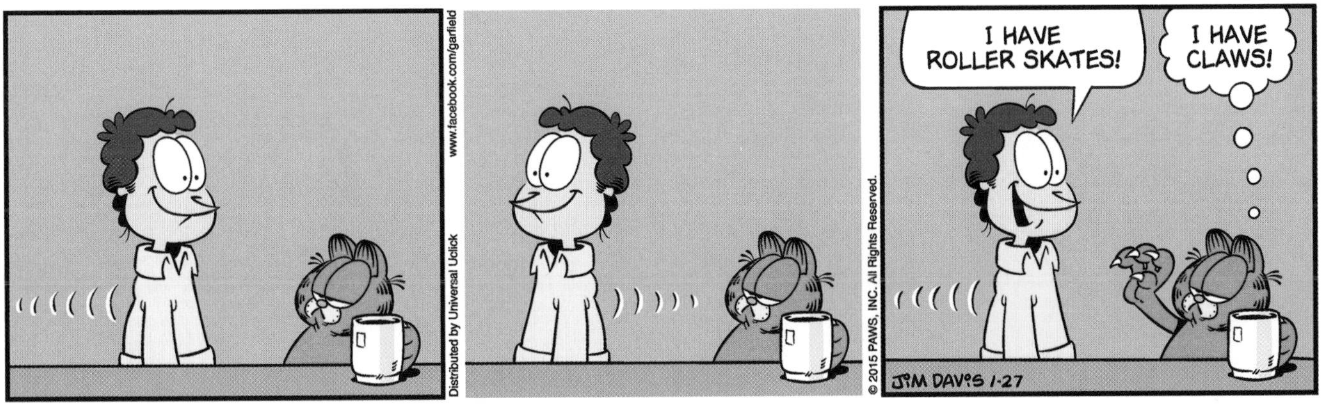
I HAVE ROLLER SKATES!
I HAVE CLAWS!
JIM DAVIS 1-27
www.facebook.com/garfield
Distributed by Universal Uclick
© 2015 PAWS, INC. All Rights Reserved.

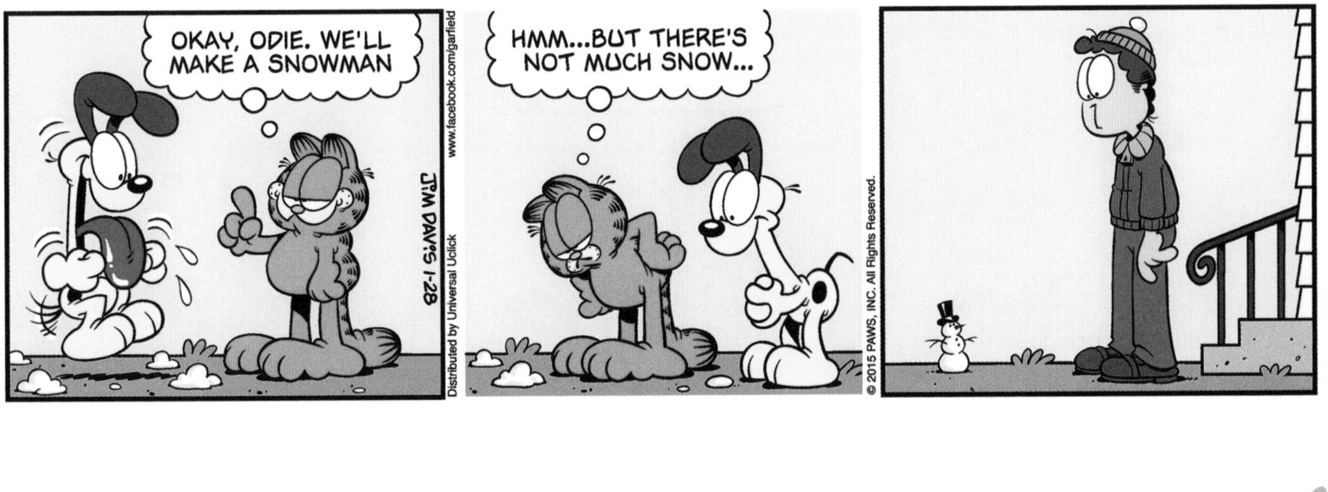
OKAY, ODIE. WE'LL MAKE A SNOWMAN
HMM...BUT THERE'S NOT MUCH SNOW...
JIM DAVIS 1-28
www.facebook.com/garfield
Distributed by Universal Uclick
© 2015 PAWS, INC. All Rights Reserved.

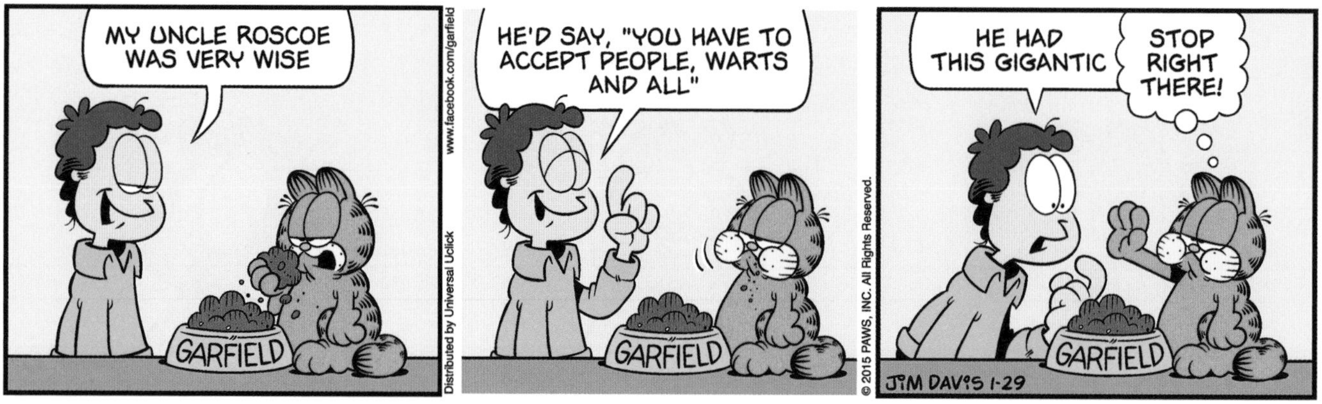
MY UNCLE ROSCOE WAS VERY WISE
HE'D SAY, "YOU HAVE TO ACCEPT PEOPLE, WARTS AND ALL"
HE HAD THIS GIGANTIC
STOP RIGHT THERE!
GARFIELD
JIM DAVIS 1-29
www.facebook.com/garfield
Distributed by Universal Uclick
© 2015 PAWS, INC. All Rights Reserved.

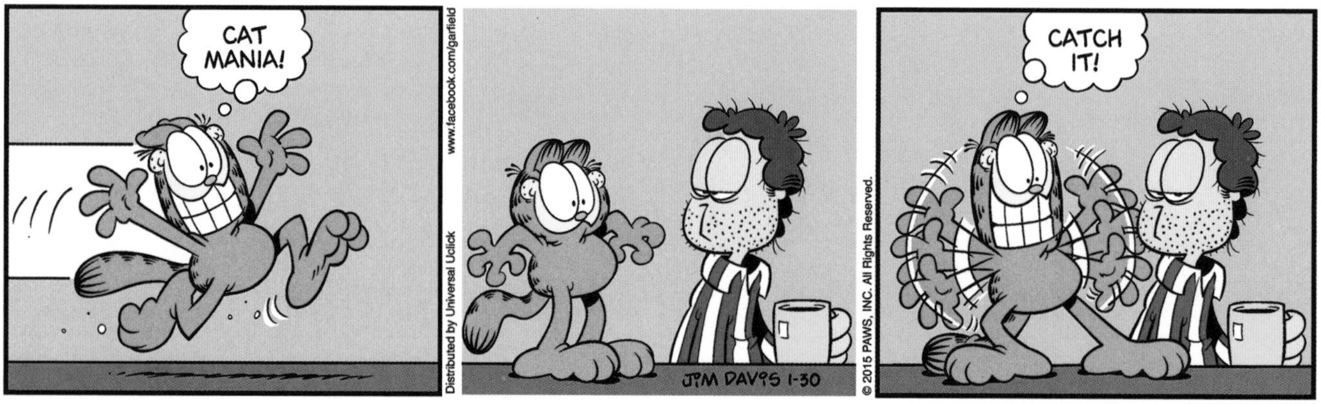
CAT MANIA!
CATCH IT!
JIM DAVIS 1-30
www.facebook.com/garfield
Distributed by Universal Uclick
© 2015 PAWS, INC. All Rights Reserved.

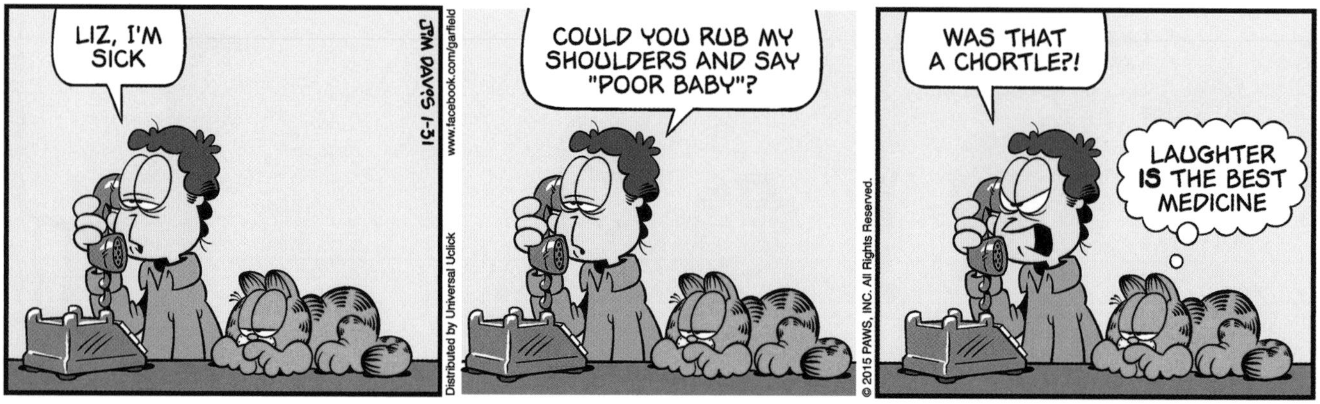
LIZ, I'M SICK
COULD YOU RUB MY SHOULDERS AND SAY "POOR BABY"?
WAS THAT A CHORTLE?!
LAUGHTER **IS** THE BEST MEDICINE
JIM DAVIS 1-31
www.facebook.com/garfield
Distributed by Universal Uclick
© 2015 PAWS, INC. All Rights Reserved.

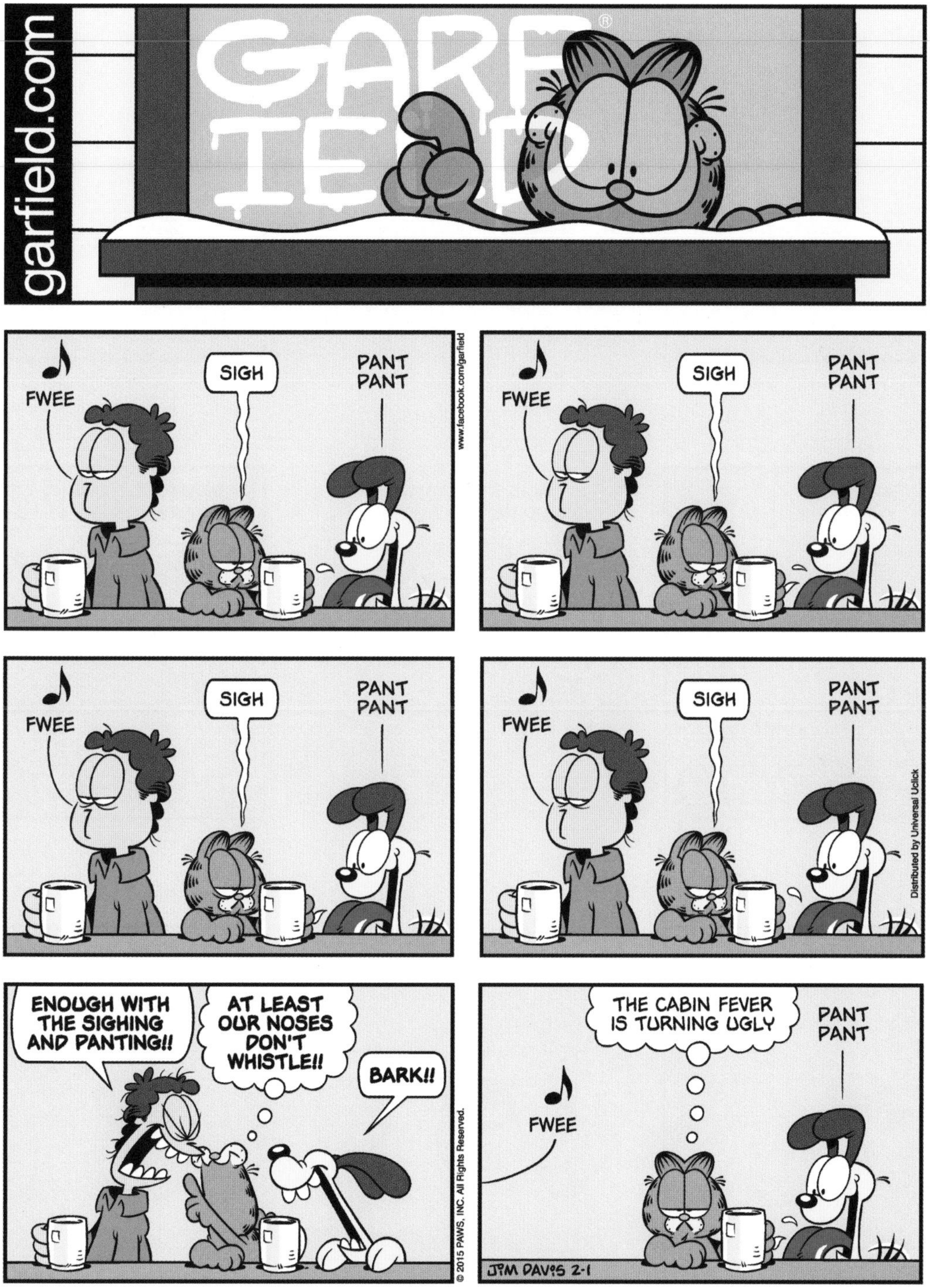
garfield.com
FWEE
SIGH
PANT PANT
www.facebook.com/garfield
FWEE
SIGH
PANT PANT
FWEE
SIGH
PANT PANT
FWEE
SIGH
PANT PANT
Distributed by Universal Uclick
ENOUGH WITH THE SIGHING AND PANTING!!
AT LEAST OUR NOSES DON'T WHISTLE!!
BARK!!
© 2015 PAWS, INC. All Rights Reserved.
JIM DAVIS 2-1
THE CABIN FEVER IS TURNING UGLY
PANT PANT
FWEE

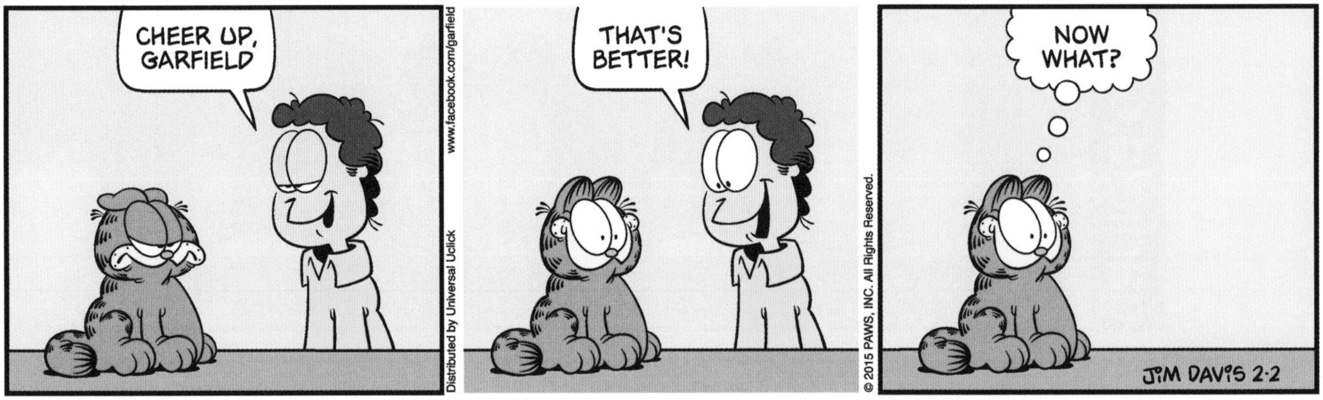
CHEER UP, GARFIELD
THAT'S BETTER!
NOW WHAT?
JIM DAVIS 2-2
Distributed by Universal Uclick www.facebook.com/garfield
© 2015 PAWS, INC. All Rights Reserved.

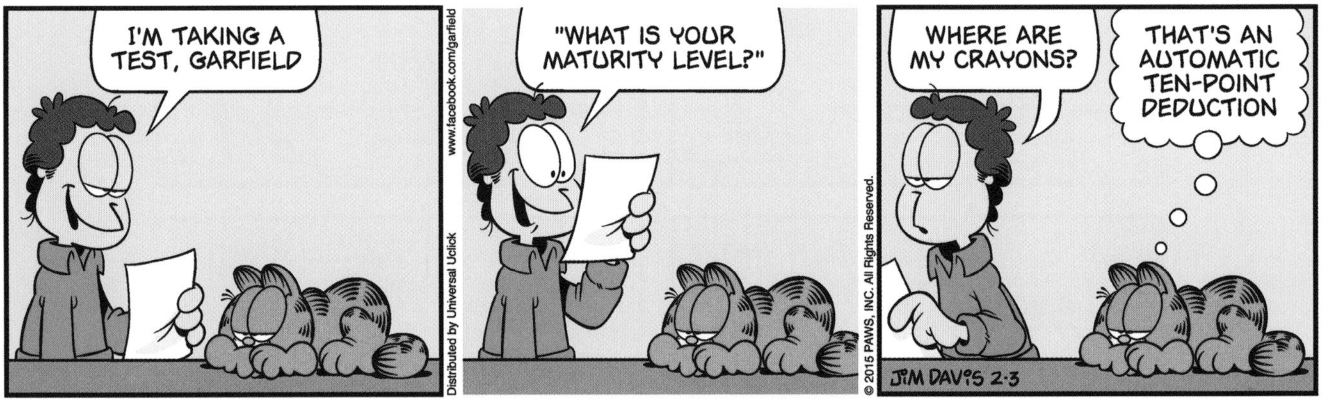
I'M TAKING A TEST, GARFIELD
"WHAT IS YOUR MATURITY LEVEL?"
WHERE ARE MY CRAYONS?
THAT'S AN AUTOMATIC TEN-POINT DEDUCTION
JIM DAVIS 2-3
Distributed by Universal Uclick www.facebook.com/garfield
© 2015 PAWS, INC. All Rights Reserved.

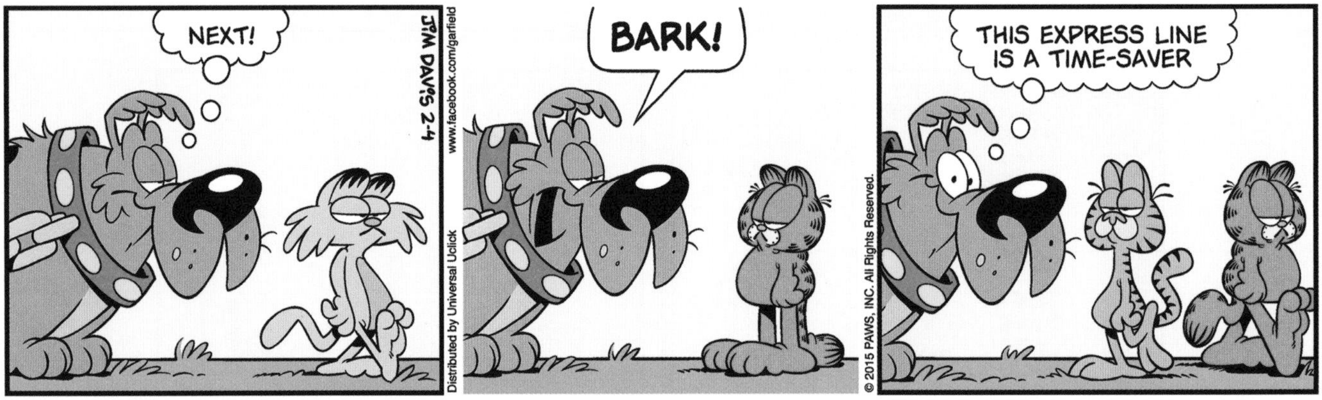
NEXT!
JIM DAVIS 2-4
BARK!
THIS EXPRESS LINE IS A TIME-SAVER
Distributed by Universal Uclick www.facebook.com/garfield
© 2015 PAWS, INC. All Rights Reserved.

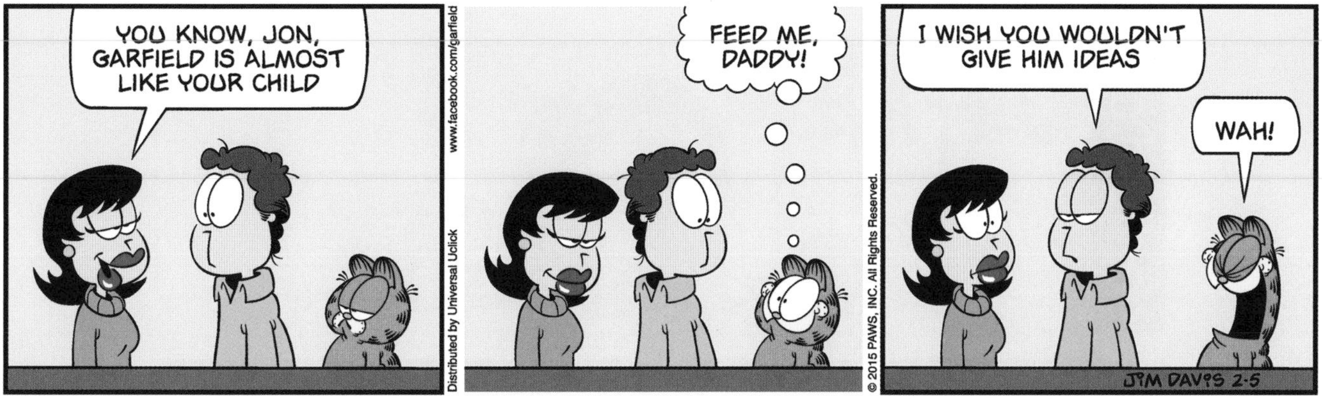
YOU KNOW, JON, GARFIELD IS ALMOST LIKE YOUR CHILD
Distributed by Universal Uclick www.facebook.com/garfield
FEED ME, DADDY!
© 2015 PAWS, INC. All Rights Reserved.
I WISH YOU WOULDN'T GIVE HIM IDEAS
WAH!
JIM DAVIS 2-5

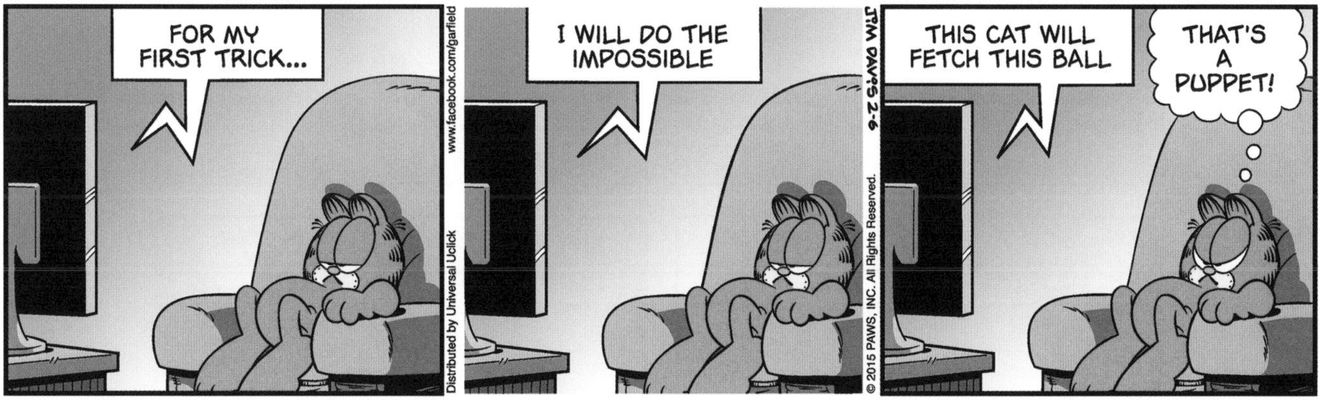
FOR MY FIRST TRICK...
Distributed by Universal Uclick www.facebook.com/garfield
I WILL DO THE IMPOSSIBLE
JIM DAVIS 2-6
© 2015 PAWS, INC. All Rights Reserved.
THIS CAT WILL FETCH THIS BALL
THAT'S A PUPPET!

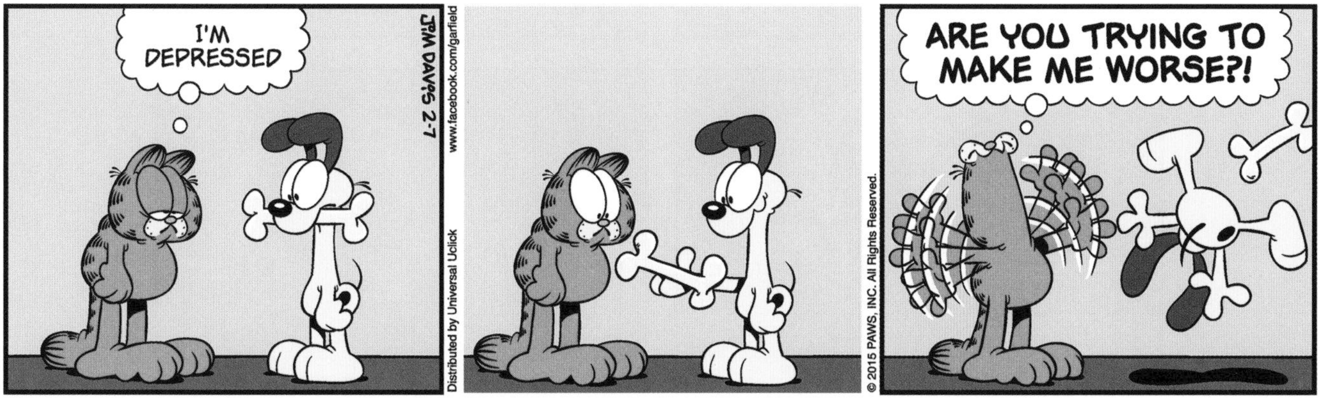
I'M DEPRESSED
JIM DAVIS 2-7
Distributed by Universal Uclick www.facebook.com/garfield
© 2015 PAWS, INC. All Rights Reserved.
ARE YOU TRYING TO MAKE ME WORSE?!

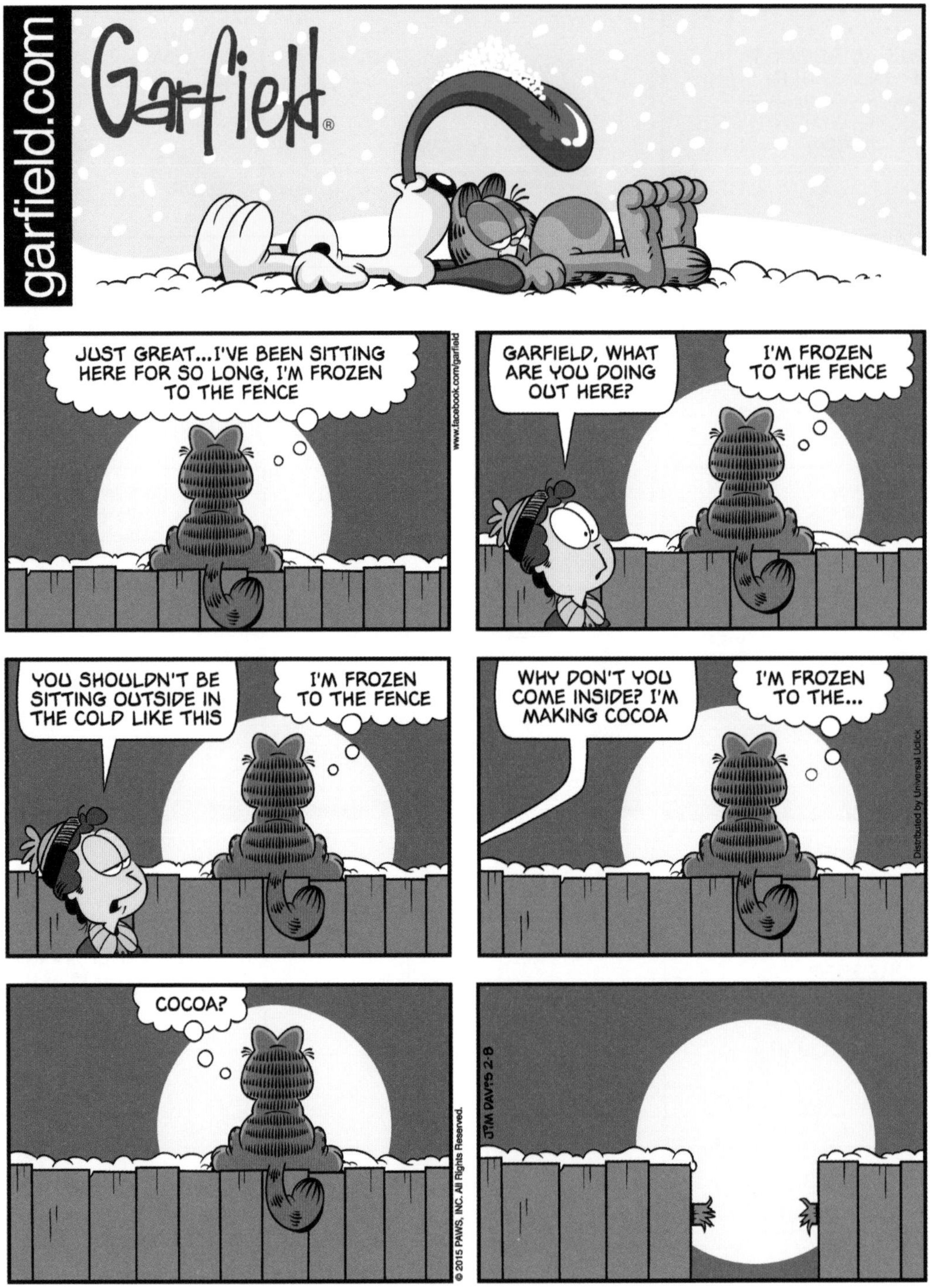
garfield.com
Garfield®
JUST GREAT...I'VE BEEN SITTING HERE FOR SO LONG, I'M FROZEN TO THE FENCE
www.facebook.com/garfield
GARFIELD, WHAT ARE YOU DOING OUT HERE?
I'M FROZEN TO THE FENCE
YOU SHOULDN'T BE SITTING OUTSIDE IN THE COLD LIKE THIS
I'M FROZEN TO THE FENCE
WHY DON'T YOU COME INSIDE? I'M MAKING COCOA
I'M FROZEN TO THE...
Distributed by Universal Uclick
COCOA?
© 2015 PAWS, INC. All Rights Reserved.
JIM DAVIS 2-8

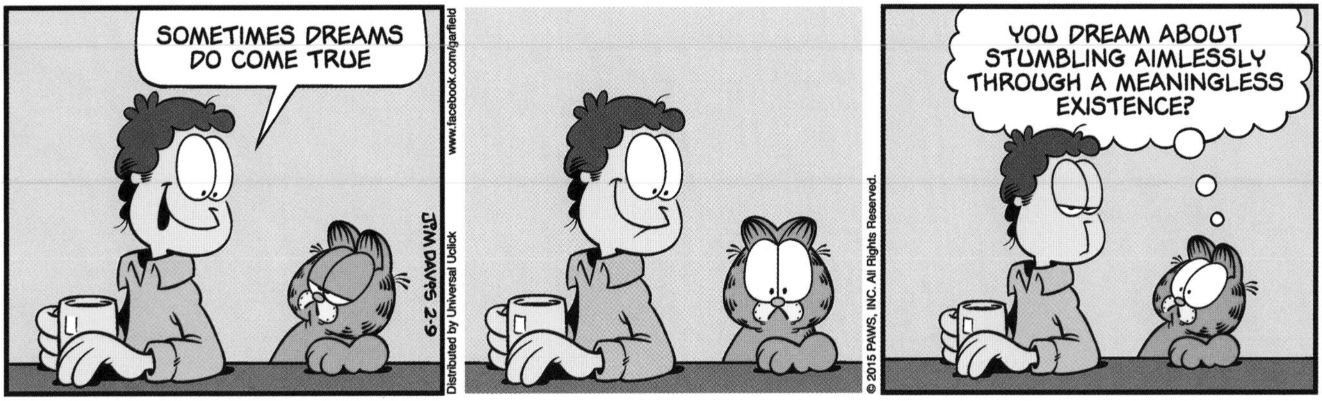
SOMETIMES DREAMS DO COME TRUE
JIM DAVIS 2-9
Distributed by Universal Uclick www.facebook.com/garfield
YOU DREAM ABOUT STUMBLING AIMLESSLY THROUGH A MEANINGLESS EXISTENCE?
© 2015 PAWS, INC. All Rights Reserved.

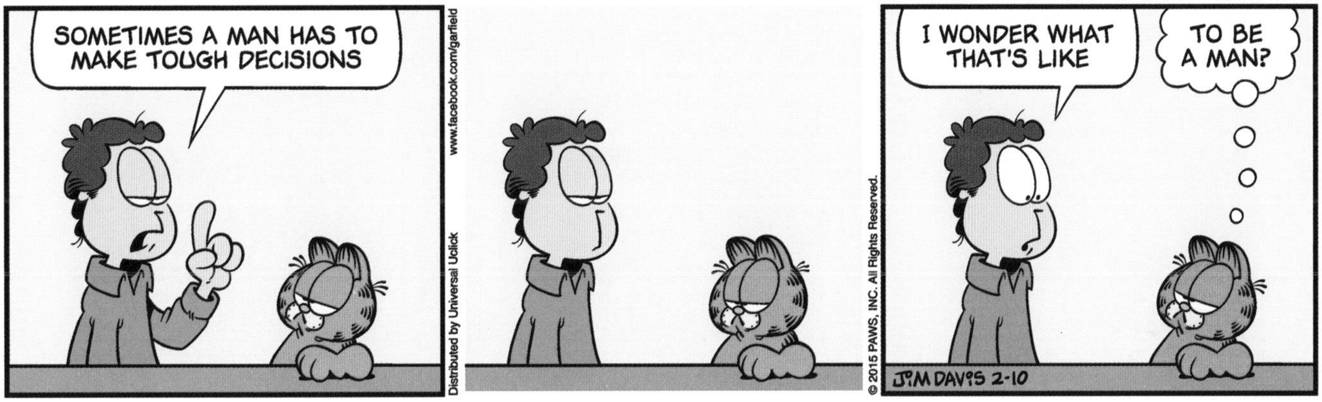
SOMETIMES A MAN HAS TO MAKE TOUGH DECISIONS
Distributed by Universal Uclick www.facebook.com/garfield
© 2015 PAWS, INC. All Rights Reserved.
I WONDER WHAT THAT'S LIKE
TO BE A MAN?
JIM DAVIS 2-10

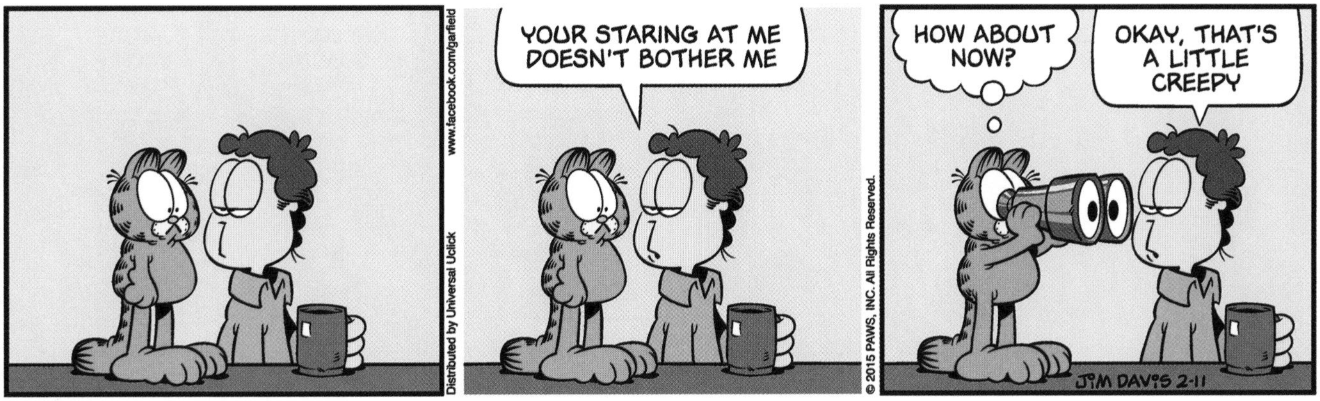
Distributed by Universal Uclick www.facebook.com/garfield
YOUR STARING AT ME DOESN'T BOTHER ME
© 2015 PAWS, INC. All Rights Reserved.
HOW ABOUT NOW?
OKAY, THAT'S A LITTLE CREEPY
JIM DAVIS 2-11

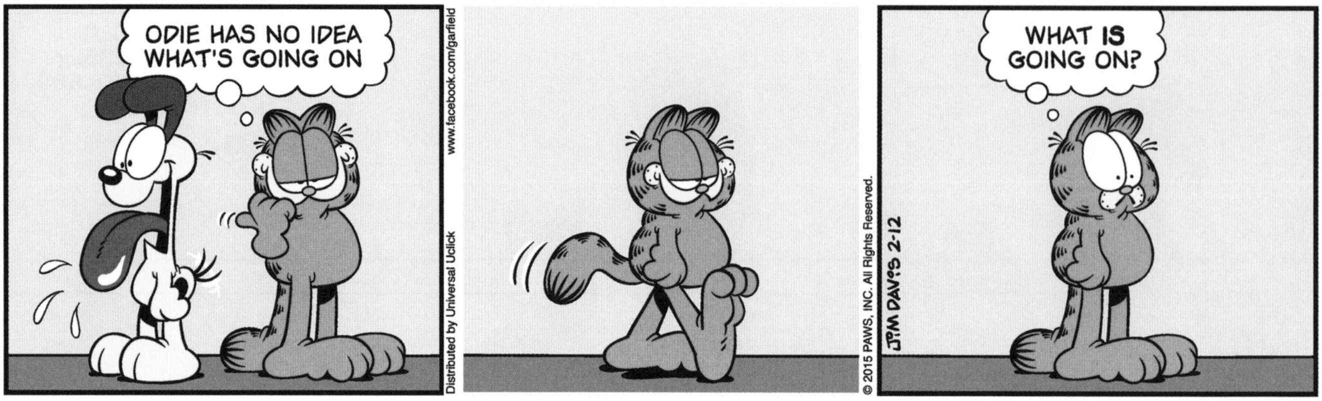
ODIE HAS NO IDEA WHAT'S GOING ON
WHAT IS GOING ON?
JIM DAVIS 2-12
www.facebook.com/garfield
Distributed by Universal Uclick
© 2015 PAWS, INC. All Rights Reserved.

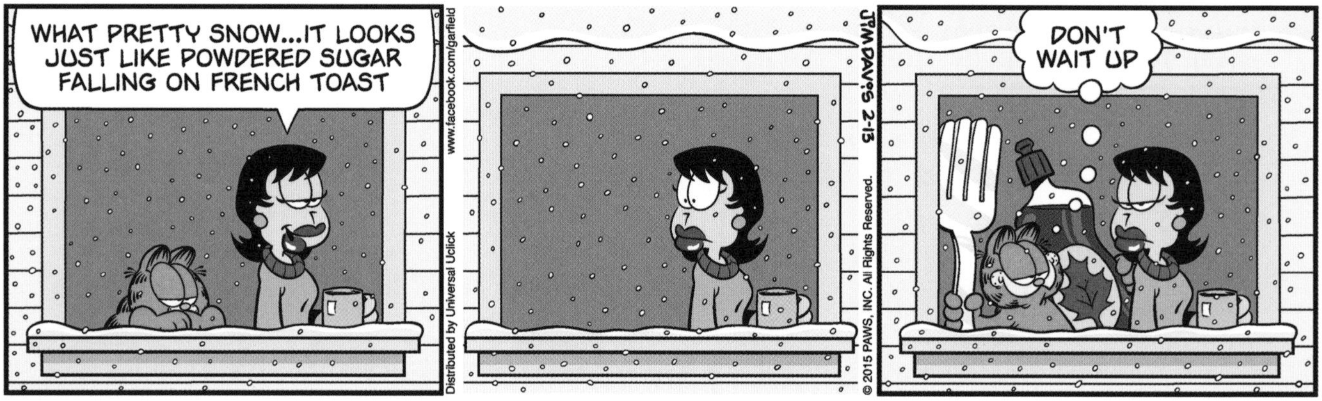
WHAT PRETTY SNOW...IT LOOKS JUST LIKE POWDERED SUGAR FALLING ON FRENCH TOAST
DON'T WAIT UP
JIM DAVIS 2-13
www.facebook.com/garfield
Distributed by Universal Uclick
© 2015 PAWS, INC. All Rights Reserved.

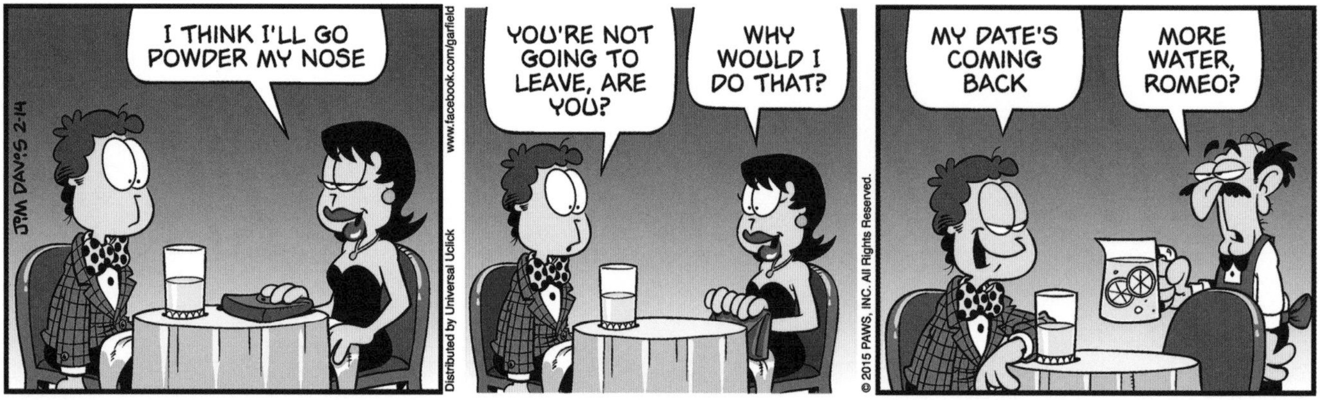
I THINK I'LL GO POWDER MY NOSE
YOU'RE NOT GOING TO LEAVE, ARE YOU?
WHY WOULD I DO THAT?
MY DATE'S COMING BACK
MORE WATER, ROMEO?
JIM DAVIS 2-14
www.facebook.com/garfield
Distributed by Universal Uclick
© 2015 PAWS, INC. All Rights Reserved.

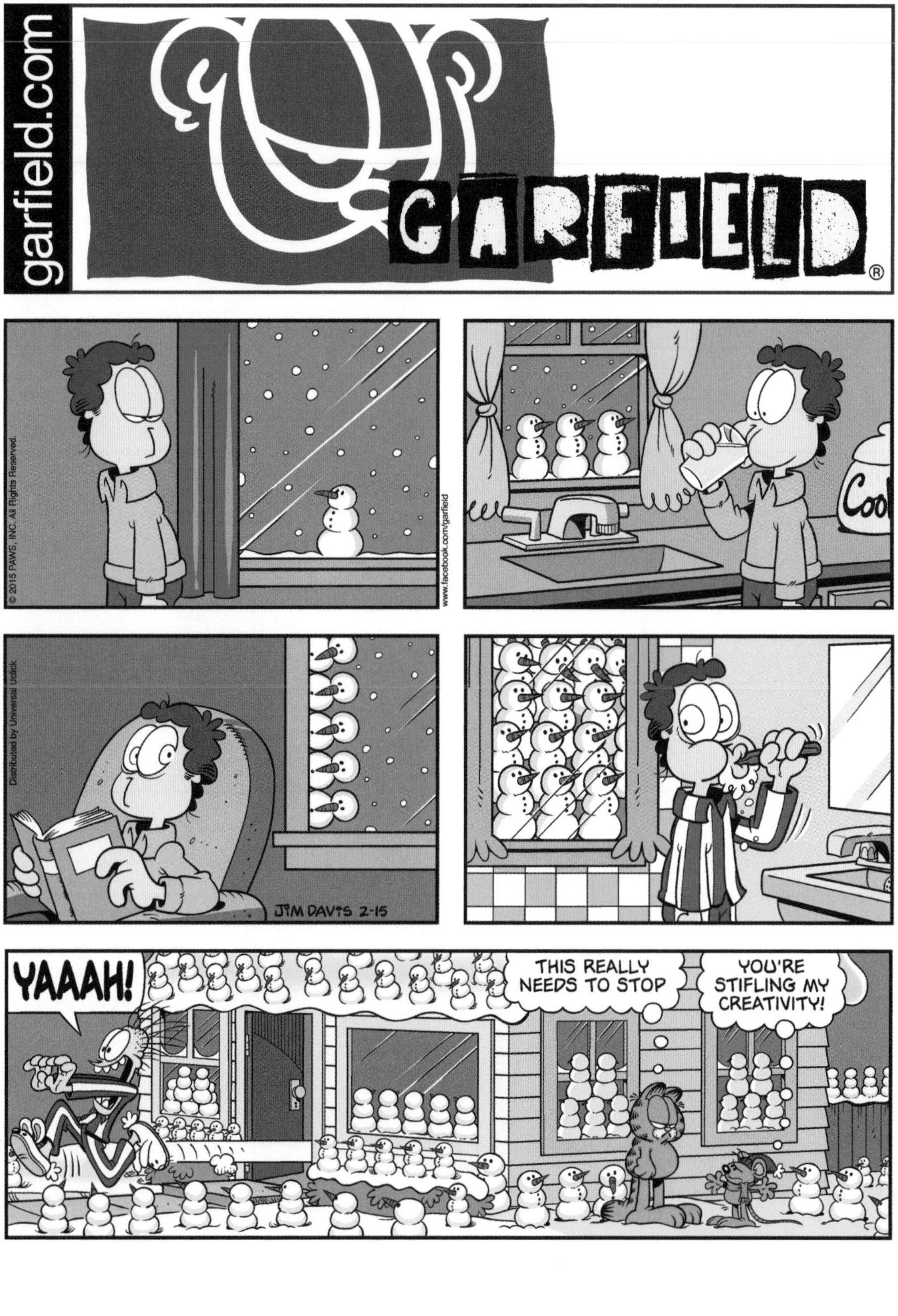
garfield.com
GARFIELD®
© 2015 PAWS, INC. All Rights Reserved.
www.facebook.com/garfield
Distributed by Universal Uclick
JIM DAVIS 2-15
YAAAH!
THIS REALLY NEEDS TO STOP
YOU'RE STIFLING MY CREATIVITY!

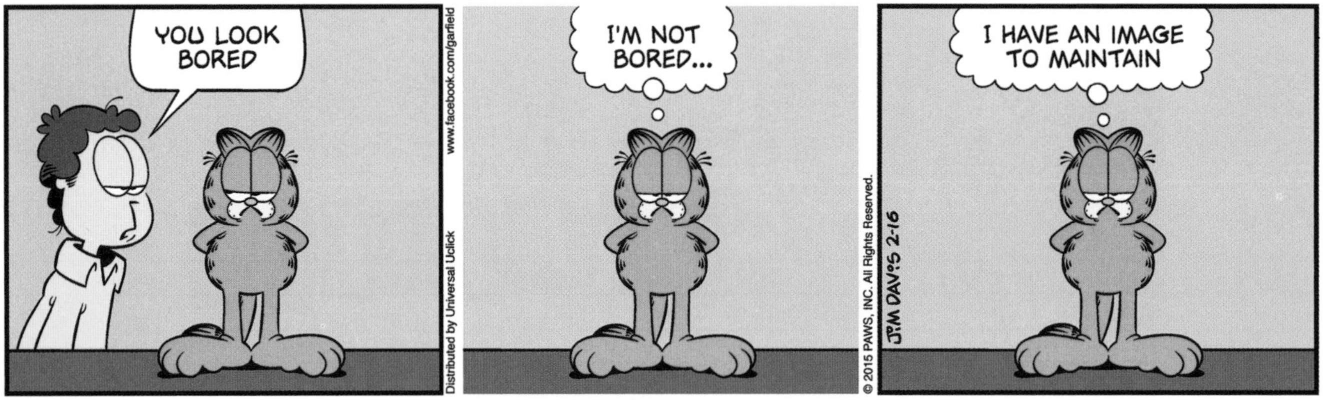
YOU LOOK BORED
I'M NOT BORED...
I HAVE AN IMAGE TO MAINTAIN
JIM DAVIS 2-16
Distributed by Universal Uclick
www.facebook.com/garfield
© 2015 PAWS, INC. All Rights Reserved.

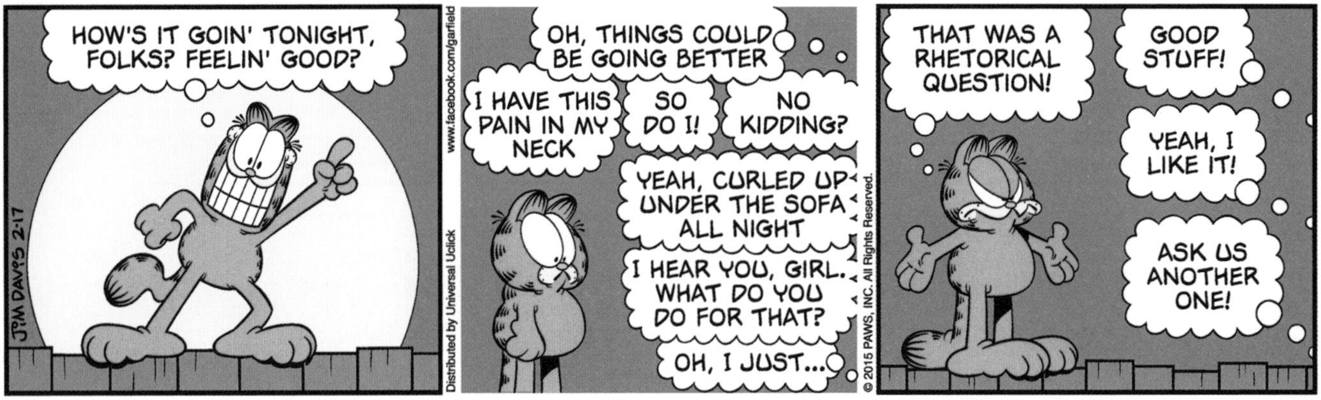
HOW'S IT GOIN' TONIGHT, FOLKS? FEELIN' GOOD?
JIM DAVIS 2-17
OH, THINGS COULD BE GOING BETTER
I HAVE THIS PAIN IN MY NECK
SO DO I!
NO KIDDING?
YEAH, CURLED UP UNDER THE SOFA ALL NIGHT
I HEAR YOU, GIRL. WHAT DO YOU DO FOR THAT?
OH, I JUST...
THAT WAS A RHETORICAL QUESTION!
GOOD STUFF!
YEAH, I LIKE IT!
ASK US ANOTHER ONE!
Distributed by Universal Uclick
www.facebook.com/garfield
© 2015 PAWS, INC. All Rights Reserved.

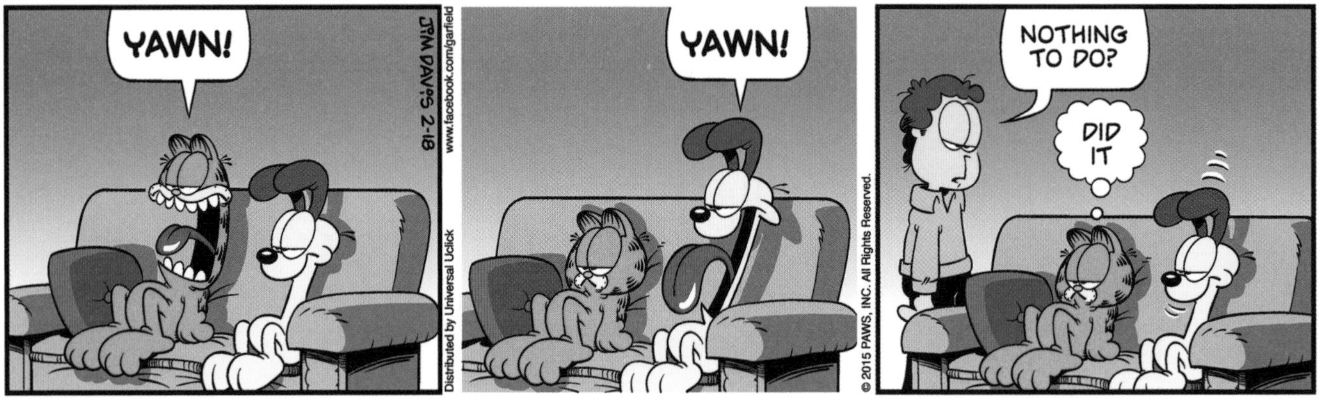
YAWN!
JIM DAVIS 2-18
YAWN!
NOTHING TO DO?
DID IT
Distributed by Universal Uclick
www.facebook.com/garfield
© 2015 PAWS, INC. All Rights Reserved.

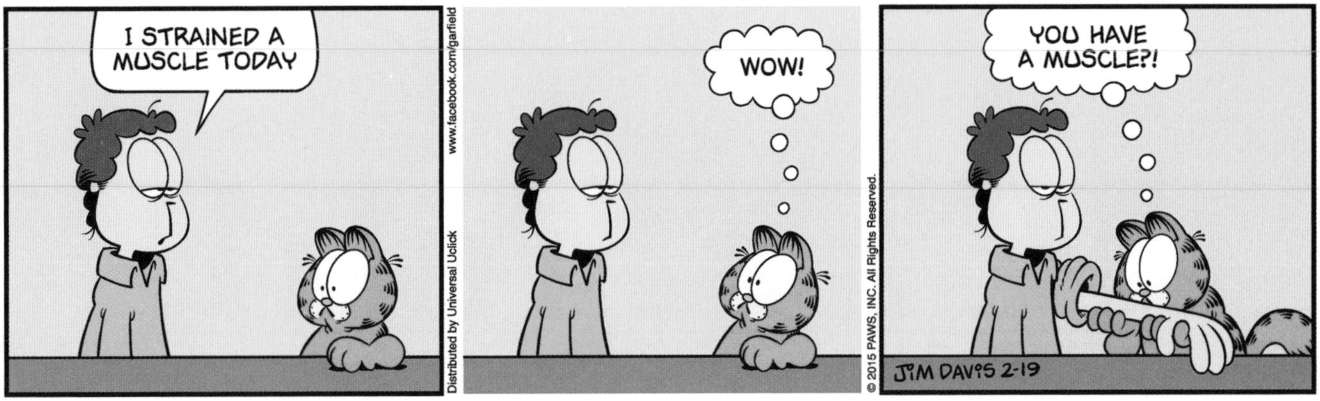
I STRAINED A MUSCLE TODAY
Distributed by Universal Uclick www.facebook.com/garfield
WOW!
YOU HAVE A MUSCLE?!
© 2015 PAWS, INC. All Rights Reserved.
JIM DAVIS 2-19

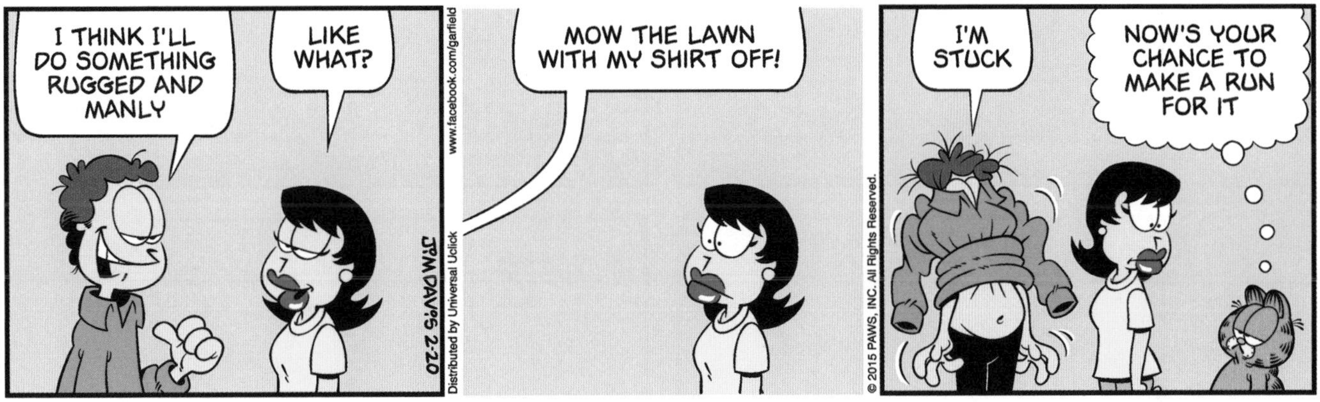
I THINK I'LL DO SOMETHING RUGGED AND MANLY
LIKE WHAT?
JIM DAVIS 2-20
Distributed by Universal Uclick www.facebook.com/garfield
MOW THE LAWN WITH MY SHIRT OFF!
I'M STUCK
NOW'S YOUR CHANCE TO MAKE A RUN FOR IT
© 2015 PAWS, INC. All Rights Reserved.

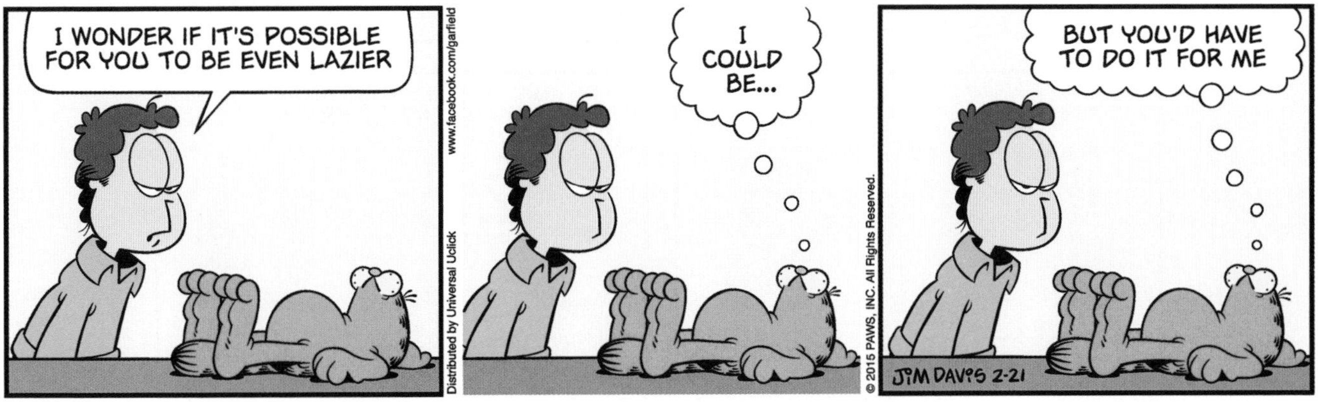
I WONDER IF IT'S POSSIBLE FOR YOU TO BE EVEN LAZIER
Distributed by Universal Uclick www.facebook.com/garfield
I COULD BE...
BUT YOU'D HAVE TO DO IT FOR ME
© 2015 PAWS, INC. All Rights Reserved.
JIM DAVIS 2-21

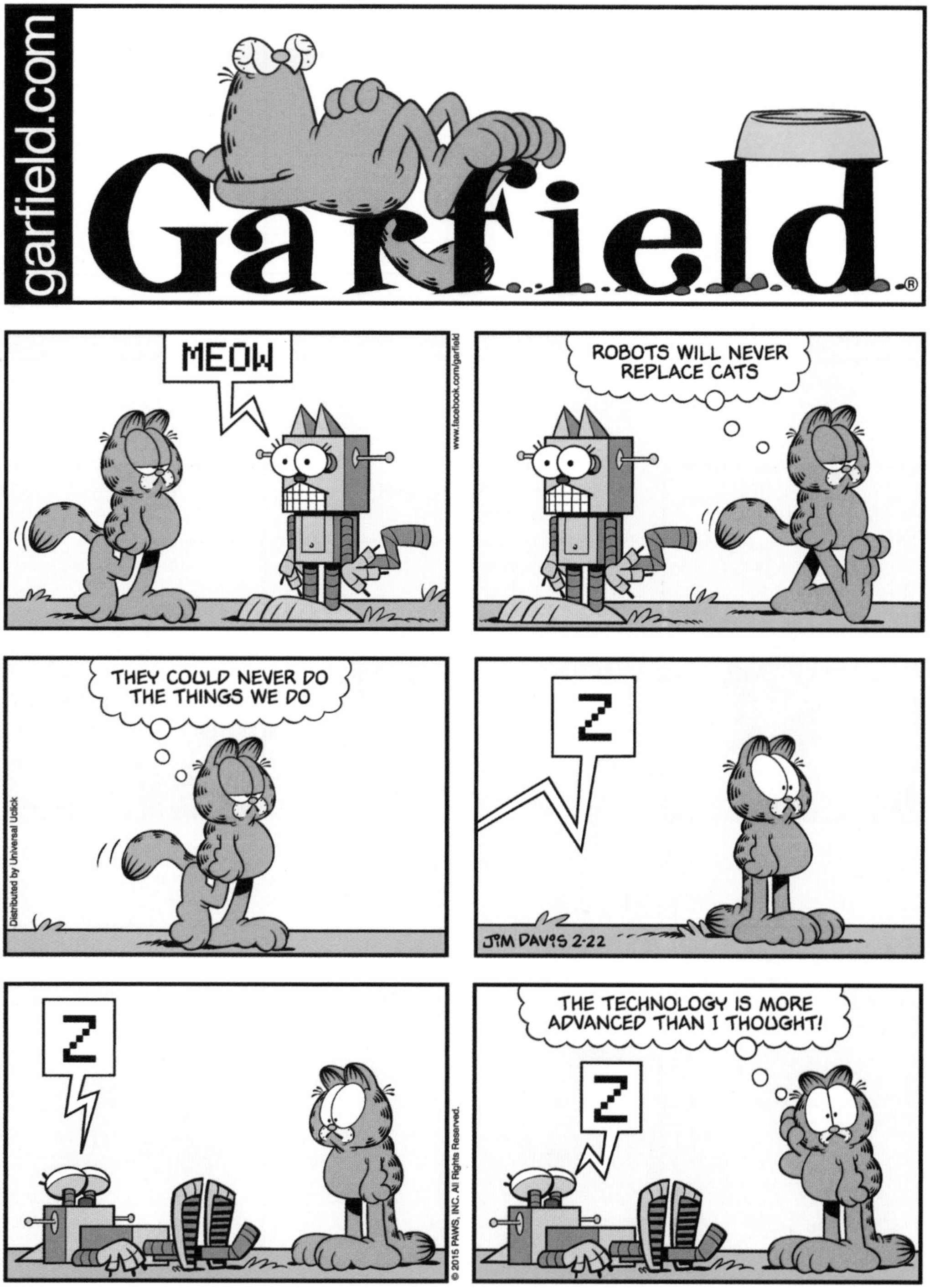
garfield.com
Garfield
MEOW
www.facebook.com/garfield
ROBOTS WILL NEVER REPLACE CATS
Distributed by Universal Uclick
THEY COULD NEVER DO THE THINGS WE DO
Z
JIM DAVIS 2-22
Z
© 2015 PAWS, INC. All Rights Reserved.
Z
THE TECHNOLOGY IS MORE ADVANCED THAN I THOUGHT!

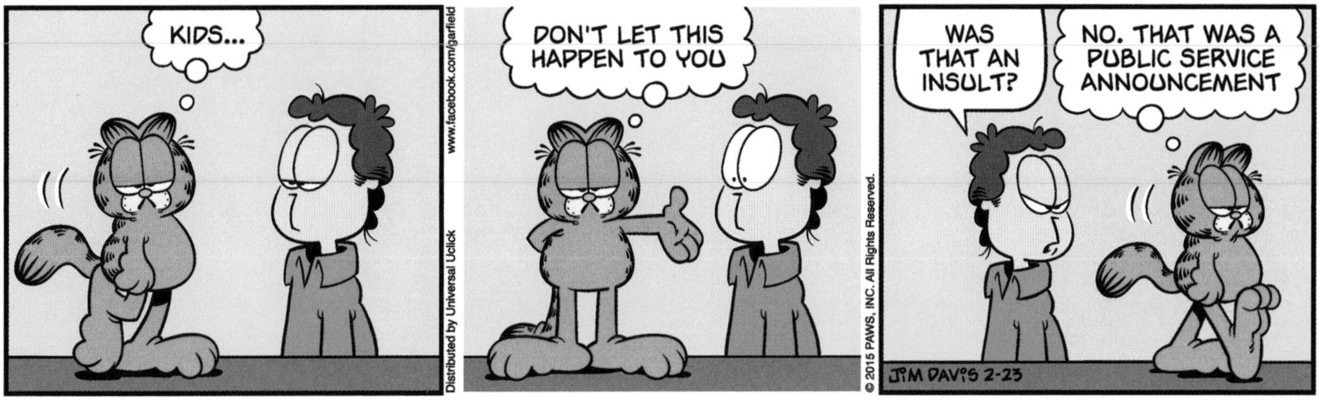
KIDS...
DON'T LET THIS HAPPEN TO YOU
WAS THAT AN INSULT?
NO. THAT WAS A PUBLIC SERVICE ANNOUNCEMENT
JIM DAVIS 2-23
Distributed by Universal Uclick www.facebook.com/garfield
© 2015 PAWS, INC. All Rights Reserved.

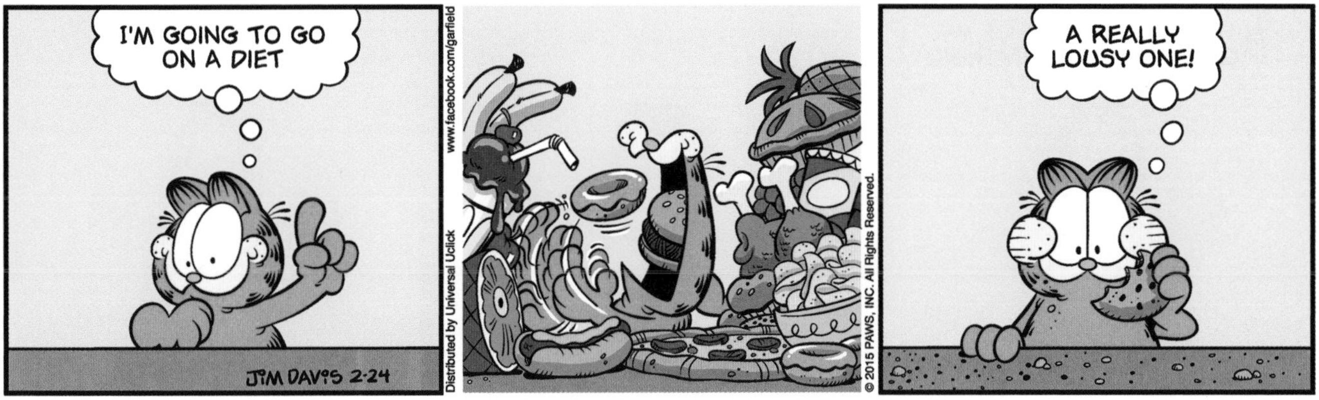
I'M GOING TO GO ON A DIET
JIM DAVIS 2-24
A REALLY LOUSY ONE!
Distributed by Universal Uclick www.facebook.com/garfield
© 2015 PAWS, INC. All Rights Reserved.

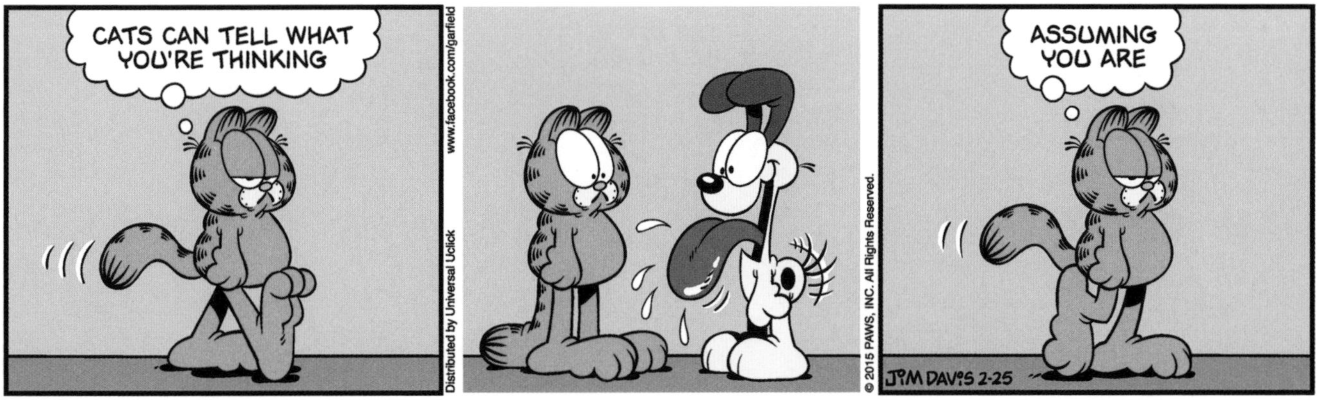
CATS CAN TELL WHAT YOU'RE THINKING
ASSUMING YOU ARE
JIM DAVIS 2-25
Distributed by Universal Uclick www.facebook.com/garfield
© 2015 PAWS, INC. All Rights Reserved.

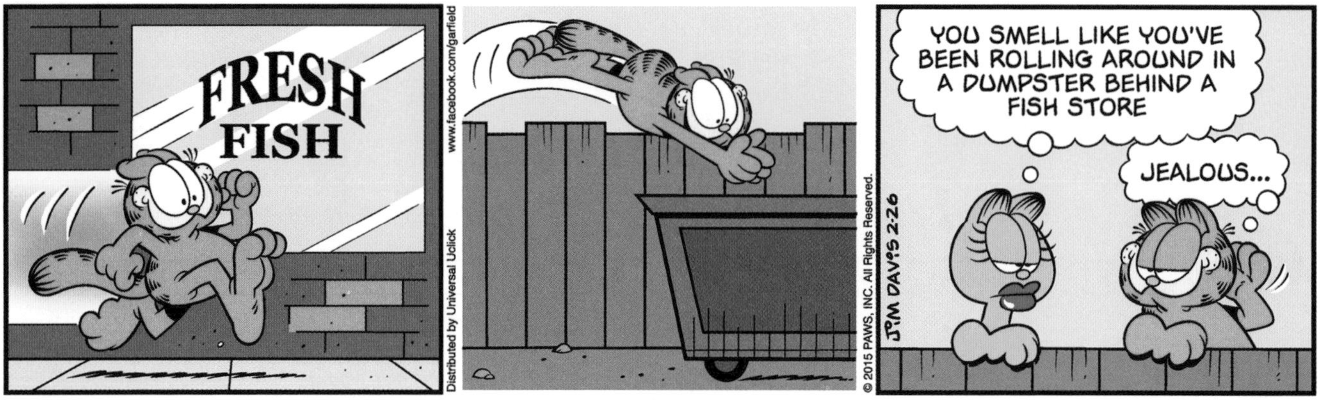
FRESH
FISH
Distributed by Universal Uclick www.facebook.com/garfield
YOU SMELL LIKE YOU'VE BEEN ROLLING AROUND IN A DUMPSTER BEHIND A FISH STORE
JEALOUS...
© 2015 PAWS, INC. All Rights Reserved.
JIM DAVIS 2-26

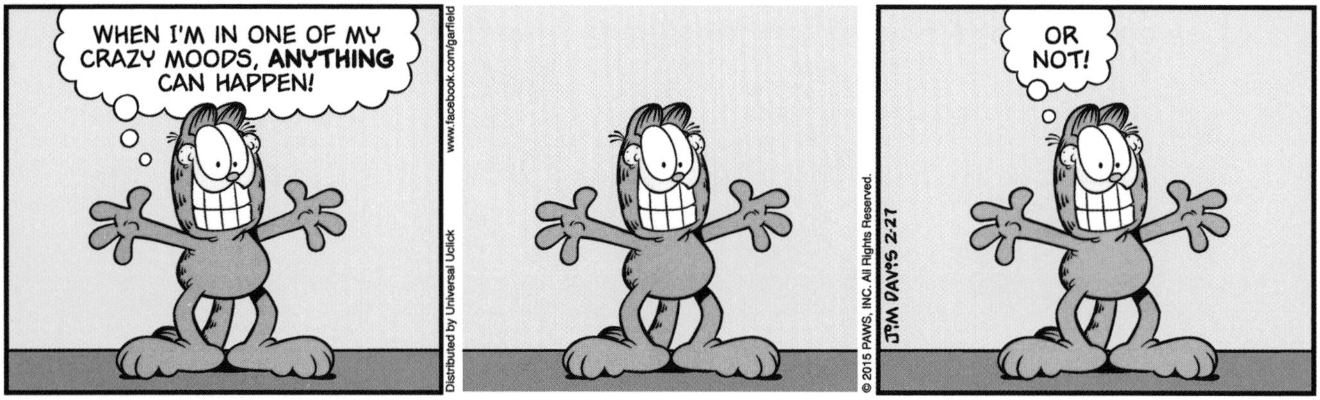
WHEN I'M IN ONE OF MY CRAZY MOODS, **ANYTHING** CAN HAPPEN!
Distributed by Universal Uclick www.facebook.com/garfield
© 2015 PAWS, INC. All Rights Reserved.
JIM DAVIS 2-27
OR NOT!

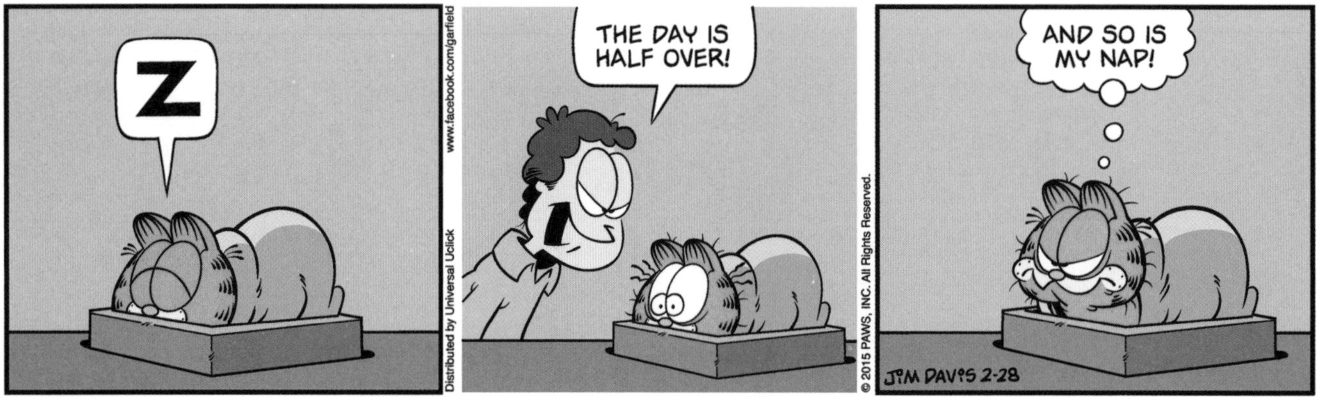
Z
Distributed by Universal Uclick www.facebook.com/garfield
THE DAY IS HALF OVER!
© 2015 PAWS, INC. All Rights Reserved.
AND SO IS MY NAP!
JIM DAVIS 2-28

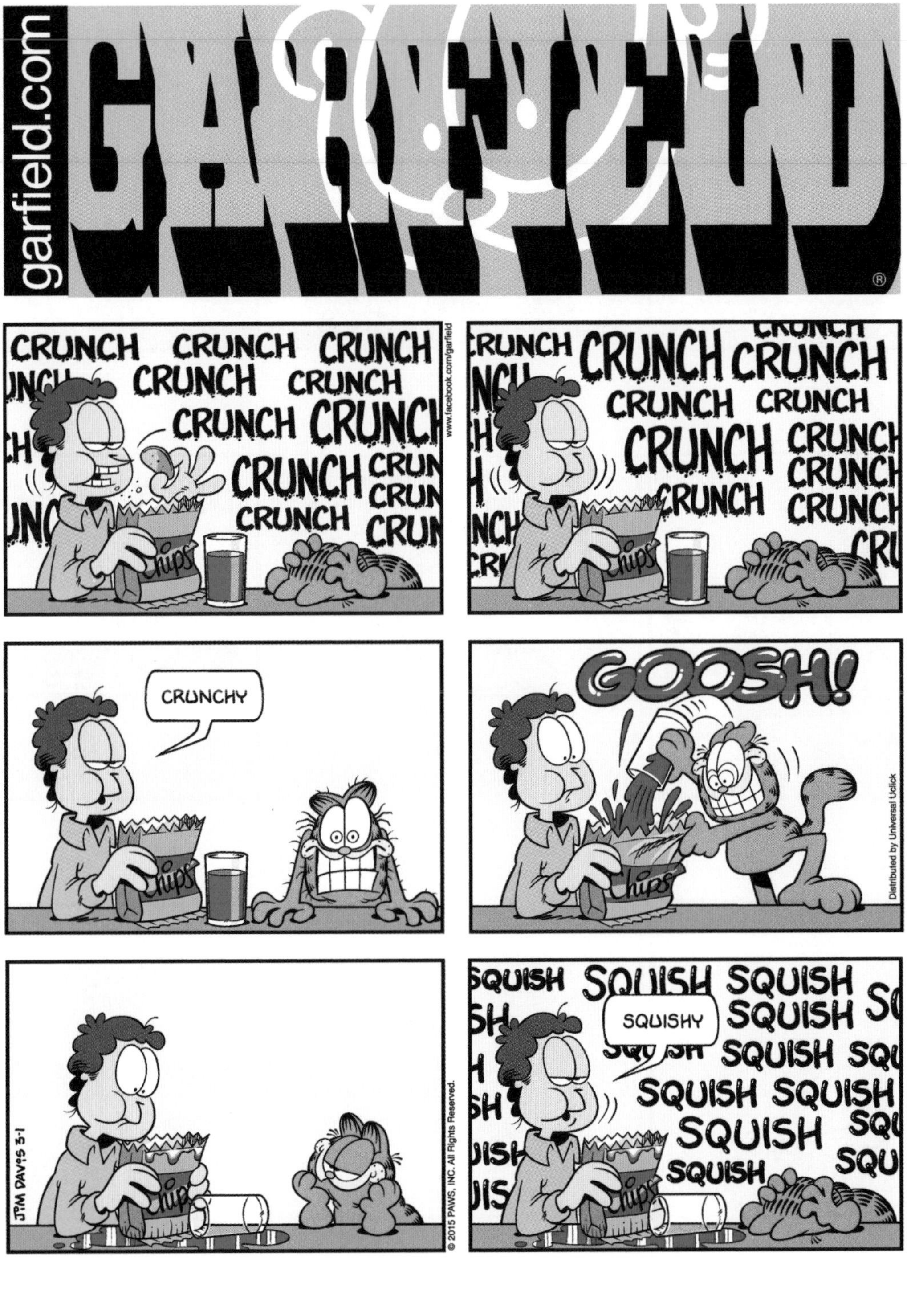
garfield.com
GARFIELD
CRUNCH CRUNCH CRUNCH CRUNCH CRUNCH CRUNCH CRUNCH CRUNCH
www.facebook.com/garfield
CRUNCH CRUNCH CRUNCH CRUNCH CRUNCH CRUNCH CRUNCH CRUNCH
CRUNCHY
GOOSH!
Distributed by Universal Uclick
JIM DAVIS 3-1
© 2015 PAWS, INC. All Rights Reserved.
SQUISH SQUISH SQUISH SQUISH SQUISH SQUISH SQUISH SQUISH SQUISH
SQUISHY

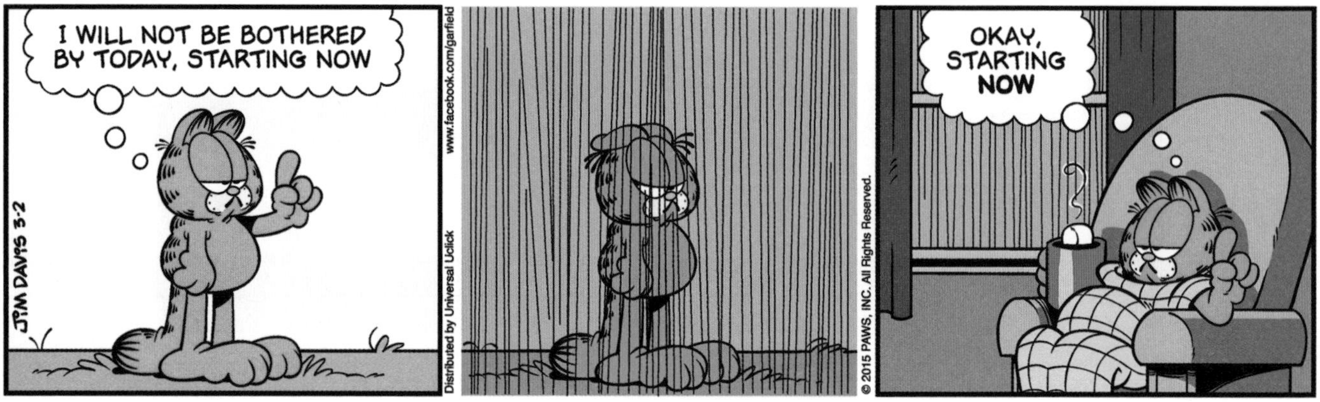
I WILL NOT BE BOTHERED BY TODAY, STARTING NOW
JIM DAVIS 3-2
Distributed by Universal Uclick www.facebook.com/garfield
OKAY, STARTING **NOW**
© 2015 PAWS, INC. All Rights Reserved.

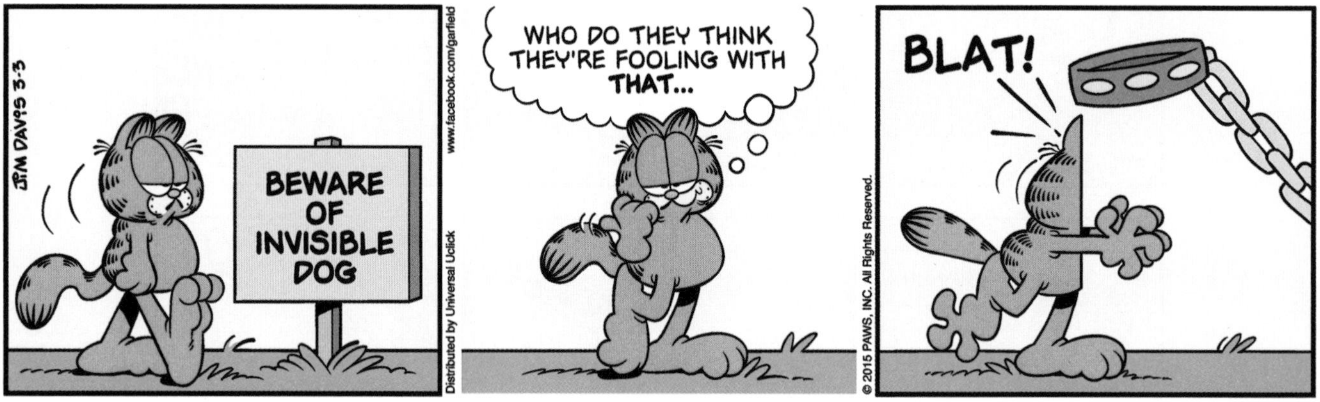
JIM DAVIS 3-3
BEWARE OF INVISIBLE DOG
Distributed by Universal Uclick www.facebook.com/garfield
WHO DO THEY THINK THEY'RE FOOLING WITH **THAT...**
BLAT!
© 2015 PAWS, INC. All Rights Reserved.

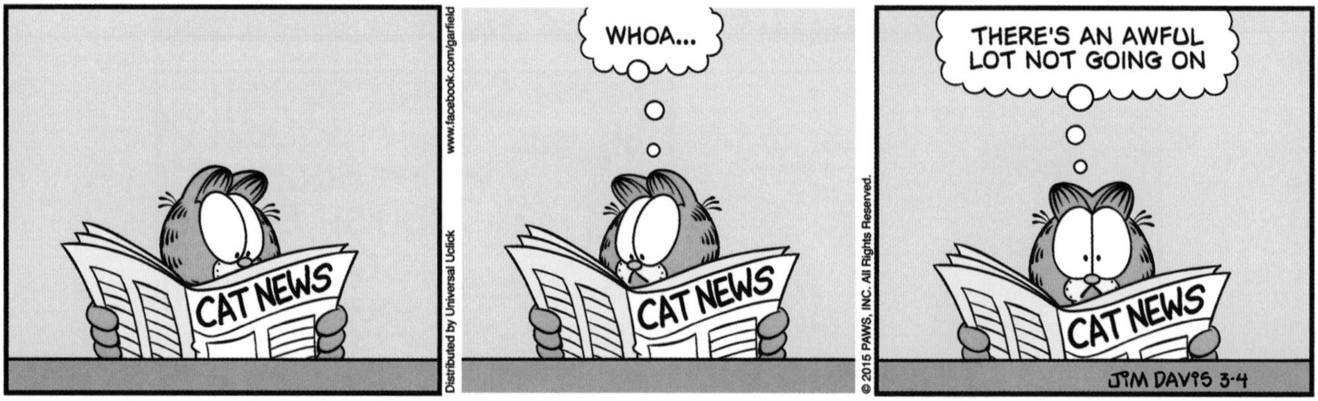
CAT NEWS
Distributed by Universal Uclick www.facebook.com/garfield
WHOA...
CAT NEWS
THERE'S AN AWFUL LOT NOT GOING ON
CAT NEWS
JIM DAVIS 3-4
© 2015 PAWS, INC. All Rights Reserved.

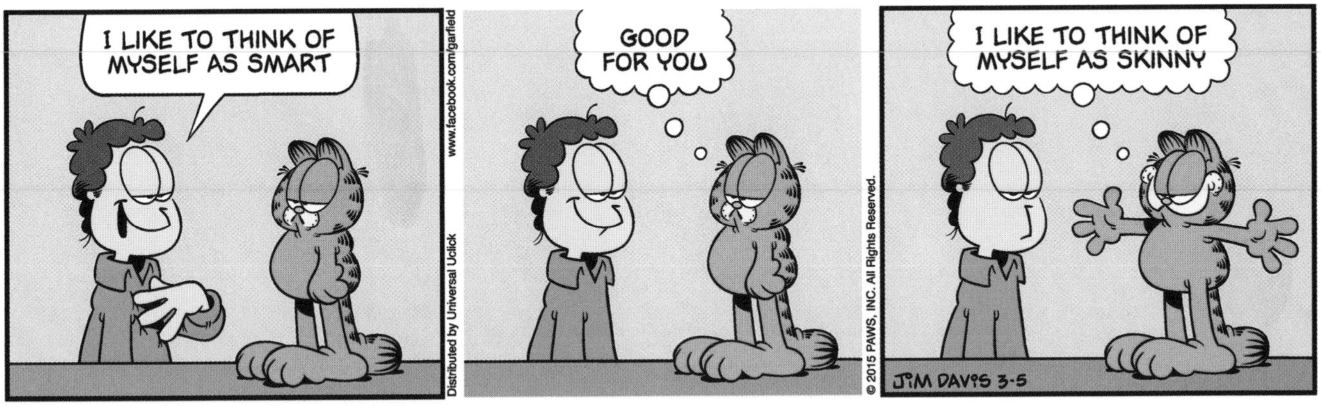
I LIKE TO THINK OF MYSELF AS SMART
GOOD FOR YOU
I LIKE TO THINK OF MYSELF AS SKINNY
Distributed by Universal Uclick www.facebook.com/garfield
© 2015 PAWS, INC. All Rights Reserved.
JIM DAVIS 3-5

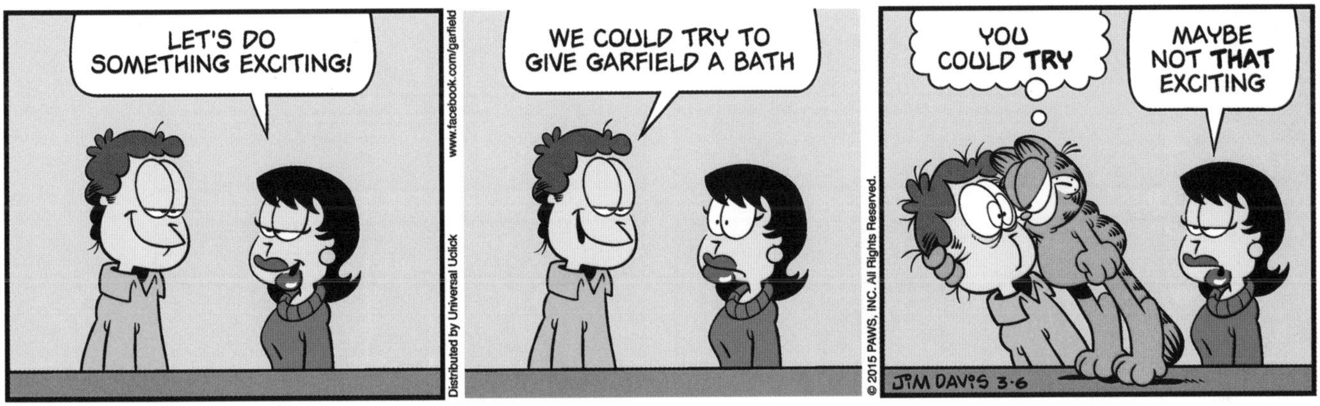
LET'S DO SOMETHING EXCITING!
WE COULD TRY TO GIVE GARFIELD A BATH
YOU COULD **TRY**
MAYBE NOT **THAT** EXCITING
Distributed by Universal Uclick www.facebook.com/garfield
© 2015 PAWS, INC. All Rights Reserved.
JIM DAVIS 3-6

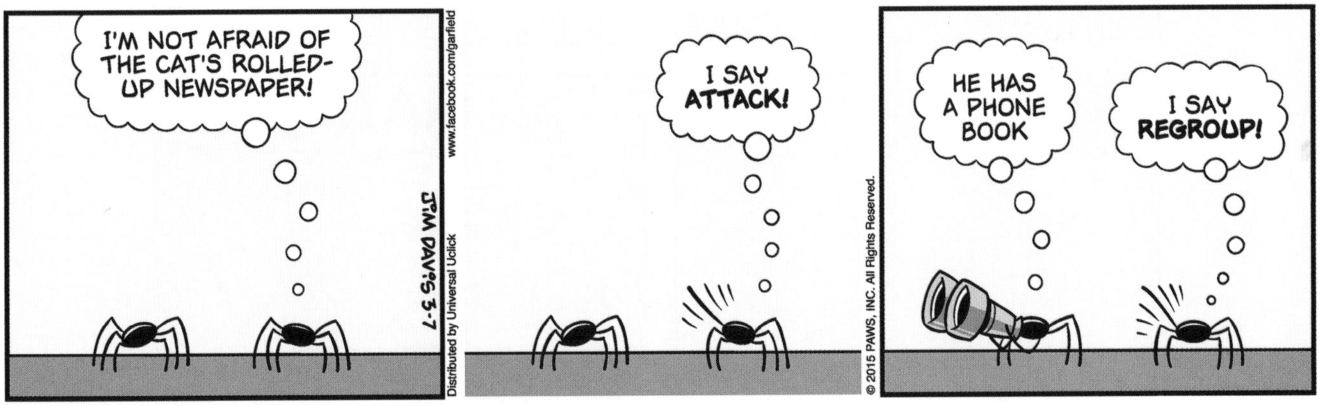
I'M NOT AFRAID OF THE CAT'S ROLLED-UP NEWSPAPER!
JIM DAVIS 3-7
I SAY **ATTACK!**
HE HAS A PHONE BOOK
I SAY **REGROUP!**
Distributed by Universal Uclick www.facebook.com/garfield
© 2015 PAWS, INC. All Rights Reserved.

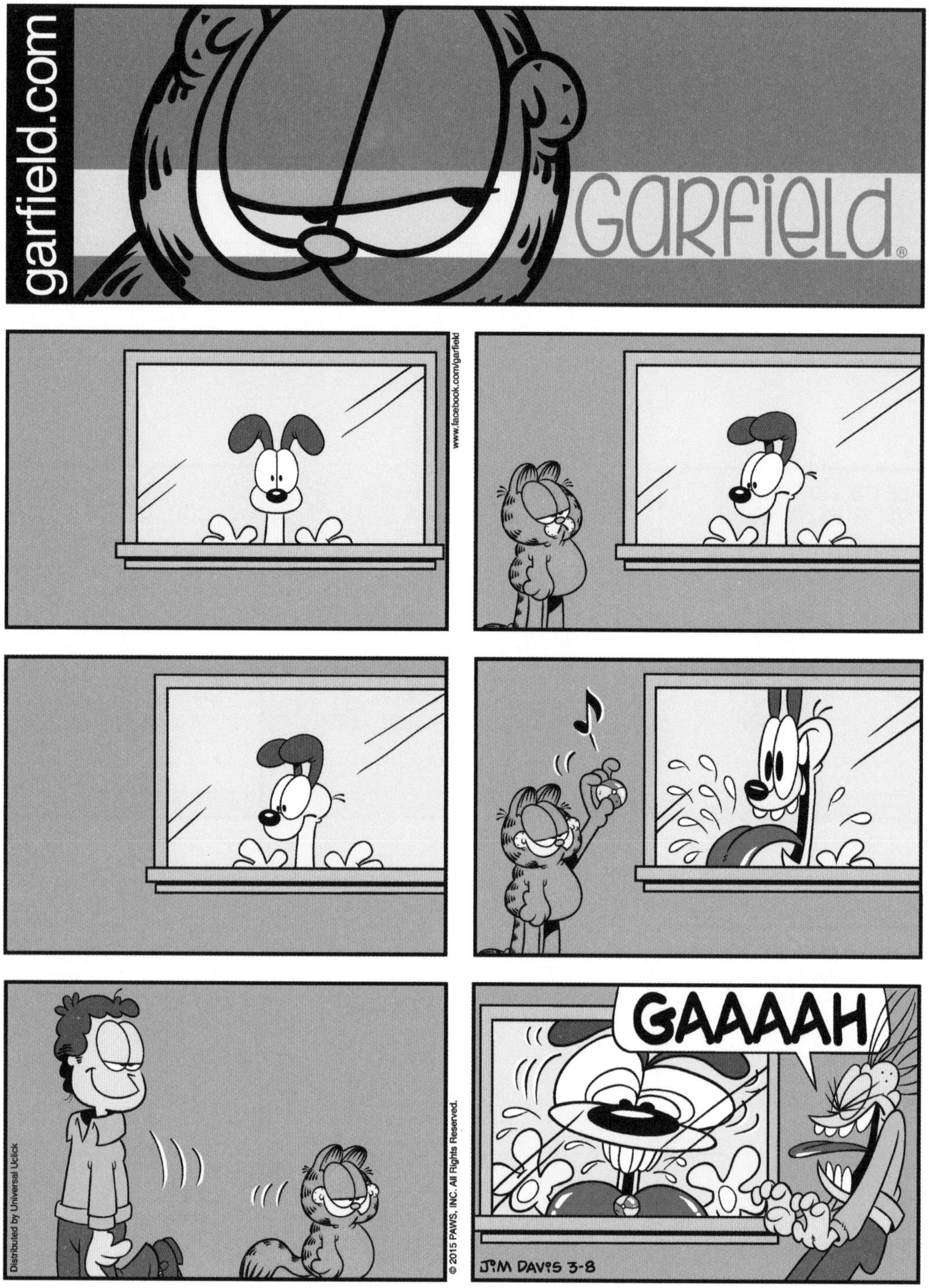
garfield.com
GARFIELD
www.facebook.com/garfield
Distributed by Universal Uclick
© 2015 PAWS, INC. All Rights Reserved.
GAAAAH
JIM DAVIS 3-8

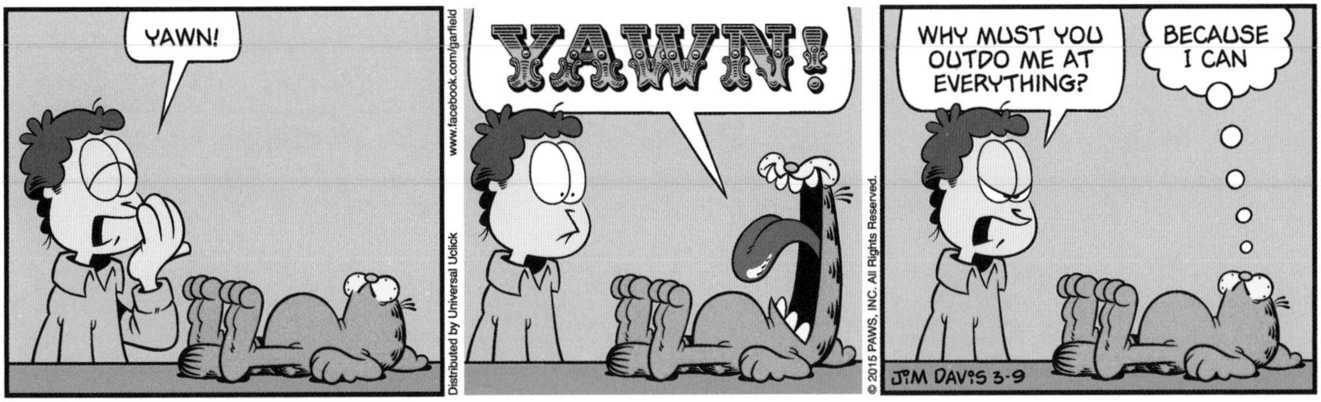
YAWN!
YAWN!
WHY MUST YOU OUTDO ME AT EVERYTHING?
BECAUSE I CAN
JIM DAVIS 3-9
Distributed by Universal Uclick www.facebook.com/garfield
© 2015 PAWS, INC. All Rights Reserved.

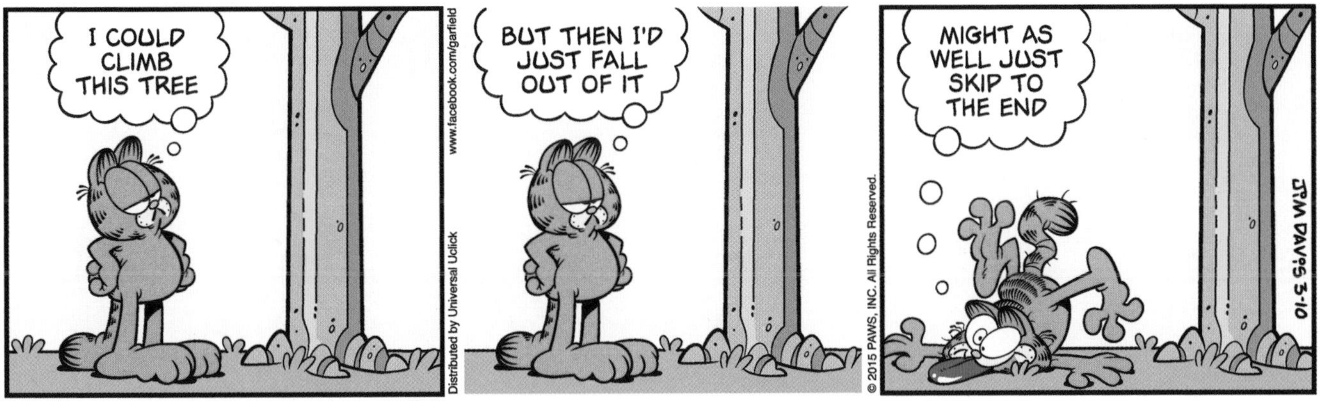
I COULD CLIMB THIS TREE
BUT THEN I'D JUST FALL OUT OF IT
MIGHT AS WELL JUST SKIP TO THE END
JIM DAVIS 3-10
Distributed by Universal Uclick www.facebook.com/garfield
© 2015 PAWS, INC. All Rights Reserved.

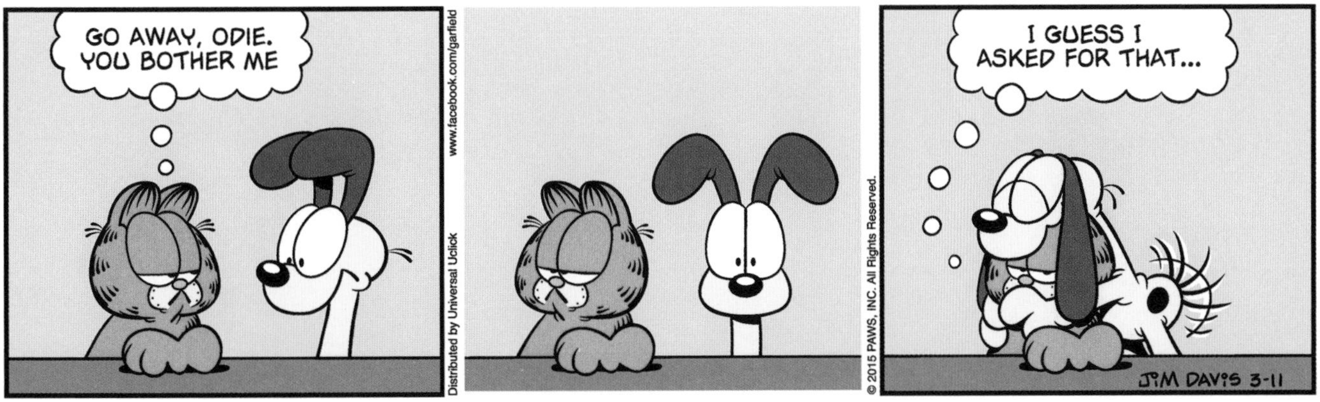
GO AWAY, ODIE. YOU BOTHER ME
I GUESS I ASKED FOR THAT...
JIM DAVIS 3-11
Distributed by Universal Uclick www.facebook.com/garfield
© 2015 PAWS, INC. All Rights Reserved.

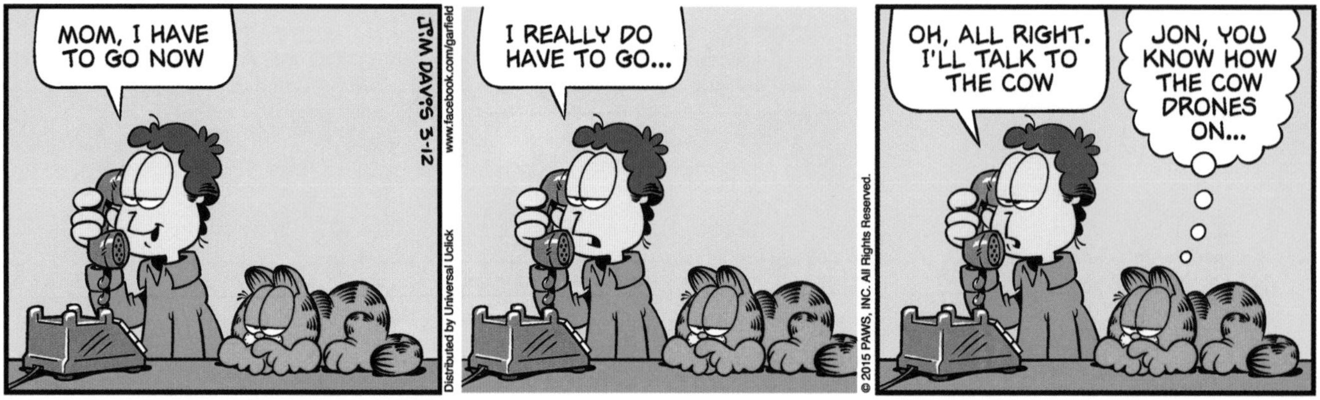
MOM, I HAVE TO GO NOW
JIM DAVIS 3-12
www.facebook.com/garfield
Distributed by Universal Uclick
I REALLY DO HAVE TO GO...
© 2015 PAWS, INC. All Rights Reserved.
OH, ALL RIGHT. I'LL TALK TO THE COW
JON, YOU KNOW HOW THE COW DRONES ON...

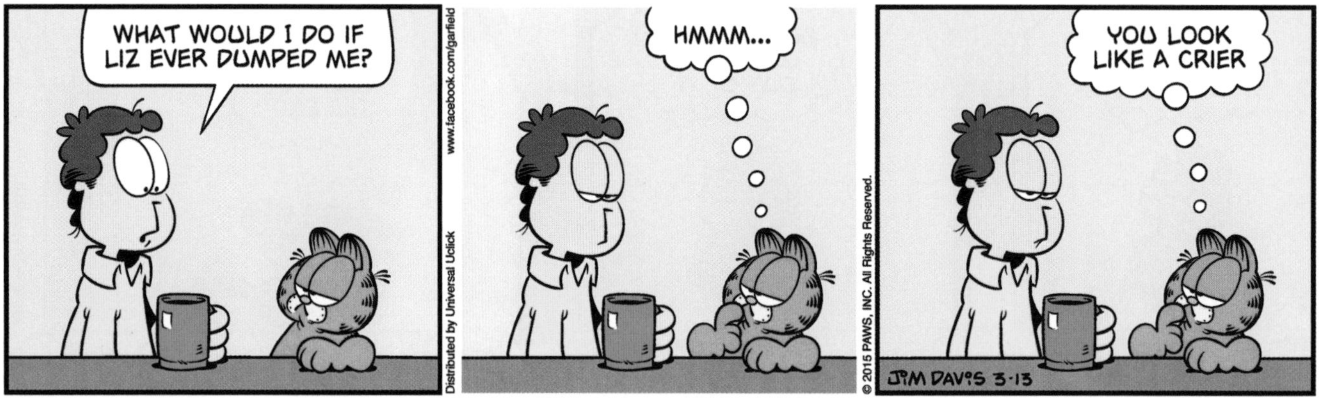
WHAT WOULD I DO IF LIZ EVER DUMPED ME?
www.facebook.com/garfield
Distributed by Universal Uclick
HMMM...
© 2015 PAWS, INC. All Rights Reserved.
YOU LOOK LIKE A CRIER
JIM DAVIS 3-13

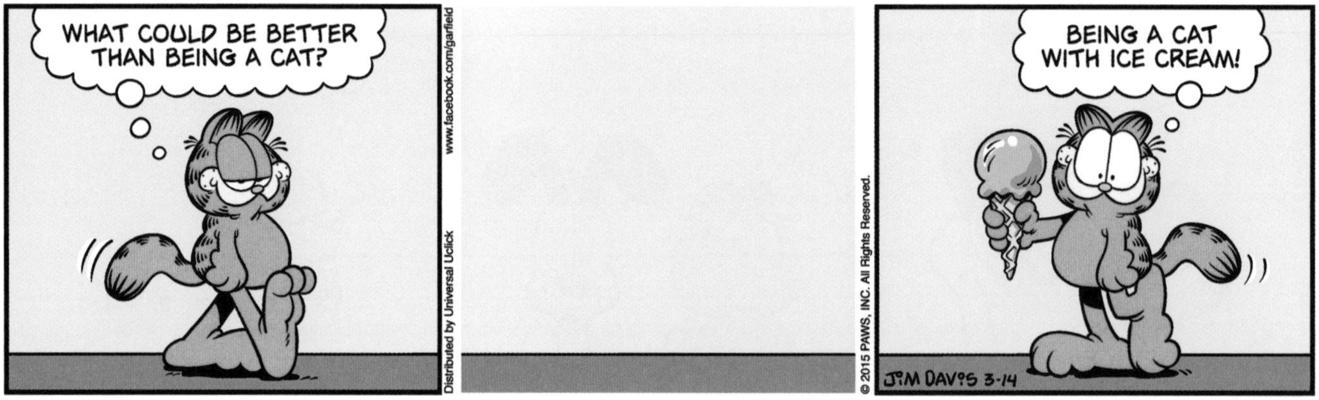
WHAT COULD BE BETTER THAN BEING A CAT?
www.facebook.com/garfield
Distributed by Universal Uclick
© 2015 PAWS, INC. All Rights Reserved.
BEING A CAT WITH ICE CREAM!
JIM DAVIS 3-14

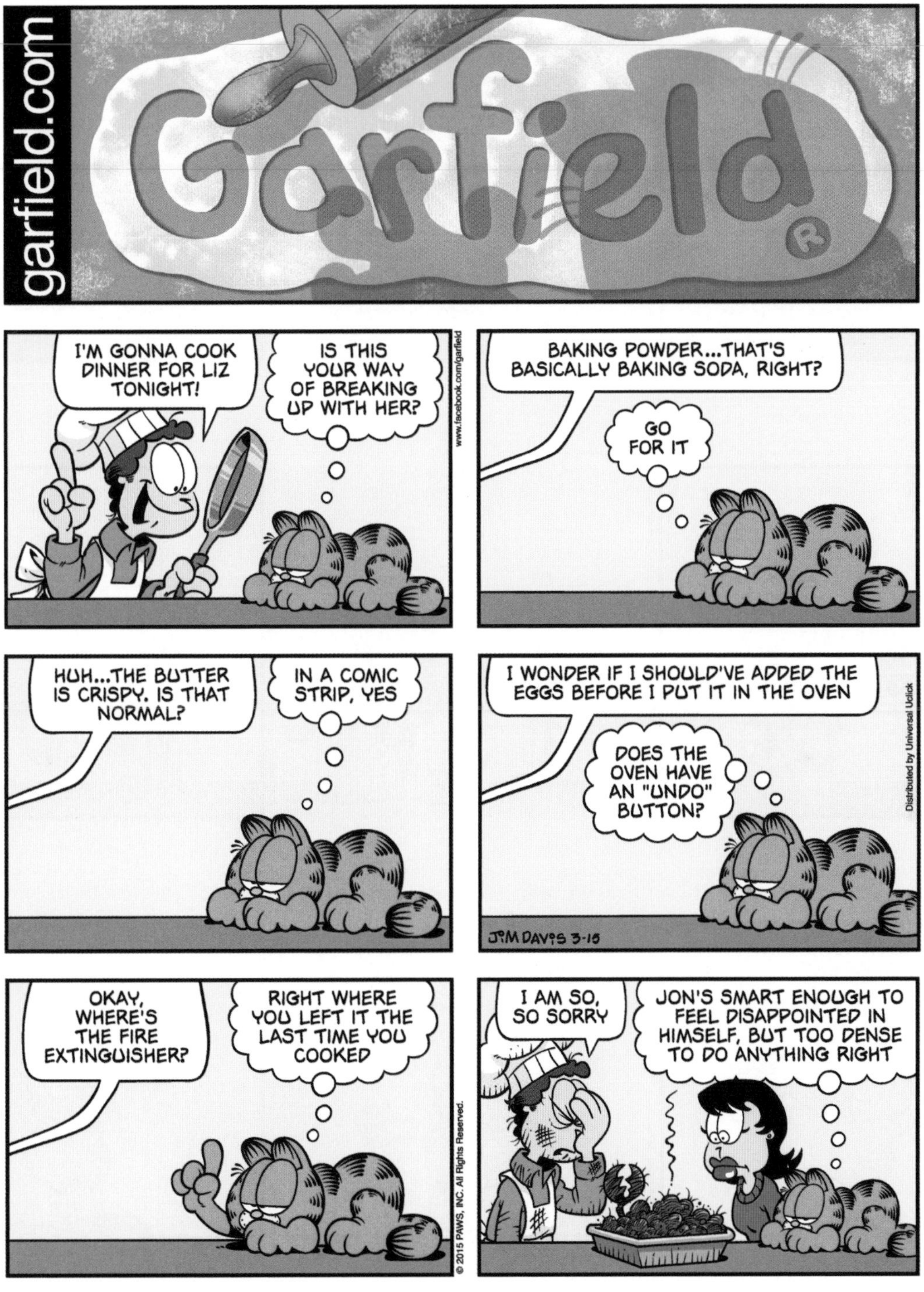
garfield.com
Garfield
I'M GONNA COOK DINNER FOR LIZ TONIGHT!
IS THIS YOUR WAY OF BREAKING UP WITH HER?
www.facebook.com/garfield
BAKING POWDER...THAT'S BASICALLY BAKING SODA, RIGHT?
GO FOR IT
HUH...THE BUTTER IS CRISPY. IS THAT NORMAL?
IN A COMIC STRIP, YES
I WONDER IF I SHOULD'VE ADDED THE EGGS BEFORE I PUT IT IN THE OVEN
DOES THE OVEN HAVE AN "UNDO" BUTTON?
Distributed by Universal Uclick
JIM DAVIS 3-15
OKAY, WHERE'S THE FIRE EXTINGUISHER?
RIGHT WHERE YOU LEFT IT THE LAST TIME YOU COOKED
© 2015 PAWS, INC. All Rights Reserved.
I AM SO, SO SORRY
JON'S SMART ENOUGH TO FEEL DISAPPOINTED IN HIMSELF, BUT TOO DENSE TO DO ANYTHING RIGHT

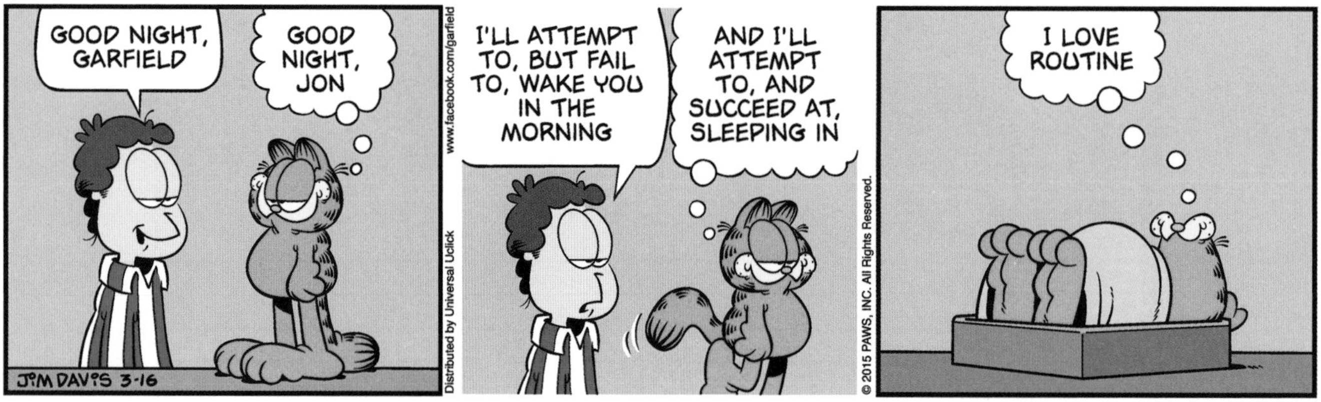
GOOD NIGHT, GARFIELD
GOOD NIGHT, JON
JIM DAVIS 3-16
www.facebook.com/garfield
Distributed by Universal Uclick
I'LL ATTEMPT TO, BUT FAIL TO, WAKE YOU IN THE MORNING
AND I'LL ATTEMPT TO, AND SUCCEED AT, SLEEPING IN
© 2015 PAWS, INC. All Rights Reserved.
I LOVE ROUTINE

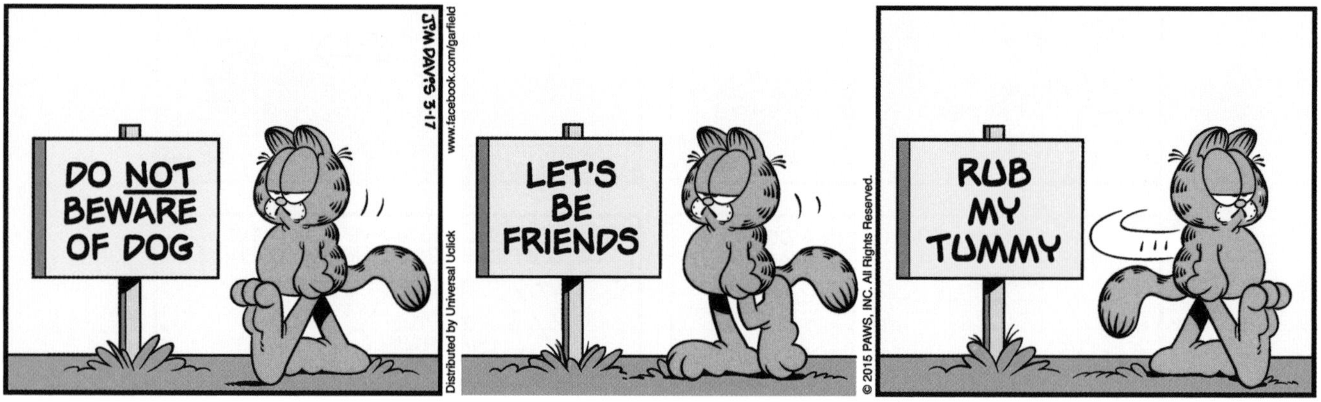
DO NOT BEWARE OF DOG
JIM DAVIS 3-17
www.facebook.com/garfield
Distributed by Universal Uclick
LET'S BE FRIENDS
© 2015 PAWS, INC. All Rights Reserved.
RUB MY TUMMY

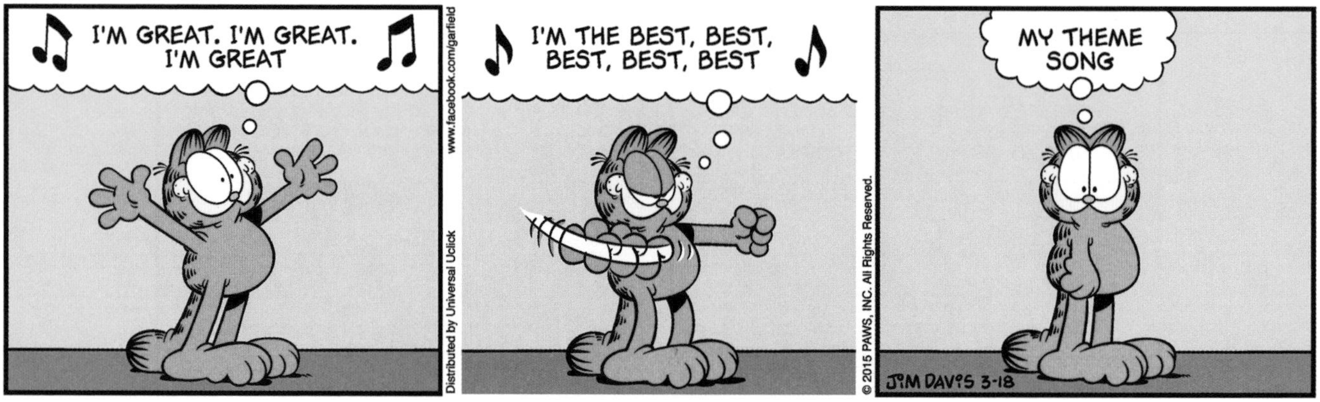
♪ I'M GREAT. I'M GREAT. I'M GREAT ♫
www.facebook.com/garfield
Distributed by Universal Uclick
♪ I'M THE BEST, BEST, BEST, BEST, BEST ♪
© 2015 PAWS, INC. All Rights Reserved.
MY THEME SONG
JIM DAVIS 3-18

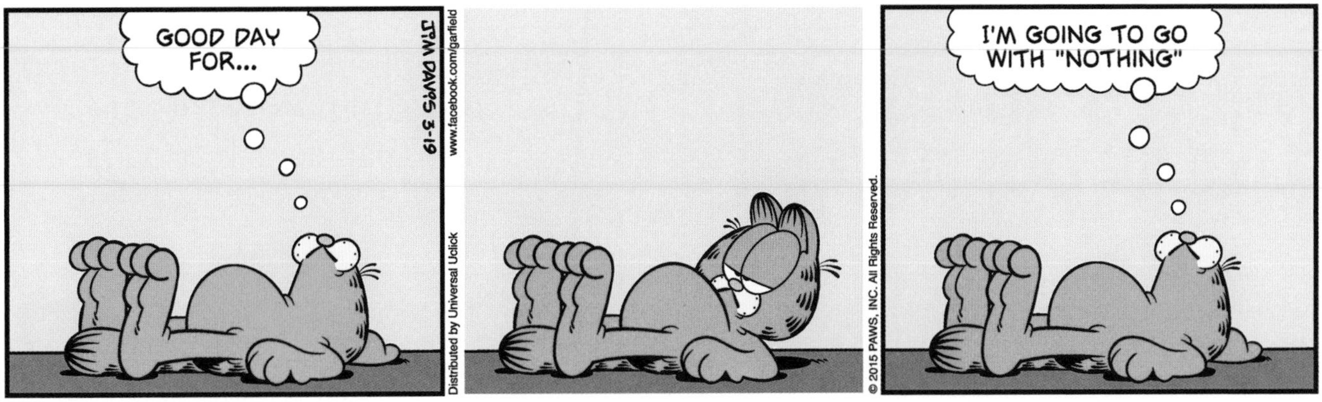
GOOD DAY FOR...
I'M GOING TO GO WITH "NOTHING"
JIM DAVIS 3-19
www.facebook.com/garfield
Distributed by Universal Uclick
© 2015 PAWS, INC. All Rights Reserved.

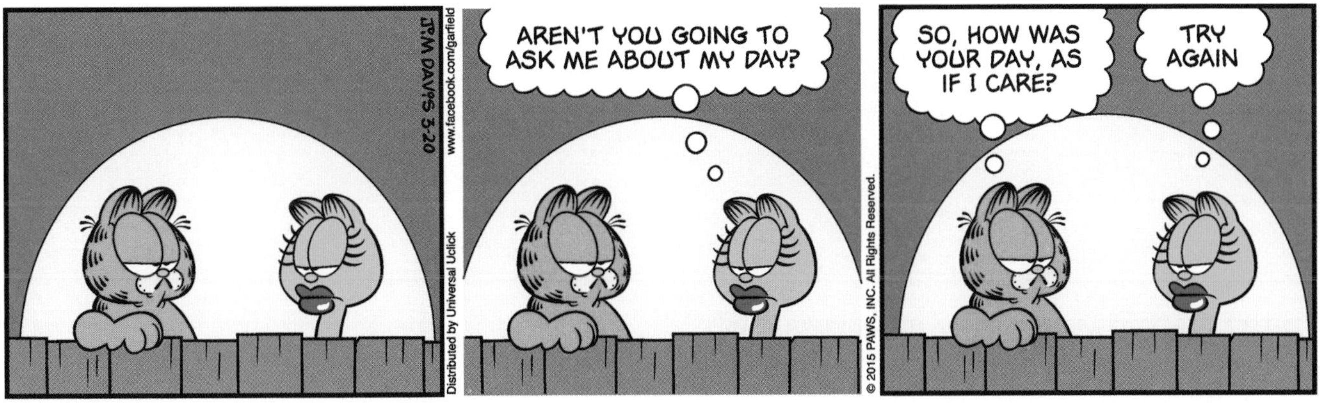
AREN'T YOU GOING TO ASK ME ABOUT MY DAY?
SO, HOW WAS YOUR DAY, AS IF I CARE?
TRY AGAIN
JIM DAVIS 3-20
www.facebook.com/garfield
Distributed by Universal Uclick
© 2015 PAWS, INC. All Rights Reserved.

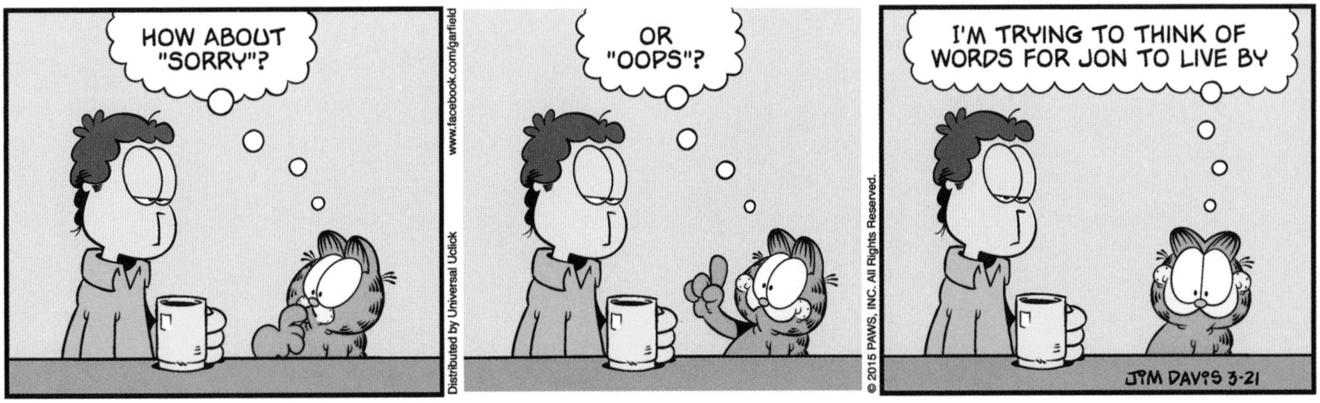
HOW ABOUT "SORRY"?
OR "OOPS"?
I'M TRYING TO THINK OF WORDS FOR JON TO LIVE BY
JIM DAVIS 3-21
www.facebook.com/garfield
Distributed by Universal Uclick
© 2015 PAWS, INC. All Rights Reserved.

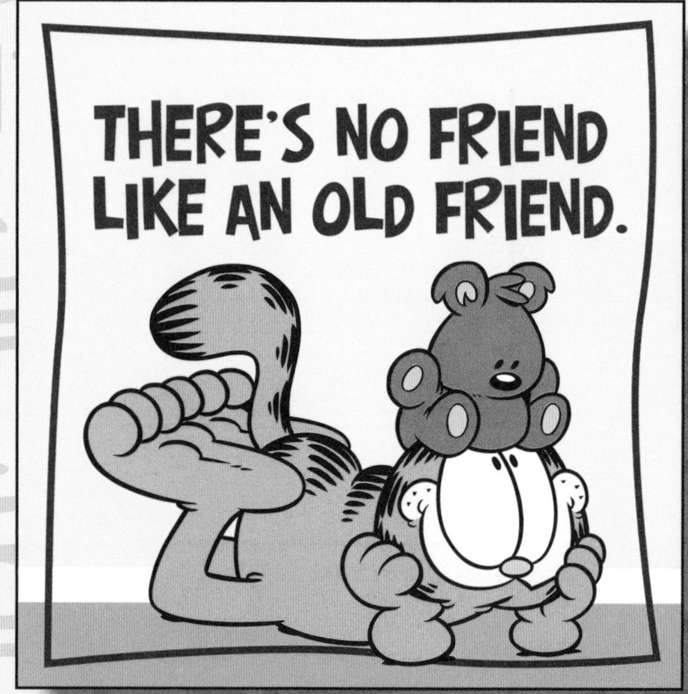
THERE'S NO FRIEND LIKE AN OLD FRIEND.

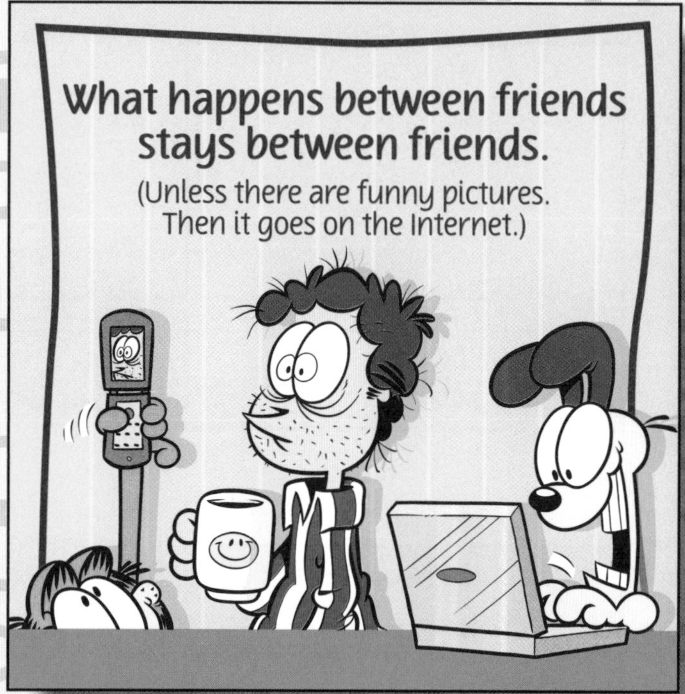
What happens between friends stays between friends.
(Unless there are funny pictures. Then it goes on the Internet.)

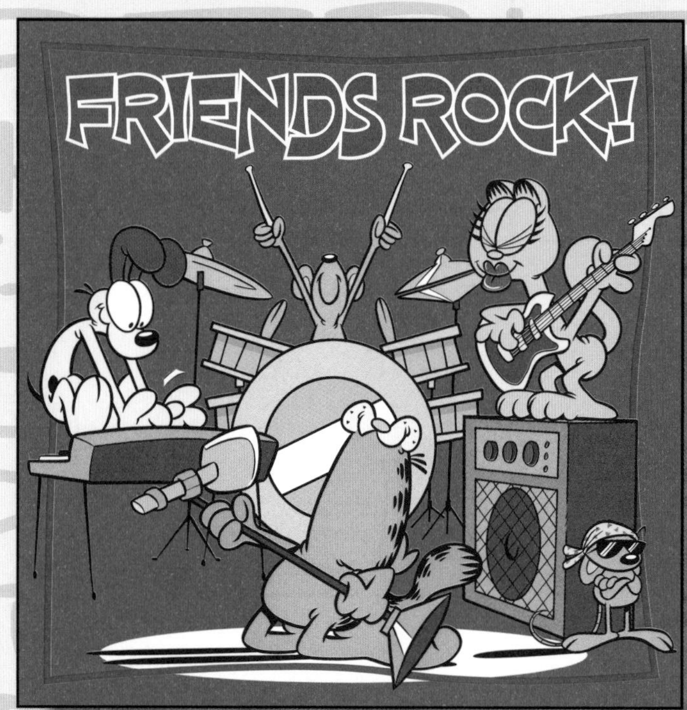
FRIENDS ROCK!

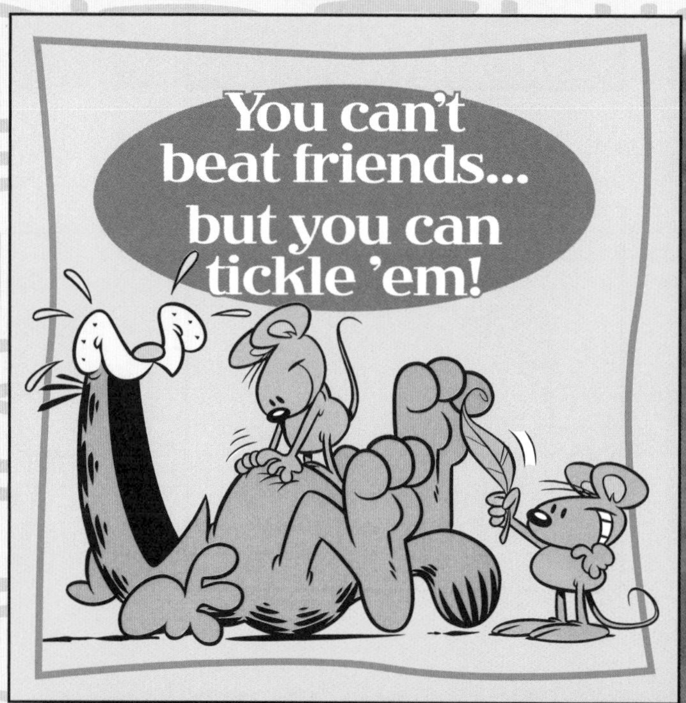
You can't beat friends... but you can tickle 'em!

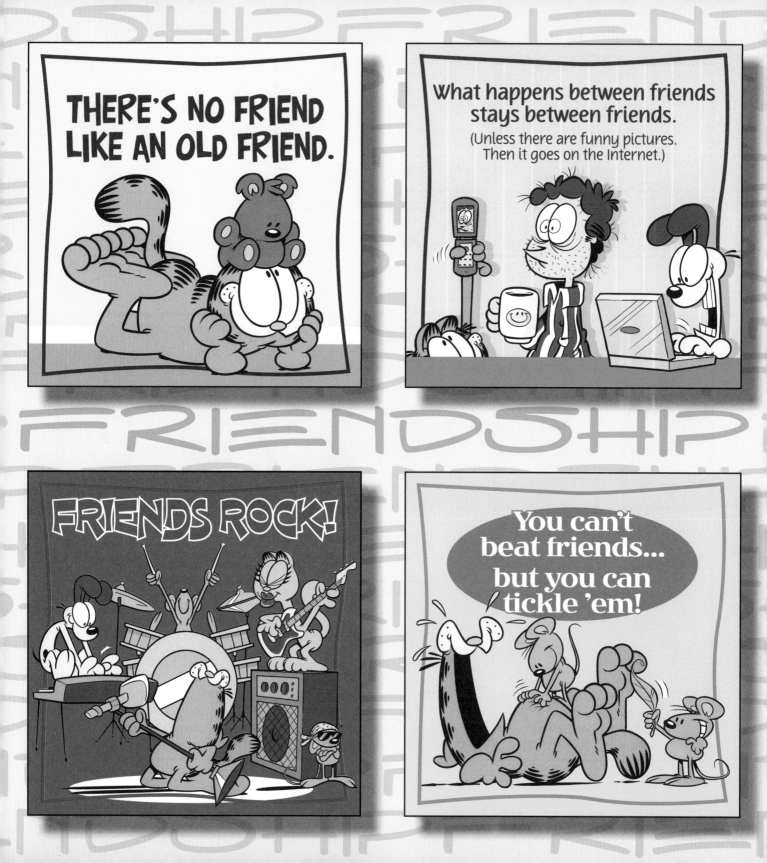

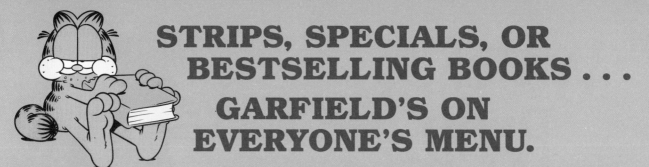

STRIPS, SPECIALS, OR BESTSELLING BOOKS . . . GARFIELD'S ON EVERYONE'S MENU.

Don't miss even one episode in the Tubby Tabby's hilarious series!

GARFIELD AT LARGE . . . . . (#1) 978-0-345-44382-3
GARFIELD GAINS WEIGHT . . . . . (#2) 978-0-345-44975-7
GARFIELD BIGGER THAN LIFE . . . . . (#3) 978-0-345-45027-2
GARFIELD WEIGHS IN . . . . . (#4) 978-0-345-45205-4
GARFIELD TAKES THE CAKE . . . . . (#5) 978-0-345-44978-8
GARFIELD EATS HIS HEART OUT . . . . . (#6) 978-0-345-46459-0
GARFIELD SITS AROUND THE HOUSE . . . . . (#7) 978-0-345-46463-7
GARFIELD TIPS THE SCALES . . . . . (#8) 978-0-345-46909-0
GARFIELD LOSES HIS FEET . . . . . (#9) 978-0-345-46467-5
GARFIELD MAKES IT BIG . . . . . (#10) 978-0-345-46468-2
GARFIELD ROLLS ON . . . . . (#11) 978-0-345-47561-9
GARFIELD OUT TO LUNCH . . . . . (#12) 978-0-345-47562-6
GARFIELD FOOD FOR THOUGHT . . . . . (#13) 978-0-345-47563-3
GARFIELD SWALLOWS HIS PRIDE . . . . . (#14) 978-0-345-91386-9
GARFIELD WORLDWIDE . . . . . (#15) 978-0-345-91754-6
GARFIELD ROUNDS OUT . . . . . (#16) 978-0-345-49169-5
GARFIELD CHEWS THE FAT . . . . . (#17) 978-0-345-49170-1
GARFIELD GOES TO WAIST . . . . . (#18) 978-0-345-49173-2
GARFIELD HANGS OUT . . . . . (#19) 978-0-345-49174-9
GARFIELD TAKES UP SPACE . . . . . (#20) 978-0-345-49178-7
GARFIELD SAYS A MOUTHFUL . . . . . (#21) 978-0-345-49179-4
GARFIELD BY THE POUND . . . . . (#22) 978-0-345-52558-1
GARFIELD KEEPS HIS CHINS UP . . . . . (#23) 978-0-345-52559-8
GARFIELD TAKES HIS LICKS . . . . . (#24) 978-0-345-52587-1
GARFIELD HITS THE BIG TIME . . . . . (#25) 978-0-345-52589-5
GARFIELD PULLS HIS WEIGHT . . . . . (#26) 978-0-345-52594-9
GARFIELD DISHES IT OUT . . . . . (#27) 978-0-345-52595-6
GARFIELD LIFE IN THE FAT LANE . . . . . (#28) 978-0-345-52600-7
GARFIELD TONS OF FUN . . . . . (#29) 978-0-345-52601-4
GARFIELD BIGGER AND BETTER . . . . . (#30) 978-0-345-52605-2
GARFIELD HAMS IT UP . . . . . (#31) 978-0-345-52606-9
GARFIELD THINKS BIG . . . . . (#32) 978-0-425-28516-9
GARFIELD THROWS HIS WEIGHT AROUND . . . . . (#33) 978-0-425-28559-6
GARFIELD LIFE TO THE FULLEST . . . . . (#34) 978-0-345-43239-1
GARFIELD FEEDS THE KITTY . . . . . (#35) 978-0-345-43673-3
GARFIELD HOGS THE SPOTLIGHT . . . . . (#36) 978-0-345-43922-2
GARFIELD BEEFS UP . . . . . (#37) 978-0-345-44109-6
GARFIELD GETS COOKIN' . . . . . (#38) 978-0-345-44582-7
GARFIELD EATS CROW . . . . . (#39) 978-0-345-45201-6
GARFIELD SURVIVAL OF THE FATTEST . . . . . (#40) 978-0-345-46458-3
GARFIELD OLDER AND WIDER . . . . . (#41) 978-0-345-46462-0
GARFIELD PIGS OUT . . . . . (#42) 978-0-345-46466-8
GARFIELD BLOTS OUT THE SUN . . . . . (#43) 978-0-345-46615-0
GARFIELD GOES BANANAS . . . . . (#44) 978-0-345-91346-3
GARFIELD LARGE & IN CHARGE . . . . . (#45) 978-0-345-49172-5
GARFIELD SPILLS THE BEANS . . . . . (#46) 978-0-345-49177-0
GARFIELD GETS HIS JUST DESSERTS . . . . . (#47) 978-0-345-91387-6
GARFIELD WILL EAT FOR FOOD . . . . . (#48) 978-0-345-49176-3
GARFIELD WEIGHS HIS OPTIONS . . . . . (#49) 978-0-345-49181-7
GARFIELD POTBELLY OF GOLD . . . . . (#50) 978-0-345-52244-3
GARFIELD SHOVELS IT IN . . . . . (#51) 978-0-345-52419-5
GARFIELD LARD OF THE JUNGLE . . . . . (#52) 978-0-345-52584-0
GARFIELD BRINGS HOME THE BACON . . . . . (#53) 978-0-345-52586-4
GARFIELD GETS IN A PICKLE . . . . . (#54) 978-0-345-52590-1
GARFIELD SINGS FOR HIS SUPPER . . . . . (#55) 978-0-345-52593-2
GARFIELD CAUTION: WIDE LOAD . . . . . (#56) 978-0-345-52596-3
GARFIELD SOUPED UP . . . . . (#57) 978-0-345-52598-7
GARFIELD GOES TO HIS HAPPY PLACE . . . . . (#58) 978-0-345-52602-1
GARFIELD THE BIG CHEESE . . . . . (#59) 978-0-345-52604-5
GARFIELD CLEANS HIS PLATE . . . . . (#60) 978-0-345-52608-3
GARFIELD CHICKENS OUT . . . . . (#61) 978-0-425-28515-2
GARFIELD LISTENS TO HIS GUT . . . . . (#62) 978-0-425-28557-2

DVD TIE-INS

GARFIELD AS HIMSELF 978-0-345-47805-4
GARFIELD HOLIDAY CELEBRATIONS 978-0-345-47930-3
GARFIELD TRAVEL ADVENTURES 978-0-345-48087-3

AND DON'T MISS . . .

GARFIELD AT 25: IN DOG YEARS I'D BE DEAD 978-0-345-45204-7
GARFIELD'S JOKE ZONE/INSULTS 978-0-345-46263-3
GARFIELD FAT CAT 3-PACK/ VOL. 1 978-0-345-46455-2
GARFIELD FAT CAT 3-PACK/ VOL. 2 978-0-345-46465-1
GARFIELD FAT CAT 3-PACK/ VOL. 3 978-0-345-48088-0
GARFIELD FAT CAT 3-PACK/ VOL. 4 978-0-345-49171-8
GARFIELD FAT CAT 3-PACK/ VOL. 5 978-0-345-49180-8
GARFIELD FAT CAT 3-PACK/ VOL. 6 978-0-345-52420-1
GARFIELD FAT CAT 3-PACK/ VOL. 7 978-0-345-52588-8
GARFIELD FAT CAT 3-PACK/ VOL. 8 978-0-345-52599-4
GARFIELD FAT CAT 3-PACK/ VOL. 9 978-0-345-52607-6
GARFIELD FAT CAT 3-PACK/ VOL. 10 978-0-425-28558-9
GARFIELD FAT CAT 3-PACK/ VOL. 13 978-0-345-46460-6
GARFIELD FAT CAT 3-PACK/ VOL. 14 978-0-345-49175-6
GARFIELD FAT CAT 3-PACK/ VOL. 15 978-0-345-52585-7
GARFIELD FAT CAT 3-PACK/ VOL. 16 978-0-345-52592-5
GARFIELD FAT CAT 3-PACK/ VOL. 17 978-0-345-52603-8
GARFIELD FAT CAT 3-PACK/ VOL. 18 978-0-399-59440-3
GARFIELD FAT CAT 3-PACK/ VOL. 19 978-0-425-28561-9
SEASON'S EATINGS: A VERY MERRY GARFIELD CHRISTMAS 978-0-345-47560-2
GARFIELD'S GUIDE TO EVERYTHING 978-0-345-46461-3
ODIE UNLEASHED! 978-0-345-46464-4
GARFIELD'S BOOK OF CAT NAMES 978-0-345-48516-8
THE GARFIELD JOURNAL 978-0-345-46469-9
LIGHTS, CAMERA, HAIRBALLS!: GARFIELD AT THE MOVIES 978-0-345-49134-3
30 YEARS OF LAUGHS AND LASAGNA 978-0-345-50379-4
GARFIELD MINUS GARFIELD 978-0-345-51387-8
GARFIELD FROM THE TRASH BIN 978-0-345-51881-1
GARFIELD LEFT SPEECHLESS 978-0-345-53058-5
MY LAUGHABLE LIFE WITH GARFIELD 978-0-345-52591-8
GARFIELD'S SUNDAY FINEST 978-0-345-52597-0

New larger, full-color format!